DATE DUE

DEMCO

THE CHANGING FACE
OF FRIENDSHIP

BOSTON UNIVERSITY STUDIES IN PHILOSOPHY AND RELIGION

General Editor: Leroy S. Rouner

Volume Fifteen

The Changing Face of Friendship

Edited By

Leroy S. Rouner

UNIVERSITY OF NOTRE DAME PRESS
Notre Dame, Indiana

Copyright © 1994 by
University of Notre Dame Press
Notre Dame, Indiana 46556
All Rights Reserved

Library of Congress Cataloging-in-Publication Data

The Changing face of friendship/edited by Leroy S. Rouner.
      p.   cm. — (Boston University studies in philosophy
and religion; v. 15)
    Includes index.
    ISBN 0-268-00804-3
    1. Friendship.   2. Friendship—Religious aspects.
I. Rouner, Leory S.   II. Series.
BJ1533.F8C44   1994
177'.6—dc20   94-15462
                                                             CIP

♾ The paper used in this publication meets the minimum requirements
of the American National Standard for Information Sciences—Permanence of Paper
for Printed Library Materials, ANSI Z39.48-1984.

Manufactured in the United States of America

For Jim Langford

Galileo scholar and Cubs fan, his imagination as our publisher has made this series possible. His own Institute lectures have been sometimes scholarly and wise, sometimes playful and hilarious, always memorable. This book on friendship salutes our publisher, our philosophical colleague, and our very dear friend.

Contents

Contents

Preface

Boston University Studies in Philosophy and Religion is a joint project of the Boston University Institute for Philosophy and Religion and the University of Notre Dame Press. The essays in each annual volume are edited from the previous year's lecture program and invited papers of the Boston University Institute. The Director of the Institute, who is also the Editor of these Studies, chooses a theme and invites participants to lecture at Boston University in the course of the academic year. The Editor then selects and edits the essays to be included in the volume. Dr. Barbara Darling-Smith, Assistant Director of the Institute, regularly copy edits the essays and prepares the manuscript for the Press. We are currently working on Volume 16, *In Pursuit of Happiness*.

The Boston University Institute for Philosophy and Religion was begun informally in 1970 under the leadership of Professor Peter Bertocci of the Department of Philosophy, with the cooperation of Dean Walter Muelder of the School of Theology, Professor James Purvis, Chair of the Department of Religion, and Professor Marx Wartofsky, Chair of the Department of Philosophy. Professor Bertocci was concerned to institutionalize one of the most creative features of Boston personalism, its interdisciplinary approach to fundamental issues of human life. When Professor Leroy S. Rouner became Director in 1975, and the Institute became a formal Center of the Boston University Graduate School, every effort was made to continue that vision of an ecumenical and interdisciplinary forum.

Within the University the Institute is committed to open interchange on fundamental issues in philosophy and religious study which transcend the narrow specializations of academic curricula. We seek to counter those trends in higher education which emphasize technical expertise in a "multi-versity," and gradually transform undergraduate liberal arts education into preprofessional training.

Our programs are open to the general public, and are regularly broadcast on WBUR-FM, Boston University's National Public Radio affiliate. Outside the University we seek to recover the public tradition of philosophical discourse which was a lively part of American intellectual life in the early years of this century before the professionalization of both philosophy and religious reflection made these two disciplines topics virtually unavailable even to an educated public. This commitment to a public tradition in American intellectual life has important stylistic implications. At a time when too much academic writing is incomprehensible, or irrelevant, or both, our goal is to present readable essays by acknowledged authorities on critical human issues.

Acknowledgments

Our first debt is to our authors, whose expertise makes this volume possible. In a number of cases they have made extensive improvements on their original lecture texts, and for this we are very grateful.

The person who does the hardest work on the manuscript is the Institute's Assistant Director, Dr. Barbara Darling-Smith. I invite the lecturers, edit their texts, and decide which ones to use, and in what order. Then I write the Introduction. But this is the fun part. The lengthy and exacting work of copy editing, which is not so much fun, is all hers, and her capacity for accurate detail is legendary. The mysteries of umlauts, diacritical marks, Sanskrit spellings, and the dark, complex truths hidden deep in *The Chicago Manual of Style* have all been revealed to her. And while copy editing may not be fun, working with her always is. She makes sure we get it right, and have a good time in the process. This year she has once again had expert help from Denice K. Carnes, who enters Barbara's corrections to the text on the computer, presides over the scanner, and adds her own lively good humor to the process.

Ann Rice, Executive Editor at the University of Notre Dame Press, oversees production of each volume. Since we have to choose a date for our annual publication party well before we begin manuscript preparation, we count on Ann's quiet authority to keep us on schedule and make sure we have the books in time for the party. And behind it all is our friend Jim Langford, Director of the University of Notre Dame Press, who was willing to take a chance on a series which most publishers would not have risked.

Finally, a salute to our friends at the Lilly Endowment. At a time when the Institute lacked funding, Craig Dykstra, Vice President for Religion, and Jeanne Knoerle, S.P., Program Director for Religion, decided to support us with a three-year grant. Like our publisher, these good friends have also become colleagues and participants in our program planning, and their intellectual and spiritual support is even more valuable than their generous financial contribution.

Contributors

ROGER T. AMES is Professor of Philosophy at the University of
Hawaii at Manoa, editor of *Philosophy East and West* and *China
Review International*, and Director of the University of Hawaii
Center for Chinese Studies. He also chairs the Board of Advisors
for the Hawaii Institute of Philosophy for Children. Specializing
in Chinese philosophy, Professor Ames has studied at the Chi-
nese University of Hong Kong, the National Taiwan University,
Osaka University of Foreign Studies, and Tokyo University of
Education. His Ph.D. is from the University of London. He is
author or editor of a dozen books, including *Master Sun: The
Art of Warfare*, and *Thinking Through Confucius*, which he co-
authored with David Hall.

EBERHARD BETHGE served as Assistant to the Director of the anti-
Nazi Confessing Church Seminary in Finkenwalde, Germany,
from 1935 until 1940. He and the Director, Dietrich Bonhoeffer,
became close friends. He has several honorary degrees and has
been Visiting Professor at Harvard Divinity School and Union
Theological Seminary. From 1961 to 1975 he was Director of the
Institute for Continuing Education for Clergy of the Evangelical
Church in the Rhineland. He is best known as the editor and recipient of Bonhoeffer's *Letters and Papers from Prison*, editor of
Bonhoeffer's *Collected Writings*, and author of Bonhoeffer's biography, *Dietrich Bonhoeffer: Man of Vision, Man of Courage*.

DAVID B. BURRELL, C.S.C., is the Theodore M. Hesburgh, C.S.C.,
Professor in the College of Arts and Letters and Professor of Phi-

losophy and Theology at the University of Notre Dame. He has been Visiting Professor at the National Major Seminary, Dacca, Bangladesh, and at the Hebrew University in Jerusalem. He is the author of *Analogy and Philosophical Language* and *Exercises in Religious Understanding*, among numerous other books. His bachelor's degree is from the University of Notre Dame. He then studied at the Gregorian University in Rome, before taking his Ph.D. at Yale University. The recipient of numerous fellowships and awards, he has also served as Rector of the Ecumenical Institute for Theological Research in Jerusalem.

ELIOT DEUTSCH is Professor of Philosophy at the University of Hawaii, and has served there as editor of *Philosophy East and West* and Director of the Sixth East-West Philosophers' Conference. He has studied at the University of Wisconsin, the University of Chicago, and Harvard University. His Ph.D. is from Columbia. He is the author of numerous books in both systematic philosophy and comparative philosophy, including *On Truth: An Ontological Theory; Humanity and Divinity: An Essay in Comparative Metaphysics; Personhood, Creativity, and Freedom;* and *Advaita Vedanta: A Philosophical Reconstruction*. He has held visiting professorships at Harvard and the University of Chicago, and has been President of the Society for Asian and Comparative Philosophy.

DAVID LYNN HALL graduated *summa cum laude* from the Chicago Theological Seminary before completing his Ph.D. on Whitehead's philosophy at Yale University. He is now Professor of Philosophy at the University of Texas at El Paso. He has twice been Visiting Professor at the University of Hawaii, and is Director of the Chenrezig Himalayan Cultural Center in El Paso. He is co-editor of the State University of New York Press series in *Chinese Philosophy and Culture* and is managing book review editor for *Philosophy East and West*. He has written books on Whitehead, Richard Rorty, and Confucius, and has published a philosophical novel, *The Arimaspian Eye*. He is also the author of *The Uncertain Phoenix: Adventures Toward a Post-Cultural Sensibility*, and *Eros and Irony: A Prelude to Philosophical Anarchism*.

EMILY ALBU HANAWALT is a Phi Beta Kappa graduate of the
College of Wooster and holds the Ph.D. from the University of
California at Berkeley. She has held postdoctoral research grants
from the Lilly Endowment, the Humanities Foundation at
Boston University, and the Bunting Institute at Radcliffe Col-
lege. She has taught at the University of California at Berkeley,
Chaminade College of Honolulu, and Boston University, where
she was Associate Professor of Classical Studies and Associate
Director of the Division of Religious and Theological Studies in
the Graduate School. She is coeditor, with Carter Lindberg, of
*Through the Eye of a Needle: Judeo-Christian Roots of Social
Welfare*, and coauthor, with Howard Clark Kee *et al.*, of *Christianity: A Social and Cultural History*.

MARY ELIZABETH HUNT is cofounder and codirector of the Women's Alliance for Theology, Ethics, and Ritual in Silver Spring,
Maryland. She did her undergraduate work in philosophy and theology at Marquette University, her Master of Divinity degree at
the Jesuit School of Theology in Berkeley, and received the Ph.D.
from the Graduate Theological Union in Berkeley. She has written numerous articles for a variety of journals and is the editor of
From Woman-Pain to Woman-Vision by Anne McGrew Bennett.
She is best known as the author of *Fierce Tenderness: A Feminist
Theology of Friendship*, which was awarded the Crossroad Women's Studies Prize for 1990. She is a member of the Board of
Directors of Catholics for a Free Choice, and serves on the Editorial Board of the *Journal of Feminist Studies in Religion*.

GILBERT C. MEILAENDER, JR., is Professor of Religion at Ober-
lin College. He did his undergraduate work at Concordia Senior
College in Fort Wayne, Indiana, and his Ph.D. at Princeton. He
serves on the editorial boards of several journals in religious
ethics, and is the author of five books, including *Faith and
Faithfulness: Basic Themes in Christian Ethics; The Limits of
Love; The Theory and Practice of Virtue;* and *The Taste for the
Other: The Social and Ethical Thought of C. S. Lewis*. Most rele-
vant to this volume is his *Friendship: A Study in Theological
Ethics*, published by the University of Notre Dame Press. He is

a member of the American Theological Society and the Society of Christian Ethics. He has also taught at the University of Virginia, and served as Assistant Pastor of the Lutheran Church of the Messiah in Princeton, New Jersey, while he was a graduate student.

JÜRGEN MOLTMANN, Professor of Systematic Theology at the University of Tübingen, is a member of the Faith and Order Commission of the World Council of Churches and the Department of Theology of the World Alliance of Reformed Churches. He was educated at the University of Göttingen where he received his Ph.D. in 1955 and his Habilitation in 1957. He is also the recipient of several honorary degrees and the Elba Library Prize. Among his many books are *The Theology of Hope*, *The Crucified God*, *The Church in the Power of the Spirit*, *The Future of Creation*, *On Human Dignity*, *The Trinity and the Kingdom*, *God in Creation*, and *Creating a Just Future*.

MICHAEL PAKALUK graduated from Harvard College in 1980. He spent two years at the University of Edinburgh, where he did an M.Litt. degree in philosophy under Ronald Hepburn before returning to Harvard for his Ph.D. He wrote his thesis there on "Aristotle's Theory of Friendship." He has been an Assistant Professor of Philosophy at Clark University since 1988, where he specializes in Aristotle, early analytic philosophy, and Hume. He has published several papers on friendship and has given a number of public lectures on this theme, including "Friendship and Individualism" at Anderson University in Indiana, and "The Importance of the Philosophical Study of Friendship" in the Distinguished Scholar Lecture Series at Broward Community College in March of 1991. He is a member of *Phi Beta Kappa* and has been a Marshall Scholar.

BHIKHU PAREKH did his undergraduate study at St. Xavier's College, Bombay, before taking his Ph.D. in Political Philosophy at the London School of Economics. He is Professor of Political Philosophy at the University of Hull, England. From 1981 to 1984 he was Vice-Chancellor of the University of Baroda, India. He chairs the Research Committee on Political Philosophy of the International Political Science Association and has been Deputy Chairman of the Commission for Racial Equality in England. He has lectured widely in India, Europe, and America, and often writes for journals and newspapers in Britain. He is the recipient of numerous awards, honors, and prizes. His books include *Hannah Arendt and the Search for a New Political Philosophy; Karl Marx's Theory of Ideology; Gandhi's Political Philosophy;* and *Colonialism, Tradition, and Reform.* He is also the editor of several works on the philosophy of Jeremy Bentham.

LEROY S. ROUNER is Professor of Philosophy, Religion, and Philosophical Theology and Director of the Institute for Philosophy and Religion at Boston University. A graduate of Harvard College and Union Theological Seminary, he did his Ph.D. under John Herman Randall, Jr., at Columbia on the philosophy of William Ernest Hocking. He edited the Hocking *Festschrift: Philosophy, Religion and the Coming World Civilization; The Wisdom of William Ernest Hocking* (with John Howie); and *Corporations and the Common Good* (with Robert Dickie). He is the author of *Within Human Experience: The Philosophy of William Ernest Hocking; The Long Way Home* (a memoir); and *To Be at Home: Christianity, Civil Religion, and World Community.* He has also edited twelve volumes in Boston University Studies in Philosophy and Religion, of which he is general editor. He has been Visiting Professor at the University of Hawaii, and was Assistant Professor of Philosophy and Theology at the United Theological College, Bangalore, India, from 1961 to 1966.

NINIAN SMART is the J. F. Rowny Professor of Comparative Religions at the University of California, Santa Barbara. He has written both technical and popular books in the philosophy of religion, Indian philosophy, the history of religions, methodology, religious dialogue, religious education, and politics. Educated at Oxford, he founded the first major department of religious studies in England at Lancaster University. He was editorial consultant for the thirteen-part television series in Great Britain on the world's religions called *The Long Search*. His many books include *The Long Search; Religion and the Western Mind; Beyond Ideology;* and *Worldviews*. He has been a Gifford Lecturer in the University of Edinburgh and has held numerous visiting professorships in places as diverse as Banares Hindu University in India, Otago University in New Zealand, the University of Hong Kong, and the United Theological College in Bangalore, India. He has served as President of the American Society for the Study of Religion, President of the British Association for the History of Religion, and President of the Oxford Society for Historical Theology.

JOHN E. SMITH, the Clark Professor of Philosophy Emeritus at Yale University, is a specialist in American philosophy and the philosophy of religion. He is the author of numerous books including *The Spirit of American Philosophy; Reason and God; Contemporary American Philosophy*; and *The Analogy of Experience*. He is also general editor of the Yale Edition of the works of Jonathan Edwards. He has filled several dozen guest lectureships in this country and abroad, notably the Dudleian Lecture at Harvard University, the Suarez Lecture at Fordham University, the Gates Lecture at Grinnell College, the Warfield Lecture at Princeton Theological Seminary, and the Winston Churchill Lecture at the University of Bristol, England. He has served as President of the American Philosophical Association, the American Theological Society, the Metaphysical Society of America, and the Hegel Society of America.

Introduction

LEROY S. ROUNER

How has our understanding of friendship changed? The question is difficult to answer, because most talk of human relationships is now sexually charged. To say that two people have "a relationship" implies that they are lovers. Nonsexual friendships are probably as important today as they ever were, but we understand them less well because there is little reflective talk about them. Sexuality dominates our talk about intimacy with one another.

So this seemed like a good place to begin a three-year exploration of fundamental human experiences which are no longer widely discussed or well understood. Jim Langford and I met with Craig Dykstra, Jeanne Knoerle, and members of their staff at the Lilly Endowment to discuss the missions of the Institute, the Press, and the Endowment, and the issues we would explore together. We agreed on three key themes: The Changing Face of Friendship, In Pursuit of Happiness, and The Longing for Home. During the spring of 1995 we will have a colloquium planning a final summary program in this series on The Good Life in a Broken World. The themes are interrelated, but friendship is clearly relevant to them all. The essays which follow do not represent a common point of view, but we hope they will help clarify what it means to be a friend, and help restore talk about friendship to our common conversation.

Eliot Deutsch begins our first section on Philosophies of Friendship with an outline of what he calls "Creative Friendship" and its place as a distinctive type in the continuum of human relationships. More than simply *friendliness*, and less than *intimacy*, friendship requires a measure of personal autonomy. Deutsch notes that *autonomy* has been interpreted in different ways in the Western philosophical tradition. For Plato it meant rational ordering of contending elements in one's nature; for Kant, the independence of rationality in morals.

1

Hegel and the later Marxists understood autonomy as identified with a larger collective society, whereas Nietzsche thought only the exceptional person of heroic will was truly autonomous. But for all their differences, these views emphasize the distinctive individuality of the self, the need for power in controlling one's life, and the freedom of self-determination.

Deutsch adds that genuine friendship also requires both a lack of self-deception and a commitment to a power which does not seek dominance. Taking his clue from Aristotle's "friendships of the good" (the "perfect friendship" of good will toward the other for his or her own sake), Deutsch argues for a "creative friendship" which finds its highest expression in relations between women and men. His view of autonomy rules out static, lonely independence. An autonomous person transforms his or her social, economic, and cultural dependencies to a care-filled relationship in which the health of one's own autonomy depends on one's care for the autonomy of others. Friendship is a commitment "to identify with the friend's welfare and at the same time to assure that one's own integrity will not only be preserved but enhanced in and through that relationship." Creativity, for Deutsch, is not the dominion of creator over the created, but a mutuality in which both creator and created are conditioned by the relationship. It therefore becomes a kind of play, a performance for its own sake. And unlike Aristotle's "perfect friendship" which is limited to a few, the playful performance of creative friendship is open to many. And in a *vive la difference* argument about relations between men and women who are truly autonomous, Deutsch notes that the *sameness* of autonomy provides a basis for enjoying all the *differences* of their experience in the creative, ritual play of community.

Jürgen Moltmann shares many of Deutsch's sensibilities in his argument for "Open Friendship." He begins with a charming children's poem in which a friend is defined simply as "someone who likes you." Friendship combines respect with affection and faithfulness. It is not an alliance for mutual advantage, as in the case of so-called "business friends." Friends promise only to "walk with each other and to be there for each other." And the necessary context for this relationship is freedom. Since Aristotle wrote so extensively and influentially about friendship, Moltmann contrasts his "Open Friendship" with the exclusiveness of Aristotle's "perfect friendship." Like Deutsch he rejects Aristotle's notion that we can be friends only with people who are like us. His resource is the New Testament view of open friendship with people who are different.

His primary example is the friendship of Jesus. He was a "friend of tax collectors and sinners," and Jesus' call to discipleship envisions a new life of friendship: "Greater love has no man than this, that a man lay down his life for his friends. You are my friends if you do what I command you." This is a friendship which stems from joy in God and in humanity. Its purpose is "that my joy may be in you, and your joy be full." Moltmann then goes on to describe "friendship with God" as the life of prayer in which our requests and God's answers are based not on the submissiveness of the servant, or the gratitude of the child, but the boldness of a friend. All this is contrasted sharply with the closed circle of friendship among peers in our society, in which friendship has become private, intimate, exclusive, and based on feeling. Moltmann calls for a deprivatization of our romantic notion of friendship, so that friendship can "once again receive the character of public protection of and public respect for others."

David Burrell focuses directly on the question of friendship with God, and compares and contrasts the views of Saint Thomas and the Muslim scholar al-Ghazali. His essay in interreligious dialogue suggests that centuries of mutual disdain between these religious communities may be overcome by remembering our common spiritual heritage in the religious faith of Abraham. He reminds us again that Aristotle regarded friendship among unequals as impossible, and hence rules out the possibility that humans can be friends with divinity. Burrell, however, notes that both Aquinas and Ghazali raise the possibility of friendship by understanding the relation to divinity as that of creator and creature, resulting from God's free activity in creating the world. Both the Qur'an and the Hebrew prophets have passages speaking of the mutual love between God and humankind, and both acknowledge Abraham to have been chosen and called "friend" by God.

Both Aquinas and Ghazali present an anthropology of the virtues which understands us as being created with the gift of charity, and thereby empowered to love and befriend the God who created us. Burrell points out that the two views are remarkably similar, even though Aquinas relies on Aristotle, and has an ontological structure undergirding his analysis, whereas Ghazali does not. While admitting that friendship with God has not regularly been understood as central to either the Christian or Muslim tradition, Burrell finds it crucial that both thinkers see human action as a response to divine initiative, and further see this response as derived from the originating creator-creature relationship. "Given that structure, and the opening to an interpersonal relationship at the divine initiative, it becomes possible to think that creatures might stand in the same relationship to God as to themselves. . . ." Burrell concludes with the hope that this exploration of common ground may offer some hope for rapprochement between two traditions which today find themselves too often at odds with one another.

Once again Aristotle rears his by-now-familiar head in John Smith's essay comparing Aristotle and Nietzsche. Smith admits at the outset that this is an unlikely comparison between the rationalism of an ancient Greek and the irony, sarcasm, and hyperbole of a romantic modern. Confident, however, that this contrast between Apollonian and Dyonisian themes may prove useful, Smith begins by contrasting Aristotle's identification with the *ethos* of the Greek city-state and its ideal of the good society in contrast to Nietzsche's criticism of European culture with its roots in Christianity. Smith takes us through Aristotle's distinction among three types of friendship—those based on pleasure, utility, and virtue—and his conviction that only good men can become friends, for only they are prepared to regard the good-for-the-other as necessary to their own good. Thus friendship, for Aristotle, belongs to the elite.

Nietzsche's view is also that of an elite, but of a very different sort. In a reversal of the Christian view of Aquinas which Burrell sketches, Nietzsche regards the self as creative only when it empowers itself to be a creator, and not when it regards itself as creature. Deutsch has already noted the self's need for power, and Nietzsche makes the will to power central to his ethic of friendship. This is Deutsch's autonomy writ large, with strong emphasis on the striving of each autonomous self to outdo the other in self-perfection. Nietzsche's "over-man" is one who is self-determined, free of pity, and ready for this competitive friendship with other men, not what Nietzsche regarded as the corrupting sentimentality of love between the sexes. Smith concludes that his two thinkers agree that true friendships are rare because people of virtue are rare. For this reason they differ from Moltmann, whose Christian ethic of "open friendship" entertains many friends. For both Aristotle and Nietzsche that is not possible.

The great difference between the two, however, is Aristotle's grounding of friendship in reason, and Nietzsche's emphasis on the will. Aristotle finds friends in the context of a common society. Nietzsche, the lonely "over-man," can be friends only with another lonely genius like Wagner—but, alas, not for long.

Our second section turns to Friendship in Various Cultures. Since Chinese philosophy has rich resources on the philosophy of friendship, we begin with an essay on "Confucian Friendship: The Road to Religiousness" by two friends, Roger Ames and David Hall. They begin with Plato's *Phaedrus* and the way in which the friendship between Phaedrus and Socrates relates to what their mutual friend Eliot Deutsch has already called "spirituality." Socrates and Phaedrus both share a desire for temperance, wisdom, and beauty, and this *eros* equips them for friendship. The *Phaedrus* concludes that true friends hold all things in common, and share a love for the transcendent Good. But Hall and Ames note that Plato seems to regard friendship as merely an instrument for attaining spirituality. They reject that view, and turn instead to Confucius.

The central virtue of classical Confucianism, *jen*, is regularly translated as "benevolence," "humanity," and "goodness." Hall and Ames quote the *Hsun Tzu* on the view that a *jen* person is one who loves oneself. But this love requires consideration of the other, and love as *ai* means "to be sparing with." So love is respectful in its regard, and circumspect in any demands it may make. It wants the other to remain fully herself in the relationship. "Hence to love another is to be sparing of her." This *jen* is related to religiousness through the continuity and interdependence between Heaven and the human being. Friendships develop among those who seek spiritual growth in those virtues which the *Phaedrus* noted: Truth, Beauty, and Goodness. Confucius argues, however, that a true friend must be better than oneself, in order to help one toward Heaven. But since the Confucius of the *Analects* is portrayed as peerless, Hall and Ames note that "there is a poignancy in the conclusion that Socrates and Confucius could not be friends. Confucius, at an early stage of his development, might seek friendship based on a perceived superiority in Socrates, while Socrates would solicit Confucius' participation in the joint inquiry after the Good. Socratic irony would not allow the inequality Confucius requires as a means of self-betterment. Confucius would not permit himself and Socrates to hold all things in common."

"An Indian View of Friendship," which Bhikhu Parekh explores through an analysis of the great Hindu epics, especially the *Mahābhā- rata*, focuses on relations between men. While Indian thinking on the topic has been reshaped by encounters with Western and Islamic cultures, the *Mahābhārata* remains a primary source for contemporary India, both metaphysically and socially. Metaphysically the Indian view of human relations with the transcendent tended to be cosmocentric, in contrast to the anthropocentric and theocentric views of the universe which have been dominant in the West. This view held that all constituent "co-tenants" in the cosmic order have equally legitimate rights to its resources. Parekh quotes a *mantra*, or prayer, which asks: "May I look upon all living beings with the eyes of a friend." On the social level, therefore, every human being owes the duty of *maitri* ("friendliness"), involving good will and help, to all others. The concept is so central that the sun, which makes everything in the universe possible, is called *Mitra*, "the Friend."

This broad-based relation to the universe becomes specific in individual friendships. The *Mahābhārata* defines a friend as one who is "good-hearted" toward others. Since the heart is the seat of both feeling and the soul, a friend is one who feels with me and for me, and who is what we would call a "soul-mate." Further, true friends in the Indian tradition, while lacking a blood bond, nevertheless forge equally strong bonds of loyalty and love, so that a friend is regularly regarded as "my brother." But because one is partial to one's friends, and loyal to them, friendship may be a source of immorality if a friend does wrong. Like Plato, Aristotle, and Confucius, however, the Indian writers on friendship argued that true friendship was possible only between men of virtue, "for only such friends did not make morally unacceptable demands on each other." Still, Parekh notes that the Indian writers admit that friendship creates islands of close relationships which threaten the structure of society. They solve this dilemma by insisting that every society must balance justice with friendship. In the *Mahābhārata*, Yudhishthira, who is the incarnation of justice, has no friends. Parekh therefore concludes that society requires a necessarily tentative balance between the demands of cold justice and warm friendship.

Thus far our accounts have shared substantial common ground. Confucius and Socrates may not be able to be friends; Nietzsche may be incapable of any long-range friendship; Aristotle may have to make do with only a few friends; but at least they share some common ideas about what makes for friendship, and why it is important to us. Emily Hanawalt's essay on "Predatory Friendship" provides an entirely new take on the issue. One could call this an instrumental view of friendship, but it is worse than that. Here friendship is often intentionally false in order to achieve power, and is regularly used to do one's enemies in. Hanawalt begins with an example from the year 1141 when the Earl of Chester takes Lincoln castle, thanks to friendship betrayed. Hanawalt quotes Orderic's evaluation of the Normans as "an untamed race," and she provides vivid pictures of a world where "treachery, deceit, and murder were everyday occurrences."

In her review of Norman histories Hanawalt notes the bleakness of twelfth-century accounts of life, and their increasingly pessimistic view of Norman heroes. Orderic Vitalis chronicles Norman cultural chaos, and adds his own philosophical reflections on the fragility of human life and the vanity of hope in worldly affairs. His contemporary Wace is equally gloomy. Norman literature shifted in the eleventh and twelfth centuries from what Hanawalt calls "the surety of epic to the anxiety of romance." How does one explain this shift? Hanawalt ventures a guess. "I have come to suspect that (this) very movement . . . is a natural progression for a society burdened with systemic uncertainties in their patterns of friendship." On the other hand, the rise of romance elevated the status of women, and afforded new opportunities for women and men to be friends.

Our concluding section on Friendship in the Modern World begins with Eberhard Bethge's reflections on "My Friend Dietrich Bonhoeffer's Theology of Friendship." This was a title I proposed to him, prompted by my friend and colleague Horace Allen, who suggested that I invite Bethge, knowing that both he and Bonhoeffer had written about their friendship with one another. His essay begins with an account of those friends who were closest to Bonhoeffer at different stages of his life, including himself. He then moves to an analysis of specific texts in Bonhoeffer's writings dealing with friendship and concludes with reflections on a poem which Bonhoeffer wrote for him as a birthday present in August of 1944, entitled simply "The Friend."

The poem speaks of a friendship which derives not from "blood and ancestry and oath" but "from free affection and the spirit's free desires." It ends acknowledging that friendship is "willing to bow to rigorous standards and rigorous reproach." For Bonhoeffer, the best fruit of friendship seems to have been the counsel of a friend, "counsel good and serious, which makes him free." The true friend is "his loyal helper to freedom and humanity." Bonhoeffer, in prison, where both his own government and those opposed to it are threats to his life, concludes his poem with a blessing after an air raid, when he says "so danger—if the omen does not lie—of every kind shall gently pass you by."

The contrast which Emily Hanawalt's essay raised about the relationship between friendship and enmity is writ large in Ninian Smart's essay on "Friendship and Enmity Among Nations." Reinhold Niebuhr used to argue that the larger the group the less it was possible for it to be moral. Since friendship is a moral relationship as well as an emotional one, Niebuhr would have regarded the idea of a "friendly nation" as a misleading metaphor at best. Smart is not so sure. He begins with the idea that nations are regularly regarded as "individuals," in keeping with what the Japanese call *kokutai* or "national substance." The nation is a great Thing of which we are a part and in which we participate spiritually. Its territory is its body, its ornaments are its national treasures, both natural and architectural, and its distinctive persona elicits loyalty and often love from its citizenry. But can nations be friends? Before answering the question directly Smart explores its opposite, the problem of enmity.

Enmities arise when oppression stimulates national feelings among the oppressed and enmity toward the oppressor, as in places like Israel, Sri Lanka, and the former Yugoslavia. He notes that racism is often cited as a cause of enmity, but he finds the notion unclear because the idea of race is not clear. Smart prefers to speak of "ethnic groupism." Large groups need their own territory, but there will always be ethnic minorities in any group, and Smart suggests that they be given a large symbolic role in national life, to offset their lack of distinctive territory. As to friendship among nations, the natural expectation is for hostility, and Smart argues that a major cause is territorial because boundaries are not clearly and agreeably marked. The spread of democracy will help, he thinks, because democracies are relatively friendly with one another. And economic cooperation gives different nations a common goal, and common interests. Finally, education from a global perspective will help temper chauvinism and give the peoples of one nation an interest in, and admiration for, the life and culture of others.

Mary Hunt's "Friends and Family Values" takes us back to personal relations of friendship, and the recent debate over "family values." Heterosexual marriage and family structure have thus far been normative for human relationships. This norm excludes many new forms of relationships, especially homosexual ones, so she defines friendship as "those voluntary human relationships that are entered into by people who intend one another's well-being, and who intend that their love relationship is part of a justice-seeking community." In the spirit of inclusivity, she proposes that this friendship of love and justice be the new normative paradigm of inclusive relationships. "Some people partner, some join communities, some remain happily single, some change their partnership, repartner, and blend families. All these are ways we know good people live which are quite other than Mr. and Mrs. Forever Amen." This affirmation of inclusivity is in keeping with her feminist persuasion that equality is a critical issue today, and that we have a "need for treating all that is, persons, animals, other aspects of nature, with the same fundamental respect, that is, in the same friendly manner."

Hunt recognizes that there are problems with the friendship metaphor, and the second half of her essay is given to exploring four of them: violence; racial/ethnic considerations; safeguards for the care/nurture of children; the cooptation of lesbian/gay friendships into couples. Her question is whether the new model of friendship can deal creatively with these issues, and her answer is cautiously affirmative, although she notes that the jury is still out on the violence issue, and that "my worst fear of a friendship norm is that it will not stem the tide of violence much more effectively than the marriage norm has." But she finally concludes that this new ethic of friendship "cannot be worse than what currently prevails, and . . . it probably will be a great deal better. . . ."

Gilbert Meilaender's concern for friendship between men and women pits Aristotle against a modern movie: "When Harry and Sally Read the *Nicomachean Ethics*." Harry argues that men can't be friends with women because "the sex part always gets in the way." Aristotle tends to agree with Harry, even though he recognizes that there can be a kind of friendship between husband and wife. For Aristotle, however, it is a friendship between unequals. Parekh finds inequality normative for classical Indian views of friendship, but the Western tradition, taking its clue from Aristotle, has generally assumed that equality was necessary between true friends. Friendship grounded in love was less than ideal for Aristotle because love is an emotion and volatile, whereas reason provides stability. Meilaender quotes C. S. Lewis on a further difficulty: "Lovers are normally face to face, absorbed in each other; Friends, side by side, absorbed in some common interest."

Meilaender takes issue with Mary Hunt's view that the difficulties facing friendship between men and women are due to economic, political, psychological, and social factors, rather than the possibility of erotic attachment. And he finally concludes that marriage can provide the balance and sanity which is the model of true friendship. Here he takes a position precisely opposite to Hunt's, and close to the "creative friendship" which Eliot Deutsch espoused at the outset. He concludes with a quote from Ben Sira: "A friend or companion is always welcome, but better still to be husband and wife."

We conclude with Michael Pakaluk's reflections on "Political Friendship." What one might call civic fraternity is clearly significant for the health of the body politic, and Pakaluk begins with the bemused observation that the issue scarcely arises in the writings of the founding fathers, even though they had a good deal to say about equality. Pakaluk's thesis is that the conventional explanation of this phenomenon—that classic political thought emphasizes virtue, whereas modern thought speaks of rights—is misguided. He argues that "political friendship, as it was conceived in classical theory, has in fact been characteristic of the American republic."

Much of his essay is concerned with a reinterpretation of Aristotle who, by this time, has become the patron saint of this volume. His concluding section on political friendship in the American republic interprets Aristotle as a resource for a coherent nation made up of different ethnic groups. This is possible because Pakaluk's Aristotle does not require a common understanding of virtue. Further, the American Declaration of Independence interprets American society as a model for the universal society of all human beings. "Can the bond which links citizen to citizen be reasonably interpreted as the universal love of humankind, or *philanthropia*, as given a concrete embodiment at this place and in this time?" He concludes, however, that political friendship is weak, and finds the reason in Aristotle's argument that political friendship is derived from friendship within the community's households. Whereas Hunt criticizes the dominance of the heterosexual family and hopes for acceptance of new and varied households, Pakaluk suspects that this kind of diversification is a threat to political stability.

Most of our authors are agreed that friendship must take place among equals, that it is more than mere friendliness, and different from the intimacies of sexual love. And most seem open to the idea that a friend is not only one who shares common goals, but one who, by being different from oneself, provides a window on a new world. That last aspect of friendship is particularly important to the Institute, since the purpose of this series is to inaugurate conversation on critical issues of common human concern. That conversation sometimes celebrates those intellectual and spiritual goods we have in common. At its most significant, however, it opens each of us, as conversational friends, to things in the other which we had not known, and hence could not value. So we present these essays in that spirit of friendship with our readers.

PART I

Philosophies of Friendship

On Creative Friendship

ELIOT DEUTSCH

And can he who is not loved be a friend?
Certainly not.

Plato, *Lysis*

EPICURUS, THE ANCIENT EPICUREAN philosopher, announces that "friendship goes dancing round the world proclaiming to us all to awake to the praises of a happy life."[1]

And even Saint Augustine, who subsequently worries about the anxieties that friendship gives rise to, states that "in our present wretched condition we frequently mistake a friend for an enemy, and an enemy for a friend. And if we escape this pitiable blindness, is not the unfeigned confidence and mutual love of true and good friends our one solace in human society, filled as it is with misunderstandings and calamities?"[2]

Friendship is among the most cherished of human goods. Yet how neglected a topic it is in philosophy. It does not even appear as an entry in the eight-volume *Encyclopedia of Philosophy*[3] or in any of the standard dictionaries of philosophy. The reason for this paucity of philosophical analysis is not entirely clear, but it seems to rest on a certain aversion in modern ethical theory to deal with particular relationships, and especially those that appear to have partiality built into them. Lawrence Blum noted that "friendship is a largely unfamiliar territory for modern moral philosophy, dominated as it has been by Kantian concerns or with utilitarianism, neither of which is hospitable to particular relationships which are both personally and morally significant."[4]

I shall want to question later the very notion that friendship necessarily involves exclusivity and hence partiality. For now, though, I think it is sufficient to note that today, from many different philo-

15

sophical sources and directions (for example, the virtue-oriented ethics of philosophers such as Alasdair MacIntyre and the "other voices" of morality set forth by many feminist thinkers) there does seem to be a growing awareness of the importance—indeed maybe even the centrality—of particularized relationships for ethics or moral philosophy. In any event, as Epicurus also observed: "Of all the things which wisdom requires us to produce for the blessedness of the complete life, far the greatest is the possession of friendship."[5] And surely *wisdom* still has something to do with what we understand *philosophy* to mean today.

Before undertaking a substantive analysis of the nature and possibilities of friendship, one important question needs to be asked. Is friendship a *universal* phenomenon or is it inherently *culture-specific*? If the latter is the case we might very well have a situation where certain conceptual schemes and/or forms of social organization could render the very notion of friendship unintelligible in principle and nonexistent in practice. In short, perhaps friendship does not "dance round the world," after all.

It is quite clear that different societies exhibit friendship in varying ways and determine in actuality who can be friends with whom. Confucius urged us to "have no friends who are not as good as yourself";[6] in dharmic-based societies such as we find in traditional India, on the other hand, where *varna*, class/caste structures, are pervasive, friendship can ordinarily be realized only among members of the same *varna*, for it is only there that certain necessary modalities of equality may obtain. If X regards Y as inherently inferior, an ideal friendship between them would be well-nigh impossible. But this does not answer the question regarding the cultural specificity of the very idea of friendship. If empirically we were to find it absent in a particular society, say, a so-called "primitive" tribe, we would no doubt be tempted to argue that the members of such a society simply have failed to develop to the full status of human beings. Philosophically, we do tend to assume the universality of the phenomenon. I ask, but I do not know how to answer, whether or not we are justified in doing so.

This does suggest to me, though, that under any circumstances we need to understand friendship within a larger context of interpersonal relationships, and that one other question needs first to be raised. The question is whether friendship is confined to a human order of experience or whether there are other inter-species forms, and indeed intra-species modes, of friendship, for example, between human beings and other animals. Our animal fables are replete with examples of this, and some people indeed refer to dogs as "man's best friend." But is this only the work of imagination, talk that is essentially metaphorical, since animals lack the kind of conscious selectivity and mutuality friendship supposedly demands? I do not know the answer; but we ought not simply assume in advance a privileged position for ourselves between ourselves regarding the possibilities of friendship.

Within the human order, however, it is clear that friendship has its place along a continuum of interpersonal relations. The continuum—with many possible refinements and further divisions—would look something like this. At one end there is *enmity* between persons, grounded on the assumption that someone is bent on doing harm to another, which attitude is reciprocated. Next is *unfriendliness*, where one disapproves of, and/or feels potentially threatened by, another. Then comes *indifference*, where one simply doesn't take notice of another with regard to possibilities of close relationship, and hence not to be confused with callous disregard. Shifting to the "positive," there is *friendliness*, the expression of approval of the other together with a general concern for their welfare, followed finally by *intimacy*, the relationship that in the most intense way lovingly binds one erotically to another, located at the other end of the continuum. *Friendship*, I should think most of us would allow, comes between *friendliness* and *intimacy* but has as well certain qualities and characteristics that we associate with them. Let us look then at the general conditions of friendship as are suggested by those qualities and characteristics.

I

First and foremost among the conditions for friendship is some measure of personal autonomy. I shall give a special reading of this concept later as it becomes a primary feature of what I will call "creative friendship," but, as a condition for friendship in general, autonomy is usually conceived as having essentially to do with self-control, or moral self-governance, or independence, or authentic self-making—with various combinations of these possible. Historically we have had many different conceptions of what it means to be autonomous, although they do share certain basic features.

For the Platonic Greek, an autonomous person was one who, through the exercise of reason, achieved a balanced integration of the disparate and contending elements in his or her nature and was thus able to act with integrity. No matter what one's social status or position was, the autonomous person was *self-controlled* and, especially for the Aristotelian Greek (with the exception of a slave and sometimes of a woman) was thus able to engage others in a community as an active participant or "citizen." To be autonomous meant then to have realized the proper human end, a rational happiness grounded in virtue.

Kant, on the other hand, conceived of autonomy as essentially the independence of rationality in morals, where, with the supreme principle of duty, reason becomes the law-giver to itself. To be autonomous meant to be *self-legislating*, allowing nothing external — civil authority, God, tradition — to determine one's will. Reason alone has the burden of imposing constraints on oneself and enabling one to act in accord with its demands. Autonomy, for Kant, has nothing to do with the rights and responsibilities of citizenship or of free choice as such.

Ever since the Enlightenment and the development of liberal thinking about human nature and society, autonomy came to be associated with free choice and individual rights. Free choice is the ability to act according to one's own interests and desires without external constraint, but with respect for the interests and desires of others. Individual rights in relation to the state have led to the popular ideas of the autonomous person as being *self-sufficient*, independent, self-reliant. I am autonomous when I am able to act properly in terms of what I perceive to be my own interests and duties.

The Hegelian and later Marxian sense of autonomy had, on the contrary, to do with identifying one's individual interests with a larger collective society. For Marx especially this meant fulfillment by means of the free expression of one's powers of action, liberated from alienation and exploitation. One is autonomous when one realizes fully one's participation in a larger community of freely constituted persons.

Standing against all rationalistic notions of personal autonomy, Nietzsche's Romanticism thought that genuine autonomy was to be had only by the exceptional person who, through willfulness and *self-mastery*, could shape himself in ways that overcame an otherwise oppressive finitude. It is thus the creative genius, the *übermensch*, who is alone the true law-giver to himself and thus truly self-governing. The rest of us can aspire to autonomy only to lesser degrees.

Now what seems to be characteristic of these differing, and by no means exhaustive, conceptions of autonomy in Western thought is first of all a view of the self as essentially nonsocial. It is certainly the case that for some views a person is said to come to full realization as a person only as she enters into community with others; but that very language still betrays the assumption of an existing self who is otherwise definable apart from others. *Independence*, then, whether as a given or an achievement, becomes part and parcel of the meaning of *autonomy*. Whatever else she may be, the autonomous person is free to and for herself.

Another common feature of traditional views of autonomy has to do with "power" — the ability to effectuate change, to acquire some degree of mastery over one's own life and, not infrequently, to exercise some measure of control over others. The autonomous person is necessarily active — "in control," as we say — the extent of the autonomy being measured by the degree of the control.

Lastly, all traditional Western conceptions of autonomy involve, in varying degrees, one's having the freedom to act in conformity with some guiding principle which one takes as one's own. Self-determination, in one form or another, is the benchmark of autonomy.

And it is, we believe, only an autonomous person who is able to establish his or her own sense of self-worth and dignity and thus able to enter into a close relationship with another. In short, it is only an autonomous person and not an individual conditioned product or one in severe psychic disarray who can have friends.

Another condition for the attainment of friendship, we believe, has to do with an openness or availability of the autonomous person. If we were to ask what kinds of persons are congenitally incapable of friendship, we might well answer, the sociopath and the sage. By definition, the sociopath closes himself off into a narrow isolation and becomes so entirely bound up with his little self that he is incapable of relating closely to the others that he recognizes. Everyone is potentially threatening to him. The sage, on the other hand, at least as conceived in traditional Indian terms — and perhaps the saint as well, as often conceived in Western terms — simply stands in a completeness without need of others. For her, there is no genuine "other" to whom she may relate. Her entire being is absorbed by her relation to a higher spiritual reality or divine being.

Friendship, then, is for those who are somewhere between the extremes of antisocial and, if I may use the expression, postsocial behavior—a place that would be dear to Aristotle, to whom we shall shortly turn.

And yet another condition for the attainment of friendship, and one that is closely related to autonomy, as it might pose a direct threat to it, has to do with self-deception. The Stoic philosopher Epictetus asks: "Do you think a man can be a friend to anything about which he is deceived?"[7] Today, we might want to go further and say that a person who is fundamentally deceived about himself in a rather thoroughgoing and intense fashion is, in the context of interpersonal relations, incapable of genuine friendship. Having a strong measure of non-self-deception is a requirement for friendship.

Now self-deception is an extremely complex phenomenon consisting of many different kinds and forms which exhibit themselves in varying degrees of intensity, and it has been analyzed philosophically and psychologically in a rich variety of ways. If we follow Herbert Fingarette in his seminal work on the subject,[8] the phenomenon of self-deception can be nicely understood within the framework of personal identity as the refusal of someone to avow or to acknowledge some aspect of one's self and one's activity in the world. The reason for this refusal is that such an acknowledgement would be, so the self-deceiver believes, unbearable in disrupting one's established beliefs and values. Self-deception becomes, then, a systematic and persistent refusal to "spell out" one's situation and to take responsibility for it.

One is very much inclined to keep one's distance from someone who announces how kind, caring, and loving a person she is while all the time exhibiting behavior exactly contrary to those qualities. One does not know what it would mean to *trust* such a person—and trust is surely an essential condition for genuine friendship.

Lastly, another condition for friendship, which we will take up again later as it becomes a pronounced feature of creative friendship, is the tacit commitment that the parties to friendship must make to the ideal of nondominance. Although there might indeed be some disparity between the relative power positions friends have within a larger social/political context, dominance as such can have no place in friendship. To dominate means precisely to subvert the other of his or her own claim to autonomy. It is, as the saying goes, to "objectify" the other as a means to one's own ends. One doesn't make friends with mere objects.

This, then, brings us to Aristotle and what he and others often identify to be the various kinds of friendship. Aristotle can, I think, point us in the direction of that other possibility which I call creative friendship.

II

In his *Nicomachean Ethics*, Aristotle distinguishes three forms or kinds of friendship where the qualities of friendliness, the mutual recognition of "bearing goodwill and wishing well to each other," obtains (1155b30).[9] These are (1) friendships of *utility* (the relationship "in virtue of some good which they get from each other" [1156a11]); and (2) friendships of *pleasure* ("it is not for their character that men like ready-witted people, but because they find them pleasant" [1156a14]). Friendships of utility and pleasure are "easily dissolved" (1156a21) and are essentially egocentric: "Those who love for the sake of utility love for the sake of what is good for *themselves*, and those who love for the sake of pleasure do so for the sake of what is pleasant to *themselves*, and not so far as the other is the person loved but in so far as he is useful or pleasant" (1156a17). (3) The last form of friendship is friendships of the *good* (the "perfect friendship" of those who wish well to each other for their own sake). Friendships of this kind are "infrequent; for such men are rare" (1156b8).

Friendships of the good require, then, "men who are good, and alike in virtue" and "their friendship lasts as long as they are good— and goodness is an enduring thing" (1156b2). This highest form of friendship, then, takes up as well "utility" and "pleasure" into itself, "for the good are both good without qualification and useful to each other. So too they are pleasant . . . " (1156a2). Aristotle goes on to note that

> for the sake of pleasure or utility, then, even bad men may be friends of each other, or good men of bad, or one who is neither good nor bad may be a friend to any sort of person; but for their own sake clearly only good men may become friends; for bad men do not delight in each other unless some advantage come of the relation. (1157a17)

And he asserts then the partiality and exclusivity of friendship of the "perfect type":

> One cannot be a friend to many people in the sense of having friendship of the perfect type with them, just as one cannot be in love with many people at once (for love is a sort of excess of feeling, and it is the nature of such only to be felt towards one person). (1158a12)

Aristotle is keenly aware of the various ways in which friendships develop during the different "stages of life," noting that "between sour and elderly people friendship arises less readily, in as much as they are less good-tempered and enjoy companionship less"; and as for the young who "live under the guidance of emotion, and pursue above all what is pleasant to themselves and what is immediately before them . . . they quickly become friends and quickly cease to be so, their friendship changes with the object that is found pleasant, and such pleasures alter quickly" (1156a30).

We might observe in passing that today we would probably characterize the different forms and contents of friendship relative to the stages of life in somewhat different terms. Young people, especially adolescents, need friends rather desperately in order to achieve their own identity and sense of self-worth. They consequently often establish intense commitments based on strong needs. These, however, often turn out to be very precarious indeed. Middle-aged persons, bent on achieving various career goals and the like, often establish friendships basically in terms of common interests. These relationships are often largely alliances, and thus, in their own way, become equally precarious. Older persons, albeit not the sour and elderly undesirous of companionship, are perhaps best equipped to have "perfect friends" insofar as they have a better, more realistic understanding of the nature and demands of friendship than the young and are not as driven by goal achievements as the middle-aged.

In any event, our primary philosophical concern is with "friendships of the good," and I would like to argue that the highest form of this higher form is what I call "creative friendship." Let me try to spell out what I see as its distinctive features and suggest that it may achieve its highest expression in, surprisingly enough, relations between women and men.

III

In our brief survey of *autonomy* I suggested that a somewhat different reading of the concept was necessary for what I call "creative friendship"—a friendship that is inherently spiritual in character in virtue of its being grounded in a kind of ritual play. Autonomy, as I understand it, does not involve in any way a static, lonely independence; rather it involves precisely the full recognition of others and the ability to establish relationships wherein one strives to bring the other with whom one is in relationship to his or her own freedom and appropriate autonomy. The autonomous person is one who recognizes various dependencies—social, economic, cultural—and transforms those dependencies into care-filled relationships where one's own autonomy is seen to be realized only as one promotes as well the autonomy of others. The autonomy necessary for creative friendship, in short, is inherently interpersonal.[10]

And with this openness and concern there comes a special intense type of responsibility. Friendship implies obligation, not in some rationalist moralistic way but as a spontaneous expression of that very caring and concern which is essential to autonomy.[11] In creative friendship my actions are always completely my own just insofar as I freely acknowledge the relationship as my own. With friendship one makes a commitment, tacit to be sure, to identify with the friend's welfare and at the same time to assure that one's own integrity will not only be preserved but enhanced in and through that relationship. If this were not the case one might be inclined simply to turn oneself over to the other and would suffer just that sort of subjugation that has characterized all too much of human (especially women's) experience. Without the deepest sort of responsibility to other and to self we do not have creative friendship but subservience.

Traditional accounts of creativity—the concept to which we now turn—both in the East and the West have been grounded in various cosmogonic speculations with creation *ex nihilo* being perhaps paradigmatic in Western theistic and later scientific thought, with various Neoplatonic emanational models being at best a leitmotif. Characteristic of these accounts and speculations has been the notion of a *separation* obtaining between creator and thing created and a subsequent *distance* between them—indeed, as existentialists were fond of noting, an *estrangement* of the one from the other. This in turn has given rise to a whole set of attitudes and beliefs, among which are those of *dominion* or *mastery over, exploitation,* and *ownership.*

When creation is regarded as a kind of "big bang" (whether theistically or scientifically understood) and human, especially artistic, creativity as an exuberant expression of individual genius, there is the natural tendency to assume creativity to be a kind of mastery over a medium or situation, a controlling of it for one's own end or purpose. For the Greeks in general creativity was understood as a making or shaping, a *techne,* a bringing to completion of what was latent therein, such as Aristotle's example of a statue as residing *in potentia* in the raw stone. In short, creativity meant a successful *exploitation* of the possibilities of a medium or situation. To exploit means "to take advantage of" (which is not always meant in only a pejorative sense) and "to assert one's superiority" (which probably ought always to be used pejoratively). One does not, in any event, then see the product of one's creativity as a literal extension of oneself. It becomes an alien object in public space. A work of art today may rightfully be owned by another, bought and sold, exchanged and even, within some legal arrangements, destroyed.

Now this does not by any means tell the whole story of what creativity has come to mean, and I have stressed certain features for purposes of drawing several contrasts, which can no doubt be readily anticipated. Nevertheless within the general structures of "modernity" these features seem altogether typical.

An alternative, and more fruitful, conception of creativity—especially as it bears on friendship—would be one that emphasized the *mutuality* that obtains between creator and created wherein each is conditioned by the relationship. One is changed in the process of creativity just as a work itself is as it comes into being. Creativity, when it is successful, is skillful, but does not demand a coercive control over some recalcitrant materiality. Rather it calls for a cooperative working with it, a celebration of its integrity. Creativity thus necessarily involves a deep care and concern for the rightness of that which is created, a nurturing of its value for its own sake. It issues then not so much in *ownership* as in *custodianship.* That which is created belongs to one only through one's obligation for care, for honoring its own being, and for striving to bring it into the fullness of its own integrity.[12]

Extending this idea of creativity to that of "making friends," it is clear that this "making" needs to be a kind of ritual play—a *participation* of the friends in a relationship that acquires a life and integrity of its own. And so a third party, as it were, is always present in creative friendship—a *presence* which the friends tacitly support and indeed bring forth in their own togetherness. Creative friendship is the creating of a power for its own sake, the exercising of a nondominant will to enhance the dignity of the other, the establishing of community.

Nondominance is a key factor here, for just as in all forms of ritual, where the parties to it each contribute in their own special way, in creative friendship equality arises by the giving of each friend fully to the relationship, however otherwise unequal they might appear to be. In other words, a full mutuality obtains no matter how different the participatory roles of the persons involved. The relationship endures without the dominance or subordination of either party; indeed it endures precisely because these features are overcome in and through the intrinsic power of the performance.

Creative friendship thus becomes a kind of *play* — an activity that is carried out for its own sake without regard for personal benefit. It is a performance which extends potentially to all who may encounter it. *Partiality* and *exclusivity* thus do not obtain in creative friendship in virtue of the availability of the friends to anyone who shares and celebrates the very idea of that relationship. In contradistinction to Aristotle, with his exclusive "perfect friends," where creative friendship obtains there is a natural extension of care, concern, indeed love, to anyone else capable of achieving it. In short, when creative friendship obtains, one is naturally disposed to have many friends.

This leads to one last consideration which may be put in the form of a question: Why is it that creative friendship is assumed to be so difficult to attain between men and women? The usual answer involves the demands of the sexual and the implicit threat of dominance which, through socialization, so often informs the relationships between men and women.

I will leave aside the sexual, having offered some reflections on that theme in this series a few years ago,[13] and note only that the socialization of both men and women regarding dominance clearly runs directly counter to that special form of autonomy that is necessary for creative friendship. But socialization can be altered, and I would want to take the matter a step further by suggesting that ideally the richest possible creative friendship might very well be had between a man and a woman where each did attain the appropriate autonomy. It would be the "richest" because, while both being human the *sameness* between them would be secure, all the *differences* in their respective experience could find a place within the creative play, the ritual of community. The challenge to remain creative, to be a participant in the relationship in ever original and striking ways, appreciative at all times of the possibilities for mutuality, would be ever-present, for something new would always be made evident in the openness given by and expressed from one to the other. Instead of instancing that perennial battle of the sexes we could have, in the relationship between a man and a woman, a paradigm for creative friendship. Aristotle thought that his model of "friendships of the good" were infrequent because of the lack of good men; had he included women he might have given witness to other possibilities—or at least he would have extended the range of possible participants.

Friendship is an elusive phenomenon, for both theoretical understanding and actual achievement. I began with an observation by Epicurus, and so let me end with one by him as well. He writes: "All friendship is desirable in itself, though it starts from the need of help";[14] and: "It is not so much our friends' help that helps us as the confidence of their help."[15]

With that bit of wisdom I thank my readers—and especially my very good friend Lee Rouner—for enabling me to better understand the potentialities of friendship.

NOTES

1. Epicurus *Vatican Collection* 52.
2. Augustine *City of God*, bk. 19.
3. Paul Edwards, ed., *Encyclopedia of Philosophy*, 8 vols. (New York: Macmillan and the Free Press, 1967).
4. Lawrence A. Blum, *Friendship, Altruism, and Morality* (London: Routledge & Kegan Paul, 1980), p. 67.
5. Epicurus *Principal Doctrines* 27.
6. *Analects* (trans. Wing-tsit Chan) 1.8.
7. Epictetus *Discourses*, bk. 2, chap. 22.

8. See Herbert Fingarette, *Self-Deception* (New York: Humanities Press, 1969).

9. As W. D. Ross, whose translations of Aristotle I use here, points out, though, "it must be remembered that the Greek word [for friendship] has a wider meaning than the English; it can stand for any mutual attraction between two human beings." See W. D. Ross, *Aristotle* (New York: Meridian Books, 1959), p. 223.

10. Allowing—indeed actively promoting—another person to be most fully their own "true self" is, I would say, the signal mark of genuine friendship. All too often one is depersonalized in the company of others in such a way that one is unable to respond to others as one knows oneself most sincerely to be. And, as social psychologists are fond of pointing out, there is a strong tendency for people to become their responses to others.

11. Much discussion about friendship gets centered on the question of what duties are morally required by the relationship. The answer, I think, ought to be "none"—insofar as "duties" and "requirements" go exactly contrary to the spontaneity that necessarily informs creative friendship. One can be disappointed by one's friend's behavior toward one, even feel betrayed by that behavior. Yet the disappointment or betrayal is not a result of some universalist moral imperative of what constitutes right behavior, but is simply due to the fact that spontaneity, which rightly addresses the particularity of the situation, was lacking.

12. I have developed this account of creativity more fully in my *Creative Being: The Crafting of Person and World* (Honolulu: University of Hawaii Press, 1992).

13. See my "Community as Ritual Participation," in *On Community*, ed. Leroy S. Rouner (Notre Dame, Ind.: University of Notre Dame Press, 1991).

14. Epicurus *Vatican Collection* 23.

15. Ibid., 34.

Open Friendship: Aristotelian and Christian Concepts of Friendship

JÜRGEN MOLTMANN

I. "SOMEONE WHO LIKES YOU"

THERE IS A CHARMING CHILDREN'S poem that also speaks to grownups. It was written by Joan Walsh Anglund, and the title of the poem and the book in which it appears is *A Friend Is Someone Who Likes You*.[1]

This poem about friendship speaks peacefully and impressively because it speaks about something that is there, surrounding everyone on all sides. It does not have to be produced; it can not be possessed; rather it waits to be discovered. The poem is about a boy, a girl, a cat, the wind, a tree, and a brook. Friendship is there in the smile of someone walking past, in the play of the wind, and in the rushing of the brook. It demands nothing from you. It likes you, whether you feel like talking now or saying nothing, whether you want to be by yourself or with someone. It is this open friendship that holds the world together. It is a delicate atmosphere. You can live in it and not notice it at all. You can live in it and spoil it continually: bringing up boys and girls, chasing away cats and mice, taking apples and pears to market, and regulating brooks. Then all you hear is the din of your own thoughts and your own machines, and you no longer find anyone who likes you or whom you can like.

The words come out of a children's book and yet express what "appears" to every grownup "in childhood, but where no one has really ever been." Ernst Bloch called it "home of identity."[2] It is the world of friendship, a friendlier world. As children we were conscious of this world. But the more grown up we become, the narrower becomes our

29

circle of friends. And there come enemies. There are competitors in the struggle for scholastic accomplishments, jobs, and careers; there are rivals in love and disappointed trust. And so we grow to be more particular about our friends, more wary with our enemies, and more unconcerned about animals, brooks, and the wind. We make friendships quickly in youth; with age it becomes more difficult, until we stop. We attach ourselves more infrequently, because we no longer open our hearts. And for all that, the radiance of childhood's friendly world remains in the grownup as a flicker of yearning, making one dissatisfied with one's unfriendly environment of jobs and functions, of roles and role expectations. So we ask, what is friendship?

Friendship is an unpretentious relation, for *friend* is not a designation of office, nor a title, nor a function one must perform from time to time, nor a role one is supposed to play in society. Friendship is a personal relation, "someone who likes you," someone you like. According to Immanuel Kant, friendship combines two things: affection and respect.[3] Friendship is more than what we otherwise call love, *eros*, or charity. "Mr. Keuner preferred City B to City A," we read in Brecht's *Calendar Stories*. "In City A they loved me, but in City B they were friendly to me. In City A they made themselves useful to me, but in City B they needed me. In City A they invited me to the dinner table, but in City B they invited me into the kitchen."[4] To combine affection with respect does not mean wanting to serve or be useful to the other person, but needing the other just as he or she is; not just at the dinner table, but in the kitchen as well.

But friendship also combines respect with affection. You may be a respected personality, enjoy awe and admiration, and still find no one "who likes you." One does not have to submit to a friend. One neither looks up to nor down at a friend. One can look a friend in the face. In friendship one experiences oneself, just as one is, readily accepted and respected in one's own freedom. When one person likes another, then the one respects the other in his or her individuality, and delights in his or her singularities as well.

Friendship is no passing feeling of affection. It combines affection with faithfulness. You can rely upon a friend. As a friend you become someone upon whom others can depend. A friend remains a friend even in misfortune, even in guilt. For between friends there rules no prejudice that defines one, and no ideal image after which one must strive. Nor is friendship an alliance for mutual advantage, as is the case with so-called business friends. Between friends there rules only the promise to walk with each other and to be there for each other; in other words, a faithfulness that has to do not with acting and possessing but with the individual person and with being.

Friendship is therefore a deep human relation that arises out of freedom, consists in mutual freedom, and preserves this freedom. It cannot be the indifferent middle-class liberality that understands nothing and excuses everything in order to have peace. We are not by nature free, but become so only when someone likes us. Friends open up to one another free space for free life. Friends are not free without each other, but only with each other. Of course that also involves being able to leave each other in peace, like a brook that lets you be in its presence, without speaking when you don't want to.

Hegel called friendship "the concrete concept of freedom,"[5] because between friends the law of reciprocity is invalidated. One trusts a friend; one confides in a friend. When necessary, one helps, without reward, but also without intruding oneself. After all, the "good turns" are not "services." We need friends, but not just in times of need; we need friends above all for the sake of joy in life. We want to communicate our joy in being and to share our happy experiences with others. Sharing in another's joy without self-interest and without envy is a good turn that cannot be regarded highly enough. Shared rejoicing creates friendship. Shared suffering follows from it, so that we say: "true friendship proves itself in misfortune." It proves itself there. But it does not originate there. And it proves itself to be simple friendship, not charitable, condescending help.

Because friendship can only exist without outward coercion and without inward constraint, it is lasting, and its gentle power is victorious over the violent power of enmity, which never has time. In enmity we freeze, inwardly and outwardly; in friendship we open ourselves and come alive. "Truly, what is rigid and unbending is the companion of death, while the soft and weak is the companion of life," says the *Tao te Ching* rightly (chap. 76); and this is true of enmity and friendship too. Because friendship is aligned towards permanence, it is ultimately stronger than enmity, which never has time.

In the long run, the future of the world will belong to open friendship. We experience this in personal relationships too. When in the family the relationship of parent to child comes to an end (because parental responsibility is finished, and the children have become

independent), friendship remains. When in society professional relationships have ceased and people meet one another simply as
people, and no longer in their social roles, then friendship can develop. When men and women overcome the privileges and slights of
a patriarchal culture, then there can be friendship between them. The
new human being, the true human being, the free human being is the
person who likes to be with other people: the friend.

Can there only be friendship between people who are alike? Is
friendship exclusive? Aristotle says that the foundation of a shared
life is *philia*.[6] *Philia* presupposes identity of nature or community of
interest. "Birds of a feather flock together," because "like draws to
like." Only what is lovable can be the object of love, and what counts
as lovable is whatever is valuable, pleasurable, or useful. This kind of
love leads to friendship only where love can be returned, and that is
impossible in the case of lifeless objects. Consequently there can only
be friendship between living things. Where utility is the motive for
friendship, people do not love each other for their own sake, but because of their mutual usefulness. Where pleasure is the aim, people
love each other for the sake of the pleasure they give to one another.
Perfect friendship is only possible where people who are alike by
nature love one another for what they are. People who are different
can become friendly for utilitarian purposes or for pleasure; but
when it is a matter of mutual esteem, only people who are alike can
be friends: freemen with freemen, slaves with slaves, Greeks with
Greeks, barbarians with barbarians, men with men, women with
women, and so forth. It is true that there are "darlings of gods," says
Aristotle, but no human being can seriously say that he loves Zeus. So
friendship in this sense means the exclusive friendship of people who
are the same: *philia*.

We find the opposite picture of friendship in the New Testament: open friendship with people who are different.

II. THE FRIENDSHIP OF JESUS

The titles employed by the Christian congregation to describe
the significance of Jesus are commonly called titles of dignity, and believers conceive of his work in terms of his divine "office." In the Old

Testament, God's will for the nation was carried out by prophets, priests, and kings. In the same way, Christ carries out his work in God's name in the congregation as a prophet who reveals the will of God, as a priest who represents the sacrifice of reconciliation, and as a king who rules his nation. Clothed in these titles of dignity, Jesus appears to the congregation with divine authority. The titles describe his uniqueness, but they also create a distance between him and his congregation, a distance that grows still wider through a piety which reveres and worships Christ and humbles itself beneath his authority.

One could say critically that all these titles come out of an authoritarian society, and that transferring symbols of state onto Christ serves only to further intensify this domination. What do images like the King of Kings, the Lord of Lords, the superstar say today in a society that, though familiar with presidents and chairpersons, hardly has a place any more for prophets, kings, and priests? Will not Christ's exalted titles serve only to justify worldly rulers in the political misery that they effect?

This is an easy criticism to make because it misses the point. Who is it who has been called the prophet of God? Who but the derided Son of Man from Nazareth, "a carpenter's son"? If he is the prophet of God, then there is an end to every pretentious prophetic posture! Who has been called the priest of God? It is the One whom the powerful sacrificed in crucifixion on Golgotha; if this sacrifice is "the priest," then who is "Reverend"? Finally, if the powerless man on the cross has all God's power, then the crowns of the mighty ones must surely lose their halos. Thus the application of the most dignified, exalted titles this society has to the crucified Son of Man from Nazareth harbors an unprecedented social-critical potential. "What the state intended to be disgrace (namely, the cross) is changed to the ideal," according to Hegel.[7] Hegel saw therein the paradox of Christian "revolution." Yet even when one understands the paradox and, in view of Christ's passion, recognizes Christ's exaltation in his humbleness, his riches in his poverty, and his omnipotence in his powerless endurance, still the distance remains. Christ stands on God's side, speaks in God's name, dies according to God's will, and rules in God's love. The exalted titles express no more than what Christ does — or suffers — for a person. They do not yet describe the fellowship he brings to men and women, new fellowship with God and with their neighbors. Whether prophet, priest, or king, whether substitute or representative, that new fellowship would be only the function of a transcendent Lord were not another "title" included, which can be no title, the name of friend.

Though in piety this name borders always on *kitsch* — "Jesus is all the world to me, I want no better friend," "What a friend we have in Jesus" — such is not the case in the New Testament. There Jesus is called "friend" in only two places; though often overlooked, these two places are important.

"The Son of man has come eating and drinking; and you say, 'Behold, a glutton and a drunkard, a friend of tax collectors and sinners!'" (Luke 7:34). The name is found in Jesus' speech about John the Baptist. John the Baptist was an ascetic and a preacher of repentance who led a legalistic life. He ate no bread and drank no wine, nourishing himself rather with locusts and wild honey. He was regarded as strange on this account. Then came Jesus. Jesus accepted public sinners — criminals — and was seen "in bad company." He ate and drank with disreputable people. So he was regarded as dishonorable and lawless. That is how the people of the time interpreted and described the striking outward differences between John the Baptist and Jesus. But what about the inner motivations? The inner motivation for Jesus' striking friendship with "sinners and tax collectors" lies in his joy in God, in the future, and in human existence. That is why Jesus celebrates the messianic feast of God's kingdom with them every time he eats and drinks with them. Jesus does not bring a dry sympathy, but an inviting joy in God's kingdom to those who are "reprobates" according to the law. Jesus celebrates the kingdom of God, which he proclaims as present in their midst, in a feast. That is why he refers to the kingdom, on more than one occasion, as the eternal "marriage feast": "Enter into the joy of your master." The respect that Jesus showed the contemptible through his affection, in that he ate and drank with them, is the right of grace, the full power of acquittal. Thus Jesus combines affection with respect. He becomes the friend of sinners and tax collectors because of his joy in their common freedom — God's future.

When "respectable society" calls him a "friend of sinners and tax collectors," however, it wants only to denounce and compromise him. In keeping with the law according to which its ranks are organized, respectable society identifies people with their failings and speaks of sinners; it identifies people with their professions and speaks of tax collectors; it identifies people with their diseases and speaks of lepers and the handicapped. From this society speaks the law, which defines people always by their failings. Jesus, however, as the Son of Man without this inhuman law, becomes the friend of sinful and sick persons. By forgiving their sins he restores to them their respect as men and women; by accepting lepers he makes them well. And thus he becomes their friend in the true sense of the word. The denunciatory, contemptuous name, "friend of sinners and tax collectors," unintentionally expresses the deep truth of Jesus. As friend, he reveals God's friendship to the unlikable, to those who have been treated in such unfriendly fashion. As the Son of Man, he sets their oppressed humanity free. Even in our society, which calls itself "humane" or "free," this kind of human fellowship with the unrighteous and with outcasts always has something compromising about it.

According to John 15, Jesus declares himself to be the friend of his disciples. When he calls them to himself, he calls them into a new life of friendship: "Greater love has no man than this, that a man lay down his life for his friends. You are my friends if you do what I command you." Here the image is not that of a priest bringing sacrifice. Here the sacrifice of one's own life for one's friends is the highest form of love. But love manifests itself here as friendship. When he cites friendship as the motive for Jesus' sacrificing his life, John means a love that sees, that is faithful unto death. He means a knowing sacrifice for the sake of friends' lives. Through Jesus' death in friendship the disciples become friends forever, and they remain in his friendship if they follow his commandments and become friends to others.

Again according to John, Jesus' friendship for his disciples stems from his joy in God and humanity. John reports Jesus as saying shortly before: "These things I have spoken to you, that my joy may be in you, and that your joy may be full." Jesus came from the overflowing joy of God and gives his life up for the joy of the world. After that, therefore, the disciples are no longer called "pupils" or "servants," but "friends." The relation of men and women to God is no longer the dependent, obedient relation of servants to their master. Nor is it anymore the relation of human children to a heavenly Father. In the fellowship of Jesus the disciples become friends of God. In the fellowship of Jesus they no longer experience God as Lord, nor only as Father; rather they experience him in his innermost nature as Friend. For this reason, open friendship becomes the bond in their fellowship with one another, and it is their vocation in a society still dominated by masters and servants, fathers and children, teachers and pupils, superiors and subordinates.

III. FRIENDS OF GOD

Knowledgeable persons hearing the words "friend of God" may think of the "Friends of God from Niederrhein," the fourteenth-century mystics. But the expression has a long history behind it. It dates back, as Erik Peterson has shown,[8] to the circle around Socrates. The truly wise are "friends of the gods" and experience the gods' friendship even if the world around them is hostile toward them. The epitaphs of exceptional men in Greece and Egypt were often ornamented with this title. Friends of the gods are "favorites of the gods." Perhaps something of that remains with us today in such expressions as "Sunday's child" or "born under a lucky star," or when we say a genius is inspired by the muses. Sober-minded Aristotle flatly refused the expression, however. According to his *Nicomachean Ethics*, friendship—*philia*—essentially unites only peers, for a friendship can be made only in reciprocity. Therefore, no free man can be the friend of a slave, just as it would be absurd for him to regard himself as the friend of the all-powerful Zeus. Only in a closed circle of peers can there be friendship, for only "birds of a feather flock together."

Hellenic Judaism, however, was familiar with exceptions to this rule. Thus the Greek Old Testament calls Abraham "the friend of God"; Moses is called the same, and according to the Book of Jubilees, every righteous man who keeps the law will be "inscribed on the heavenly tablets as the friend of God." This is echoed in the New Testament when James writes: "Abraham believed God, and it was reckoned to him as righteousness; and he was called the friend of God" (James 2:23). As Abraham has the place of "father of the faithful" in the New Testament, he certainly has the place of leader of the multitude of the "friends of God" as well.

In classical Christianity, then, the expression "friend of God" has had two meanings. First, it was used in a narrow, exclusive sense. Abraham believed the God of the promise, and he went out from his country and lost all that he had; therefore, it is the Christian ascetics, who forsake everything and go out poor, homeless, and solitary, who are the true friends of God. Again, Moses became a friend of the God who "spoke with him face to face" on the mountain; therefore, it is those who pray, who constantly speak with God face to face, who are the true friends of God. Finally, Christ himself gave up his life for his friends; therefore, the Christian martyrs were called the true friends of God. In this narrow and exclusive sense Christians have been regarded as friends of God only under extraordinary circumstances. Indeed, at times Christianity has even been divided into three ranks: the servants of God who are the unawakened believers, the children of God who are the awakened believers, and the friends of God who consistently have faith and follow. But at the same time, a broad, inclusive formulation has always been there too; that is, that through Christ's friendship, all Christians have become friends of God. Where is it that this new, so disrespectfully familiar-sounding relation to God in friendship is revealed?

According to Luke and John, friendship with God manifests itself especially in prayer. In their obedience to the commandments of God, men and women perceive themselves as servants of the Lord God. In their faith in the gospel of God, they see themselves as children of God the Father. But in prayer, they speak to God as a friend. The parable Luke appends to the Lord's Prayer speaks of a quite ordinary request to a friend for bread. Although it is of course inconvenient for the friend due to the lateness of the hour, he complies just the same; because he is a friend he cannot ignore the urgency of the request. Whenever prayer is made in the name of Jesus, God is called upon as friend and importuned in the name of that friendship. Again in John, the disciples' new friendship leads them to the certainty in prayer "that whatever you ask the Father in my name, he may give it to you" (John 15:16).

Request and answer are the two sides of friendship with God. And friendship with God gives prayer the certainty that it will be answered. This can be expressed more simply in the words of Karl Barth: "God listens."[9] There is room enough in God's divine freedom for human freedom. In the world government of God there is the possibility of human impact and participation. In the form of a friend God encounters men and women as the "answering God." He calls them not only to the submissiveness of a servant, and not only to the gratitude of a child, but to the familiarity and boldness of a friend.

After obedience and faith, therefore, prayer must come to be seen as the highest expression of human freedom in God. By bringing before God the sighing and groaning out of the depths of the world, men and women call upon God's friendship for the suffering. And God shows friendship by hearing them. Prayer and answer are what constitute human friendship with God and divine friendship with human beings. It seems to me important to place both the praying and the answering on the plane of friendship. For then it is a relation of mutual affection and of respect for freedom. It would be servile to beg without certainty of answer; that would be respect without affection. It would be childish to try to force an answer with prayer; that would be affection without respect. A friend asks out of affection, but at the same time respects the other's freedom, trusting in God's friendship. Thus prayer is not a servant's desperate begging, nor is it the insistence of a demanding child. Prayer in Christ's name is the language of friendship. And the hearing in Christ's name is hearing by the one "who likes you."

IV. CLOSED AND OPEN FRIENDSHIP

In the notion of Jesus' friendship we find a summary of what the previously used exalted titles had to say with regard to society: as prophet of God's kingdom for the poor, Jesus becomes the friend of sinners and tax collectors; as high priest he sacrifices himself for the life and salvation of others and consummates his love through his death in friendship; as the exalted lord, he liberates men and women from servitude and makes them friends of God. In theological doctrine concerning Christ's threefold office his work has always been described in highly exalted and official terms, concealing his simple friendship in the process. The corresponding official church has therefore always maintained an exalted air as well, becoming in the process a "church without fellowship." When Christ lives and works, however, as prophet of the poor, as sacrifice for the many, and as freedom leader, then he lives and works as friend and brings about friendship. It would be well if the church, church officials, and those taken care of by them finally recalled that together they are no more and no less than a "fellowship of the friends of Jesus." In this regard, however, we must direct a final critical look at the phenomenon of friendship.

The expression *friendship* is of course just as misleading today as the old exalted titles were. Friendship always stands in danger of becoming exclusive. That was already the case with Aristotle. When only "birds of a feather flock together," then there may well be "honor among thieves," but it need be extended no further. It is true that the Greeks eulogized friendship as the central bond of their community. Because justice remains sterile if there is no harmony among the citizens, friendship satisfies the spirit of justice and is itself the most just of all. But it can unite only peers, for it can be made only in reciprocity. Because of this peer and parity principle, the Greek ideal of friendship tended toward exclusivity.

It is not much different in our society today. Every time we come to a social evening, we find people who are alike, who feel, think, and talk the same way. When people different from one another come together, they often split apart: men with men, women with women, young people with young people. We tend toward a closed society. Quite aside from how hurtful it is for those who remain "out in the cold," it is also terribly boring for those "inside": always the same faces, the same stories, the same dull jokes! When Emperor Joseph of Austria wanted to open the Prater as a park for the people of Vienna, the nobility protested; surely he would remain among his own kind. At that, the elderly emperor responded that if that were the case he would have to spend all his remaining days and nights in the Capuchin crypt alone with his dead ancestors.

The closed circle of friendship among peers is broken in principle by Christ, not only in relation to the despised humanity of "bad society," but in relation to God. Had he abided by the peer principle, he would of necessity have had to stay in heaven. But his incarnation and his friendship with sinners and tax collectors break through the exclusive circles. For this reason Christian friendship also cannot be lived within a closed circle of the faithful and pious — of peers, in other words — but only in open affection and public respect for others. Through Jesus, friendship has become open. It is forthcoming solidarity.

In the Old High German language friend and enemy were still public terms derived from the protection and mutual assistance pacts.

Friendship was made through pacts and preserved publicly through allegiance. But with the modern separation of the private sphere of life from the public sphere, these terms came to be assigned differently. The enemy—the enemy of the state, the enemy of society, the enemy of the people—has remained a political term, while friendship has shifted into the private sphere and there been internalized. The friend has become a personal friend, an intimate friend, a bosom friend, and friendship has become a matter of feeling. Because the individual becomes increasingly lonely through the separation of public and private life, he or she needs friends. But they do not substantially break through his or her loneliness. They bring only a two-party loneliness. "Blessed is he who, forsaking the world without hate, holds to his bosom a friend, and with his friend delights," wrote Goethe.[10] That is romantic friendship in the seclusion of privacy. Jesus' friendship for his disciples, for sinners, and for tax collectors, does not know the privacy and intimacy of modern friendship. To live in his friendship today requires that the romantic notion of friendship be deprivatized. Friendship must once again receive the character of public protection of and public respect for others. Is that possible? In this world of professions, functions, and businesses, can friendship be publicly lived and proffered?

We have models. The Quakers, for example, have been calling themselves "the Society of Friends" for centuries. Their open social work in the English slums and their political fight for the abolition of slavery in the United States provide exemplary demonstrations of Jesus' open friendship. What would it be like if Christian congregations and communities were no longer to regard themselves only as "the communion of the saints," or as "the congregation of the faithful," but as such a "community of friends"? Then they would have to overcome the much-lamented disconnectedness among churchgoers (ironically termed church visitors in German), and make it possible for a person to feel at home in their community. Then they would have to break through their unconscious and sometimes, unfortunately, also very deliberate exclusivity with respect to the "evil world" and "unbelievers"—and be ready for friendship with the friendless. Then they would have to assemble in grass roots communities that would live close to the people and with the people in the friendship of Jesus.

Talk will not bring about this change from dominion to friendship and from closed society to open fellowship, particularly if the talk takes on a threatening tone of morality: that it "has to happen." It does not "have to happen" at all. It happens wherever men and women are seized by joy in God, in people, and in the world. It is not by sympathizing with others but by rejoicing with them that they will be won; and with them will be celebrated the "feast of the earth." We saw how Jesus, out of that joy in God called by the old word *gospel*, became a friend. His celebration was not only the "wedding of the soul with God," as the old hymn has it, but the "feast of heaven and earth," namely, the celebration of that coming kingdom which will restore heaven and earth. This celebration makes friends and brings friendships to light everywhere.

There is a divine and a cosmic friendship which precedes personal friendship and invites us to personal friendship. In an environment viewed as hostile, we can only form exclusive friendships for mutual protection. In a community of creation experienced as friendly, we form open friendships. In open friendships we do not surrender our identity. We expand the relationships in which this identity can be experienced. If we believe in the community of creation in the life-giving Spirit of God, we discover the "sympathy of all things," and make ourselves consciously a part of it.

NOTES

1. Joan Walsh Anglund, *A Friend Is Someone Who Likes You* (New York: Harcourt, Brace & World, 1958).

2. Ernst Bloch, *Das Prinzip Hoffnung* (Frankfurt: Suhrkamp, 1959), p. 1628.

3. Immanuel Kant, "The Metaphysical Principles of Virtue," in *The Metaphysics of Morals*, pt. 2, par. 46f. (Indianapolis: Bobbs-Merrill Co., 1964), pp. 135ff.

4. Bertold Brecht, *Gesammelte Werke*, vol. 12, p. 389.

5. G. F. W. Hegel, *The Philosophy of Right* (Oxford: Clarendon Press, 1952), p. 228.

6. Aristotle *Nicomachean Ethics* 8.3–8.

7. G. F. W. Hegel, *Lectures on the Philosophy of Religion*, vol. 3 (New York: Humanities Press, 1974), pp. 89ff.

8. Erik Peterson, "Der Gottesfreund: Beiträge zur Geschichte eines religiösen Terminus," in ZKG, vol. 42, new ser. 5 (1923): 161–202.

9. Karl Barth, *Church Dogmatics*, 3.3, trans. G. W. Bromiley and R. J. Ehrlich (Edinburgh: T. & T. Clark, 1961), pp. 285–88.

10. Johann Wolfgang von Goethe, *Goethes Werke* (Wiesbaden: Insel-Verlag, 1949–52), vol. l, p. 74.

Friendship with God in al-Ghazali and Aquinas

DAVID B. BURRELL, C.S.C.

IT IS FASCINATING IN OUR TIME to reach back over centuries of mutual disdain to a time in which, from our view, religious intolerance can be contrasted with a quest for understanding on the part of each of the three traditions of "the book" which found their thinkers moving on parallel and often intersecting trajectories. Having explored the more metaphysical issues connected with the relations between the universe and its creator, and more recently between free creatures and the free creator of all, I should like here to reflect on friendship, a theme closer to our hearts and to theirs.[1] More specifically, I wish to explore friendship with God, something deemed impossible by Aristotle, and certainly considered unseemly for Muslims, given the stereotype which has accumulated during the centuries of disdain. Yet I shall try to show not only that friendship with God is rendered possible by the revelation of a free creator in the Bible and Qur'an, but that it delineates a paradigmatic way of free creatures relating to that creator in both Islam and Christianity. After all, the spiritual ancestor of both, Abraham, the one whom "God chose for friend" (4:125), "was called 'the friend of God'" (James 2:23).[2]

I. SOME COMMON FACTORS

It is notoriously difficult to speak for traditions so varied as Christianity and Islam, yet it will suffice to show that a thinker given central place in each not only finds room for friendship with God but indeed makes that theme the axial point of his exposition of the relationship between the creator and free creatures. Such an exploration will also allow me to commend the writings of two colleagues and friends, Paul Wadell and Marie-Louise Siauve. Wadell's recent *Friends of God: Virtues and Gifts in Aquinas* is a masterful condensation of a ten-year inquiry, and Marie-Louise Siauve's *L'amour de Dieu chez Gazālī* presents an integrative study of that thinker which complements her translation of his book devoted to "love [*mahabba*], ardent desire [*shawq*], intimacy [*uns*], and perfect contentment [*ridā*]" in his magnum opus, *Ihyā' 'Ulūm ad-Dīn*.[3] I am currently engaged in translating the book preceding this one in the *Ihyā'*, and have found that Siauve's study of the role which love plays in Ghazali's presentation of the relation of creatures to creator can help us reassess his philosophical acumen. And while Aquinas' role as a philosopher may not be in question, the angle of vision and appreciation to which Wadell introduces us can remind us how decidedly theological was his appropriation of Aristotle. Moreover, there is little evidence of "influence" of Ghazali on Aquinas, who was apparently acquainted only with his extended introduction to his celebrated attack on "philosophy" as he knew it (the *Tahāfut al-Falāsifā*). Published separately as the *Maqāsid al-Falāsifā*, this work presented the positions of the Islamic *falāsifā* so fair-mindedly that Western readers like Aquinas mistook Ghazali for one of them.[4]

So we have here a fascinating parallel treatment of two religious thinkers, each concerned to present his respective tradition in a way which underscored its capacity to serve as a more comprehensive vehicle of the creator-creature relationship than the current philosophical syntheses could deliver. Indeed, the perspective was not a merely speculative one for either of them; Aquinas' treatment in the *Summa Theologiae* delineates the manner of creatures' return to their source and origin in the God who freely creates them, while the entire structure of Ghazali's *Ihyā'* reflects his conviction that faithful practice alone confirms and explicates the meaning of what one might manage to state conceptually.

While there is no evidence that Ghazali was directly beholden to Aristotle, as Aquinas was, the philosophic climate in which his thought moved was redolent of both Aristotle and Plato. So it would be best to begin with some reminders from Books 8–9 of the *Nichomachean Ethics*. This is particularly useful for moderns, whose notions of friendship tend to be romantic in character, and who imagine relations to terminate directly in the individuals concerned, as the simplest parsing of "John loves Mary." For Aristotle, by way of contrast, friendship is endemically triadic: if John indeed loves Mary, then they must each be oriented to an overarching (and penetrating) *good*, in which they can both share. And that orientation to the *good* in each of them is what constitutes their proper character, so that he can insist not only that "friendship is a kind of partnership," but that one "stands in the same relation to his friend as to himself" (1172a1). It is this image of the individual as one who is "in relationship" which suggests that a recasting of Aristotle's *Ethics* in the light of these books would yield an ideal quite different from "the magnanimous man" (1124b4). For that one was deemed to be "self-sufficient [and hence in] no need of friends" (1169b5), but when we adjust our view to "happiness as a kind of activity" (1169b32) rather than something which can be attributed to a person, we are prepared to see ourselves as inherently relating beings. The culmination of this turn of argument sees "a friend [as] by nature desirable for a good man" (1170a12). "By nature," we know, is Aristotle's most telling argument; in this case it also seems to be the one which he invokes not quite knowing how to emend his earlier substance anthropology, in which individuals acquired virtues.

Aristotle's remarks in this context on self-love recall the Platonic divisions within the self— "the good man in relation to himself . . . is completely integrated and desires the same things with every part of his soul" (1166a12)—so there is already at work an inwardly relational view of human subjects. Something similar was invoked at the end of Book 5, where he asks whether one can treat oneself unjustly or not; "in a metaphorical and analogical sense there is such a thing as justice not towards oneself but between certain parts of the self [wherein] the rational is contrasted with the irrational part of the soul" (1138b10). What the Bible and Qur'an add to this discussion, however, is the requirement of intentional creatures relating to the source of their very being, their creator. Once God is revealed to be the originating source of all that is, and intentional creatures are invited to respond to the One as the source of their existence, the meaning of *divinity* is substantially altered from Aristotle's use of the term. So while the inequality factor (which made friendship between humans and gods impossible for him [1158b28]) is pushed to infinity, the question of the possibility of friendship is posed anew by the fresh terms used to name the *relata*: creator and creature. Hence Aquinas will state that the very to-be of creatures is to-be-related to the One from which their existence derives: created to-be *is* a relation to its un-created source, to-be itself (cf. ST 1.44–45). While Ghazali does not articulate his metaphysics in so lapidary a fashion, he takes his stand on the implications of Islamic *tawḥīd* ("faith in divine unity"): "There is no activity outside of God, who has brought forth and created all that is . . . without assistance of any sort."[5]

Islamicists will detect echoes of al-Ashʿari in the precise use of *activity* here. We may bracket that complex question for the moment in the interest of comparing these two thinkers and of focusing on their shared legacy from the doctrine of free creation of the universe: human beings, created in the image of the creator, are called upon to live a wholehearted response to the gift of life which they are. For the doctrine of free creation entails that our life *is* gift, not *a* gift which we were somehow around to receive; it is we ourselves who are gift, and so are called upon to return all that we are to the giver. Hence the in-sistence in Islam that the goal of human life consists in the ongoing practical recognition that God is Lord of all, while the elaborate struc-ture of the entire second part of the *Summa Theologiae* of Aquinas is designed to show how we can return our whole selves to the One who is our source. And if Ghazali seems to put the heart first in his anthro-pology, while Aquinas stresses the role of intellect and of understanding, that intellect is ever for Aquinas at the service of this inner imperative of *return*, so the very structure of the *Summa* itself displays what is for him the existential context of human understanding.

But such a requirement to return all that we are to the One from whom we derive could easily seem like total submission, which is also usually offered as a translation of *Islam*. If that is the case, how can either tradition speak of friendship with this creator-God, much less make of it the apogee of the human-divine relationship? Or to return to Aristotle's objection to the very possibility of friendship with divinity, what of the now "infinite qualitative difference" (as Kierkegaard phrased it) between creator and all creatures, including intentional ones? Friendship demands reciprocity, and both of these implications of the doctrine of creation emphatically rule that out. Or so it seems. Yet the same revelation which introduces the arresting assertion of free creation also asserts (in the Qurʾan): "God will bring a people whom He loves and who love Him" (5:54), and "God loves those who turn unto Him" (2:222); while the Hebrew prophets resonate with such language: "I shall betroth you to myself for ever . . . in uprightness and justice, and faithful love [*ḥesed*] and tenderness" (Hos. 2:19), and Jesus himself says to his disciples on the eve of his death: "I shall no longer call you servants; . . . I call you friends" (John 15:15). Moreover, both traditions, biblical and qurʾanic, acknowledge Abraham to have been chosen and called "friend" by God. The implication seems to be that the same initiative which created "the heavens and the earth and all that is between them" can also see to it that we are constituted in a reciprocal relationship with our creator.

The philosophically minded can detect here the impulse to secure a supernatural status for those creatures offered a reciprocal relationship with their creator, for otherwise it would be quite impossible for them to effect a commensurate response. That was indeed Aquinas' strategy, as we shall see, while Ghazali's is less clearly articulated. What remains true for both, however, is that the divine initiative makes reciprocity possible, much as the Hebrew scriptures insist that the covenantal relationship is founded on the gift of Torah. Indeed, it will be illustrative to watch each of our thinkers negotiate this Scylla and Charybdis, for the Hebrew picture seems to structure their discussion, even though covenant itself remains a background notion for each. Aquinas' treatment is cast explicitly in the Aristotelian anthropology, of passions (or desire) and virtues, to which he adds a third level: gifts of the Spirit.[6] Ghazali, at least in the *Ihyāʾ*, relies on the anthropology at work among Sufis, according to which human beings can become increasingly responsive to the providential action of God at work in the world, and through that very response allow the activity of the creator greater and greater sway in their lives, so that they may, in the stage of intimacy with God (*uns*) "act with the very action of God" (AD 263). This latter phrase will characterize human actions in Aquinas' third level, inspired by the gifts of the Spirit, so discrepancy in anthropologies may not entail great differences in description of the stages in this relationship of creatures to creator whose paradigm lies in friendship.

II. AQUINAS' SCHEME:
PASSIONS, VIRTUES, GIFTS OF THE SPIRIT

What is remarkable in reading Aquinas today is the way in which we are able to acknowledge his sources in scripture, underscored in the opening question of the *Summa* and detailed in his commentaries on diverse books of the Old and New Testament. This treasure had been virtually ignored by Thomists, anxious to celebrate their mentor's philosophical acumen. It was also minimized by Aquinas himself in the structure and execution of his best-known *Summa Theologiae*.[7] So we need to see that his use of Aristotle is in the service of explicating Jesus' words in his final discourse to his disciples: "I call you not servants but friends" (John 15:15). Aristotle noted three characteristics of authentic friendship: a wish for the other's well-being, a genuine reciprocity, and a shared good. Moreover, Aristotle's anthropology of passions and virtues offered a serendipitous groundwork for Aquinas' elaboration of the dynamics of human beings' responding to such an invitation. For the hunger of the heart for what is good lies at the basis of what it is to be a human being for Aristotle, inherited from Plato. The more transcendent that good, the more need we have for reason to discern for us the path to take to arrive there, since we are invariably presented with many contenders. This fact introduces choice, while the roots of human freedom lie in the hunger itself.

That hunger of the heart for what is good is evidenced for Aristotle in the passions, which Aquinas adopts wholeheartedly. Wayward as they may be, the passions are the root of all activity for an end in human beings, whose task is to channel them to activity which will carry us to authentic rather than illusory goods. That task is entrusted to reason but executed by the virtues which deliberate actions can develop in us. And the role of virtue is to allow our native passions an expression which permits us to do the right thing in the right way at the right time with an alacrity and spontaneity befitting one whose heart hungers for what is good. Yet since the passions possess a natural order, following that of the constitution of the self imaged in Plato's *Phaedrus*, the virtues will be ordered as well. Temperateness, for example, is at the service of courage, even though in certain situations we may need to call upon courage to assist us in moderating food, drink, or sex. The ease with which we will be able to call upon virtues to assist each other, however, depends on their being properly ordered and so available. Here is where Aquinas sees God's promise of friendship, made effective in and through Jesus' words, offering a fresh focus to Aristotle's insistence that the virtues be ordered. Much as Plato saw justice to consist in the harmony of the three virtues which directed the three parts of the self—prudence, courage, and temperateness—

so Aquinas saw God's love for us evidenced in the promise of friendship, charity, to offer a new ordering for all the other virtues in one whose life would become a wholehearted response to the creator's invitation (ST 2.2.23.8).

This ordering is made possible by a gift which becomes an immanent disposition, as the virtues must be in order to facilitate action as they do. That gift is the theological virtue of charity, which empowers us to respond to Jesus' invitation. It is a created participation in God's love which, orienting us to the source of all existence, thereby orders all our other dispositions to become responses to that same invitation, since "each instance of [its] activity expresses the ruling interest of the will."[8] This account offers a fresh focus to Aristotle's account of character, the complex of virtues available to persons and exhibited in their *characteristic* ways of acting. It also assures that creatures and creator share in the same good, which in this case is the loving activity of the creator. By virtue of that sharing, it allows human creatures to reciprocate by returning that creator's love, thus making friendship possible between such radically disparate beings. So the story usually goes. Yet there is a further step in Aquinas, which completes Aristotle's picture of a friend being present to and indeed shaping the very relation by which one relates to oneself.

That relation, in a Christian trinitarian conception of God, is the Holy Spirit. So the complex of virtues which facilitates our wholehearted response to the creator of all strains towards a kind of "connaturality" with that divine activity, whereby we would be acting by the very activity of God. If we were not created agents to begin with, this final stage would seem to be *ecstatic* in an alienating sense of the term: carrying us out of ourselves so that it was no longer we who act. Yet as created agents, already aware of God as the source of our being, it is to come complete circle to full possession of that being if we allow God to be what God indeed is: the principle of all our activities. If the disposition to love God above all things, which is the created gift of charity, allows us so to relate to God, the gifts of the Holy Spirit indicate how one so related acts. That is, we act as so related and, so related, are thereby present to the very relation by which God relates to God's own self, which is the Holy Spirit.[9]

We cannot shape that uncreated relation, it is true, but so acting can certainly shape our relation to ourselves, disposing us perfectly to fulfill the desires of our friend as the way of becoming more truly who it is we are called to become. In this way, the manner of acting which Aquinas dubs "the gifts of the Spirit" is the perfection of the love of friendship in us. They do not replace our will so much as they manifest that harmony of wills to which friendship aspires. And since the one from whom we take our cue is the very Love of God, to respond to which is the goal inscribed in our very nature, we are in no danger of alienation by allowing the Spirit to execute that response in us. As Wadell summarizes this final stage, "the paradox of Aquinas' account of the virtues is unflinching: our greatest moral possibility is not to act, but to let ourselves be acted upon by God, for it is when we suffer the divine love that we become most like it" (132). That is what it is to be moved by the Spirit, whose gifts complete the entitative empowerment of the infused virtue of charity by allowing us to be empowered by the personal power and love of God.

Aquinas can exploit Aristotle's anthropology of the virtues in a quite specific way, given the Christian doctrine of a triune and incarnate God. Yet we shall see that al-Ghazali will present a remarkably parallel account, although with far less immediate reliance on Aristotle and little or no ontological infrastructure. What does link the two, however, is a robust account of the free creation of the universe, attributable to God alone, without intermediaries of any sort — an untrammeled initiative on the part of the One from whom all that is comes forth, to which all human beings have been invited to respond by the gracious gift of God's own word. For Aquinas that Word was made flesh in Jesus, while for Ghazali it offers a "straight path" in the Qurʾan given to Muhammad to recite. Yet that same Qurʾan, heard and recollected, will also empower us to respond in a way befitting the gift, as we shall see.

III. GHAZALI'S PATTERN

Human love for God (desire) is transformed by God's love for us, leading to intimacy with God (*uns*) and perfect contentment (*ridā*), the state of friendship (*wilāya*), in which the creature acts freely with the very freedom of the creator, according to Ghazali. Aristotle's dynamic of passion and virtue is all implicit in Ghazali, if present at all. What is central in his anthropology is the heart, with its desires. It is the heart which recognizes the voice of its creator in the recitation of the Qurʾan, and the heart which responds to that voice, albeit erratically. The discipline which the heart needs is found in the same recitation, whose verses point to and constitute a "straight path." The ninety-nine names of God, culled from the Qur'an, constitute a pattern to which faithful servants of God are called to conform their lives, imitating as best they can the One from whom their existence and activity derives.[10] So Ghazali need not contend with a list of human perfections taken over from Hellenic thought, whose ordering would need to be transformed in the light of divine revelation. He begins rather with what Kierkegaard called "the infinite qualitative difference": the "distinction" of creature from creator, and proceeds to delineate how human beings may be led, by the Qur'an, to traverse that chasm by a journey leading to "intimacy with God."[11]

The guides along this way are largely Sufi masters, who identify the stations along the way and display by their lives the transformations possible to human beings who set out resolutely along this path. Without having recourse to anything so explicit as a "supernatural elevation," Ghazali nonetheless presupposes that God's love can bring creatures to a greater and greater proximity to the creator. The point of encounter is the human heart, and the divine action is invariably described as "removing the veil from one's heart, in order that one can see with one's heart, so be elevated to God's own self along with those who are already near to God" (LA 156). The progressive stations are then described as successive unveilings of the heart, and the dynamic is summarized as follows: "In this way the love of God for His servants brings them closer to Himself, removing their negligences and sins from them by purifying their inner self (*bāṭin*) from the filth of this world. God removes the veil from their hearts, in such a way as they contemplate what they see in their hearts" (LA 159). He proceeds to distinguish this transforming love of God from the servants' response, which consists in "the desire which animates them to seize hold of the perfection which they lack" (LA 159). There lies the lack of symmetry in the two loves: God's is transforming and ours seeks transformation. Yet the dynamic of "the way" is to bring us to the point where our response is a perfect reflection of God's initiating love: "the one who has entered into intimacy with God is one who acts with the very action of God" (AD 263).

But in what does such intimacy consist, and would one be correct to assimilate it to friendship? To be sure, Ghazali has no Aristotelian analysis to rest his account upon, yet his assemblage of living examples from a vast repertory of Sufi masters displays people who live in a kind of exchange with God quite similar to Aristotle's account of friendship. Indeed, that must be what makes the stories so attractive. Since this exchange takes place within, one needs signs which will discern the genuine article from ever-present pretensions. Signs that God loves a person begin with the paradoxical one that the person is subjected to trials (LA 160), which is complemented by the assurance that God cares for such persons, taking charge of their external affairs as well as their inner life (LA 160). Signs that one responds to that love are generally more conventional in nature, and can be summarized as showing that one loves God above all other things (LA 163–206), yet all the while "keeping that love hidden and refraining from proclaiming or otherwise manifesting one's joy" (LA 198).

Yet what characterizes the accounts which inform Ghazali's treatment is an utter assurance that the person is loved and cared for, and so treated by God as God's friend, even though the dimension of trials reminds us of Teresa of Avila's celebrated retort that if that was how God treated his friends, it was no wonder he had so few of them! Moreover, Ghazali is scrupulous in avoiding any hint of the propensity of some Sufis towards "annihilation [*fanā*]" in God, which could only conceive of broaching the given "infinite qualitative difference" by dissolving it, and thus absorbing the human protagonist into the divine unity. He does indeed insist that the linchpin of Islam, faith in divine unity (*tawḥīd*), entails that none truly exist but God, by whose existence all else exists. And those who have reached the stage of intimacy with God appreciate that grounding fact better than most, and so realize that "they act with the very action of God" (AD 263). Indeed, "servants of this sort are no longer aware of existing on their own" (AD 263), but by the free disposition of God, and so can be said to be "annihilated [*faniya*] in the oneness of God," but in this carefully delineated sense: "the loss of awareness of oneself as an autonomous agent" (AD 262).

Marie-Louise Siauve finds that "such intimacy is no longer 'with God' but 'in God'; God acts in the person and by the person. Those who are intimates of God are no longer aware of existing by themselves, but only of being servants of God" (AD 263). This state is certainly comparable to Aquinas' final stage of acting by the Spirit and being moved by the gifts of the Spirit. For Siauve, this culminating state offers a key to the unity of Ghazali's thought: "God is one, omnipresent and the only [full-fledged] agent in creation. Those who are intimates of God's not only progress indefinitely, by the élan of his love, towards an ever greater intimacy with God, but if they should attain God, their encounter [*wajd*] with God allows them to live in intimacy with God, taking joy in what gives joy to God, acting with the very action of God. They become aware of neither existing nor acting except by the act by which God gives them existence and movement. One could then say of them that they have let themselves be 'annihilated', in order to be nothing but the act of God in the creature. In their intimacy with God, their hearts are enlarged to the measure of the Generosity of God" (AD 267–68).

Ghazali's reliance on the example and stories of Sufi masters allowed him to finesse some of the conceptual difficulties involved in characterizing a relationship across the "infinite qualitative difference." The full-blooded characters in the Sufi stories, however, certainly belie any caricature of the goal of the Sufi path as "existential monism" (Massignon) or "unity of existence [*wahdat al-wujūd*]". What seems to emerge is a lived familiarity which needs to respect "the distinction" in such a way as to grant that however reciprocal things may be, the source of all remains just that, so that the reciprocity is ever a divine gift. Human action for both Aquinas and Ghazali will ever be created action, and paradigmatic human initiative will be a response to an invitation freely offered by the One whose free action initiated it all, so that one can say that human creativity will be, at its best, created creativity. That perspective remains an affront—an "offense," Kierkegaard would say—to other conceptions of the *humanum* which trade on "autonomy," but in that offense lies a challenge: which account offers a better rendition of something immensely valuable to all human beings, that is, friendship?

IV: CONCLUSION: PARALLELS, FUNCTIONAL EQUIVALENCIES, DIFFERENCES BETWEEN GHAZALI AND AQUINAS

That human beings are destined for friendship with God is hardly the impression which observers have either of Christianity or of Islam, although this development in Christianity might not be found untoward, given that the Word of God was made flesh. In Islam, however,

where the Word was made Arabic, the watchword has long been submission to the "straight path" delineated therein, by way of obedience
to the law (*sharīʿa*) derived from it. That a theologian as central to
Islam as al-Ghazali would propose that reciprocal love between Muslims and the one God is the paradigmatic form of Islam challenges both
those stereotypes and the commonplace translation of *Islam* as "submission." And while there is no doubt that his Ashʿarite tendencies may
have facilitated his manner of articulating the mutuality of divine and
human love in this exchange, it remains that his anthropology was more
clearly derived from the Sufis. It is here that the parallels emerge
between his dynamic and that of Aquinas.

What seems crucial is that neither thinker had to secure human
dignity in the face of the creator by pure initiative. Both see human
action at its best as a response to the divine initiative, and this response
character of human activity as a corollary of the originating creature-
creator relationship. Given that structure, and the opening to an
interpersonal relationship at the divine initiative, it becomes possible
to think that creatures might stand in the same relationship to God as
to themselves, and that God, the partner, would stand in the same relationship to a creature as to God's own self! This is indeed the most
acceptable formula for an intimacy which not only allows but demands
that each be itself, while acknowledging and celebrating that each lives
by the life of the other. Aquinas saw in the very terms of this description a demand for an entitatively supernatural status, both to permit
reciprocity in the creature-creator interaction and to secure the integrity of the creature's response. Ghazali's reliance on the Sufi notion of *heart*, on the other hand, proffers a more continuous path of
"drawing near to God," punctuated by discrete stages yet culminating
in a freedom bestowed by God to created responders so that their
hearts may respond wholeheartedly.

Ontologies apart, however, these seem to be two complementary
ways of articulating a paradigmatic way of relating that is available to
creatures of a creator who makes the divine initiatives known. In that
respect, they stand together against all Pelagian forms of Christianity
as well as all forms of Islam which must open and close their presentation with the *sharīʿa*. And since variant Pelagian readings of Christianity are arguably dominant, and the same could be said for *sharīʿa*
Islam, this comparative sketch of two religious thinkers central to each

tradition may offer some hope for a rapprochement, at least in understanding, in the face of stereotypes reinforced by majority attitudes.

NOTES

1. See David B. Burrell, *Knowing the Unknowable God: Ibn-Sina, Maimonides, Aquinas* (Notre Dame, Ind.: University of Notre Dame Press, 1986); and *Freedom and Creation in Three Traditions* (Notre Dame, Ind.: University of Notre Dame Press, 1993).

2. See also Gen. 18:17, Wis. 7:27, Isa. 41:8, 2 Chr. 20:7.

3. See Paul Wadell, *Friends of God: Virtues and Gifts in Aquinas* (New York: Peter Lang, 1991); and Marie-Louise Siauve, *Friends of God* (New York: Peter Lang, 1991) (*L'amour de Dieu chez Gazālī* [Paris: Vrin, 1986]). Hereafter referred to as AD. See also Muhammad al-Ghazali, *Livre de l'amour*, trans. Marie-Louise Siauve (Paris: Vrin, 1986). Hereafter referred to as LA.

4. Thomas Hanley, "St. Thomas' Use of Al-Ghazali's *Maqāsid-al-falāsifā*," *Medieval Studies* 44 (1982): 243–70.

5. Richard Gramlich, trans., *Muhammad al-Gazālīs Lehre von den Stufen zur Gottesliebe* (translation of bks. 31–36 of Ghazali's *Ihyā' 'Ulūm ad-Dīn*) (Weisbaden: Franz Steiner, 1984), p. 524.

6. I am indebted to Wadell, *Friends of God*, for this scheme.

7. Eugene Rogers, Jr., has effectively made this point in "A Theological Procedure in the *Summa Theologiae*: 'Sacra Doctrina est Scientia' in Question 1 of the *Summa* and Chapter 1 of the *In Romanos*, with a Comparison to Karl Barth" (Ph.D. diss., Yale University, 1992).

8. Wadell, *Friends of God*, p. 106; cf. ST 1–2.12.2.

9. Stanza 38 of the *Spiritual Canticle* of John of the Cross shows how one trained in the thought of Aquinas will put it, speaking of the spouse: "Besides teaching her to love purely, freely, and disinterestedly, as He loves her, God makes her love Him with the very strength with which He loves her. Transforming her into His love, . . . He gives her His own strength by which she can love Him. As if He were to put an instrument in her hands and show her how it works by operating it jointly with her, He shows her how to love and gives her the ability to do so" (Kieran Kavanaugh and Otilio Rodriguez, trans., *Collected Works of John of the Cross* [New York: Doubleday, 1964], p. 554).

10. David Burrell and Nazih Daher, trans., *Al-Ghazali on the Ninety-Nine Beautiful Names of God* (Cambridge: Islamic Texts Society, 1992).

11.   "The distinction" is Robert Sokolowski's key expression in *The God of Faith and Reason* (Notre Dame, Ind.: University of Notre Dame Press, 1982); "infinite qualitative difference" may be found, *inter alia*, in Soren Kierkegaard, *The Sickness unto Death*, ed. and trans. Howard and Edna Hong (Princeton, N.J.: Princeton University Press, 1980), p. 99. For "intimacy with God," see Siauve, LA, 207–14; Ghazali, AD, 246–68.

Two Perspectives on Friendship: Aristotle and Nietzsche

JOHN E. SMITH

YOU WILL NO DOUBT WONDER about this unlikely combination of philosophers, backgrounds, and beliefs. On the one hand, Aristotle appears as the living embodiment of the Greek conception of the human as a "rational animal" motivated by, in his own phrase, "the desire to know." Knowledge for Aristotle means a clear-headed grasp of the *logos* of things — what makes things what they are and explains what they do. Although motivated by desire, pursuit of knowledge for Aristotle requires a dispassionate inquiry, an apprehension of measure and form in the universe represented in Greek art and mythology by the figure of Apollo, who shoots arrows from a distance and is not himself involved.

On the other hand, Nietzsche appears as a philosopher-poet, a master of irony, of sarcasm, of hyperbole, and as a man of many masks who liked to hide. I resist the temptation to call Nietzsche an "irrationalist," because I agree with the best informed of his interpreters in their rejection of this term as inaccurate. There is plenty of *logos* in Nietzsche's writings; it is just difficult to find. The reason, apart from his well-known tendency to prevent us from doing so — his wisdom must not be attained without suffering — is that his thought is filled with the contradictions, ambivalences, and even the absurdities which he encountered in his own life. If Aristotle is the thinker of Apollo, Nietzsche is the thinker of Dionysus for whom there is no thought at a distance. Knowledge is to be gained only through participation, engagement, passion, and total immersion in the murky waters of human existence. We shall see what a difference is made by these two divergent approaches in their treatment of friendship.

There is a second difference between them to be taken into account, and that is the different situations in which they developed their philosophies. Aristotle was thoroughly familiar with the meaning of *ethos*, the characteristic feature of a people, the spirit of a community embracing customs, ideals, beliefs, and all the invisible bonds of loyalty and dedication which bring many individuals into a unity of life. Aristotle, moreover, understood the nature of a community; that it is no mere collection and, even less, a crowd, but a distinctive level of being which has a life and a history of its own. Nietzsche, by contrast, represents one of the last outworkings of the eruption of individual subjectivity, starting with Descartes and culminating with the primacy of self-consciousness in the thought of Hegel. Nietzsche is the radical individualist striving to become himself in what appeared to him to be a time of leveling, of mediocrity, a time when the anonymity of the masses thwarted his every attempt to achieve what he called greatness of spirit or self-mastery. Aristotle knew little of the labyrinth of self-consciousness about which Nietzsche appears to have known too much — so much, in fact, that he plumbed the depths of its *negative* side (self-diremption and alienation). Thus most of what Nietzsche has to say is filtered through his own consciousness of self-deception, of finding the other only as a form or stage of himself, of hiding to avoid disclosing what he did not want others to see.

As we shall see again, these fundamental differences in approach and situation separating the two thinkers had a decisive effect on their understanding of our basic topic. And if Royce was right, as I think he was, when he said that "contrast is the mother of clearness," we may expect to profit from this juxtaposition of two philosophers who would most likely appear to an ideal observer as coming from different planets.

The difference in what I am calling their prevailing situations involves yet another factor, one that puts us in touch with their underlying aims. The society Aristotle presupposes when he is describing the social value of friendship is assumed to be a *good* society — the *ethos* of the city-state — in which there prevails a concern for the common welfare. He was not unaware of the rivalries that developed between the most powerful city-states, nor was he unfamiliar with tyranny where the best interests of the government came before those of the people as a whole. In his *Politics* he set forth the outlines of a "right constitution" whereby all the Greek states might be united in one commonwealth. In all this, however, Aristotle was no prophetic critic of either society or the state, since he sought to give clear and rational expression to the *best*, the virtues both individual and social upon which Greek civilization was based.

Nietzsche's situation is far different. He was the *staunch critic* of European society, especially of its real or supposed roots in the Judeo-Christian tradition. He saw all previous morality as the morality of the "herd" and the "slave," and denounced its mediocrity, sham, and self-deception. Nietzsche, in short, like Zarathustra, philosophized with "the hammer." In every direction he was bent on destroying the idols that stood in the way of the development of the "over-man" — the strong individual of self-mastery through suffering, of nobility, of heroism and, above all, of honesty. All that Nietzsche has to say must be understood in the light of his role as the critic, even in the role of the nihilist. He might have made it easier for us to see him in this light if he had been more willing to acknowledge the fact that his passion for destruction, his willingness to cast himself as an "immoralist," were means he adopted in the name of a *higher morality*. His reluctance in this regard stemmed from his fear that, in revealing this underlying motive, he would become yet another "moralist." That is the reason, too, why he attacked the idea of *morality* itself and posed as one who is "beyond good and evil"; he wanted to suggest that the self-discipline necessary for the species of "higher men" goes far beyond morality as conventionally understood.

It is impossible here, even if it were germane, to present all of the points made in Aristotle's two books on friendship, the many fine distinctions drawn and the morals pointed. The same is true for Nietzsche, where the terrain is not well charted and we face irony, masks, and indirect communication. Nietzsche could rarely make even the simplest assertions without reflecting on who he would be if he said that, who would he be if he didn't, how this might be taken by those of inferior rank, and so forth. Moreover, whereas in Aristotle we can easily find chapter and verse for his arguments and conclusions, Nietzsche's views on friendship are spread through paragraphs in a number of his works and his letters, in addition to the well-known brief sections in *Zarathustra* on "Friends" and "Neighbor-Love." In order to manage this protean situation I shall follow the advice of Aristotle himself, who suggested that whenever we need to encompass a multitude, we can do so only with a principle. Accordingly, I shall first focus in the case of both thinkers on what I take to be their fundamental conception of friendship so that we shall have some grasp of each perspective. Then, being guided by some ideas which I shall purposely select from Aristotle's view, I shall attempt to see where he and Nietzsche overlap and where they diverge.

I begin with Aristotle's distinction between three types of friendship, based in order of importance on *virtue, utility,* and *pleasure.* Aristotle, as always, first notes general opinion, goes on to cite some "more profound" opinions—which usually means citing the ideas of previous philosophers and poets—and ends with his own analysis, which he describes as an investigation into the "human aspect of the matter" (that is, friendship) as opposed to the speculations of the philosophers. The principle Aristotle follows here is fundamental to his thought as whole: whatever is intrinsic, essential, and enduring is superior in worth to what is "accidental," transient, and a means to some further end. Thus the friendship based on virtue is the highest form because each party wishes the other to be more virtuous in and for him- or herself, while in the case of utility there is the wish for the other to be useful, and in that of pleasure there is the wish for the other to be pleasant. In both these cases, Aristotle says, the relation is dependent on something other than love of the person and his or her intrinsic character, which is to say that it is dependent on what Aristotle calls "accidental" or a *changing* quality, use, and pleasure. Here Aristotle expresses one of the most pervasive beliefs of ancient Greek culture: the abiding and the permanent—virtue—cannot be dissolved as so often happens in the other two types.

Two points are noteworthy here. First, Aristotle does not suppose that in friendships based on virtue the friends may not be useful to each other or take pleasure in each other's company. It is simply that their friendship is not rooted in the expectation of either of these benefits. The second point is that Aristotle did not regard the permanent element as something static, but rather as a disposition or a tendency to act in a certain way which continues even when the person is not realizing this disposition in action.[1] Aristotle does, however, attach a time limit to these dispositions in the sense that they can atrophy if not exercised. This leads him to say that permanent friendships need to be sustained through friendly relations, for if the two are apart for long periods of time, they may forget each other.

Time is important for Aristotle because intimacy between friends takes time. The wish "to be friends quickly," he says, is not friendship, not least because the two need time for each to admit the other to the relationship. I am reminded of a remark made by Paul Tillich not long after he came to America, in which he said that here people have become "friends" five minutes after they have met. He preferred to call these "friends" by the name of "acquaintances."

Aristotle repeats over and again the belief that only *good* men[2] can be friends for what they are in themselves, and he appeals for support to actual practice in the use of the term *friendship*. He acknowledges that it is used in the case of friends related by pleasure and utility; even states, he says, can be friends in the latter sense. But he insists that these can be said to be friends only in an analogical sense. That is, their relationship merely *resembles* friendship between good men who are friends for each other's sake. This leads Aristotle to the view that it is "inferior people" who will make friends for pleasure or for use, in contrast to virtuous people. The word for "inferior people" in the text is an old form of what is better known as the *oi polloi* or the low-in-rank, ordinary, common, and uneducated people. True friendship thus belongs to the elite; an elite of virtue, to be sure, but an elite nevertheless. As we shall see, this view readily invites comparison with Nietzsche's understanding of friendship, a comparison that will throw light on both thinkers.

Another focal point is Aristotle's claim that it is not possible to have many friends of the true sort. His main reason is that the affection of friendship is exclusive and certainly not indiscriminate. Moreover, the intimacy required must be established and nurtured over a long time. The virtuous man finds that he cannot distribute himself, so to speak, over many people. His contention becomes even more plausible when we consider that he thought of a true friend as a sort of second self. It seems obvious that the number of such selves an individual could sustain would have to be limited.

Although Aristotle discusses at some length what he calls "friendships of inequality," it is clear that the best relationship in his view is one of equality between the parties. Friendship, he says, cannot continue, even that based on virtue, if one of the friends becomes too far above the other in wealth, power, or virtue so that inequality results. In a nice display of candor, Aristotle asks whether it is true that we really wish for our friends their greatest good. He answers that in wishing this good for a friend for his own sake, we are being a true friend. But we cannot wish that he should become other than he is (for example, that he become a god), because we can wish for him only those goods consistent with his remaining a human being. Otherwise we should lose him as a friend. We shall press this point later, for Nietzsche, being Dionysus, often appeared to need no less than gods for friends.

Aristotle, like most people, reveals his firmest convictions by repeating them. Such is the case with his belief that true friendship exists more in giving than in receiving. Nevertheless, he insisted on the importance of justice in friendships, which meant mutual rights for the partners. On this tack, Aristotle is making his way to introducing the social dimension of friendship and its being situated in the wider community of the state. Declaring that "community is the essence of friendship," Aristotle goes on to say that associations of all kinds, including friendship, are parts of the association we call the state. Associations such as those of seamen and tradesmen exist for some particular advantage, but the political association is for the advantage of all, since the aim of lawgivers is the good of the overarching community. All associations are subordinate to the political community which "aims not at a temporary advantage but at one covering the whole of life." We shall have to see whether Nietzsche has any place for community within the confines of his powerful individualism.

One of the advantages of Aristotle's dispassionate approach is that it allows him to confront difficult questions in a way that is not always possible for the engaged thinker who has a personal stake in the answer. Aristotle asks whether a friendship should be broken off when the friends do not remain the same.[3] In considering his reply, we need to bear in mind one of his essential doctrines concerning the nature of the person, namely, the priority of *intellect* together with the subordination of both desire and the power of choice. We know that this is his view from other writings, but in the *Ethics* he makes a special point of saying that individuals in general regard their real self as identical with the intellectual faculty they possess. The good man, he says, always strives to sustain this element in himself. For a person to remain the same means continuing to be committed to, and guided by, the ethical principles grasped by *nous* through what has come to be called the "active intellect." Suppose, he says, we have admitted to our friendship a good man who has become a bad man. Are we still bound to love him? Aristotle's direct answer is that perhaps it is *impossible* to do so, but in any case it would be *wrong* to do so because we are to direct love only toward the good. Feeling the full force of the dilemma, Aristotle claims that the friendship under these circumstances should be ended only when we are sure that the friend's condition is *incurable*. If, however, it appears that the other is capable of reform, we are morally obligated to help the other regain his real self. No one can read this passage with Nietzsche in mind and fail to see that it goes to the heart of the problem in his relation to Richard Wagner, a friendship which, while it lasted, was the commanding influence in Nietzsche's life.

Those familiar with Christian ethics, especially the commandment to "love thy neighbor as thyself," are well aware of the many discussions that have taken place about the proper way to fit self-love into the equation. Aristotle, in pursuing his analysis of friendship, raises the question directly: "Should one love oneself or someone else most?" In his typical fashion, he appeals first to what is commonly said or thought. According to this general opinion, to call someone a "lover of self" is a reproach because it is the sign of a bad man to consider himself first in all things. Aristotle, however, claims that the facts "do not accord with those theories," and goes on to present the other side of the picture. We admit, he says, that we should love our best friend most. But the best friend is the one who wishes a person's good for its own sake and this condition is most fully realized in our regard for ourselves. In solidifying his point, Aristotle claims that all the feelings that constitute friendship "are an extension of regard for self," and since a man is his own best friend, "he ought to love himself most."[4]

Which of the two views, Aristotle asks, should we adopt, since there is some plausibility in both? A conflict of opinion requires that we first become as clear as possible about the meaning of the alternatives. The matter turns on what each side means by "self-love." Two distinct meanings are involved, according to Aristotle. The first is the self-love that we reproach, and the second is what he calls "noble" self-love. The former involves assigning to oneself the larger share of wealth, honor, and bodily pleasures. Those who take more than their share are said to be following their passions or the irrational part of themselves. Aristotle concludes that "love of self" as a reproach stems from the bad kind of self-love and is "rightly censured."[5]

Noble self-love is found in the person who is always aiming to outdo others in acting justly, temperately, and in other virtuous ways. Appealing to the *ethos* of the people, Aristotle says, "No one charges such a person with bad self-love." On the contrary, the person of moral nobility is to be called a lover of self "in an exceptional degree"[6] precisely because he loves the dominant part of himself—the intellect—which is most worthy to be loved. Self-restraint, Aristotle continues, is restraint by the intellect. Thus "the intellect is the man himself" so that in valuing that dominant part the man loves himself to the highest degree. Noble self-love means a life according to principles, while the bad self-love aims only at what is expedient. In a conclusion that nicely embraces both the individual and the community, Aristotle writes:

> If all men vied with each other in moral nobility and strove to perform the noblest deeds, the common welfare would be fully realized, while individuals also could enjoy the greatest of goods, inasmuch as virtue is the greatest good.[7]

Further, the good man should love himself because he will benefit himself by acting nobly and at the same time aid his fellows. The bad man, on the contrary, should not love himself because he will follow his base passions and thus bring harm to himself and his neighbors. This consequence is obviously in accord with all that Aristotle has been saying about self-love, but it does not at all prepare us for the heroic note which he strikes in the next paragraph. There he declares that the virtuous man will surrender everything, even his life if need be, to secure nobility for himself. Such a man "would prefer an hour of rapture to a long period of mild enjoyment, a year of noble life to many years of ordinary existence," and, above all, he would prefer "one great and glorious exploit to many small successes."[8] It might seem as if Aristotle were merely trying to glorify the noble individual, but the context points to something else. The noble man gives his life for others, his friends, and is ready to forego both wealth and honor that his friends may benefit from his sacrifice. Nobility of spirit is his return.

In all this we must, of course, bear in mind that Aristotle was taking for granted a belief that was dear to the hearts of many Greek philosophers, namely, that the intellect is the best part of the person and that its excellence always consists in exercising it in connection with what is best—virtue and truth. That belief, however, has been called seriously into question not least because of the neat division of the human faculties which it involves. On the classical view, the intellect invariably appears as unambiguously good while the passions and desires provide a convenient way of accounting for the evil that men do.

As Augustine was to point out, the very possibility of pride and concupiscence requires the intellect no less than the passions since these attitudes stem from the way we understand and evaluate our deeds and aims. By Nietzsche's time other voices had been raised against the intellectualistic conception of the self and the identification of the real self with the mind.

The final topic discussed by Aristotle in connection with friendship is whether it is necessary for happiness, by which he means a sense of well-being (*Eudaimonia*) and not simply pleasure. Again, Aristotle begins with "what people say" about the question as a prelude to his own analysis. The conventional wisdom says that the supremely happy are self-sufficient and have no need of friends. Friends, moreover, are meant to supply things we cannot obtain ourselves, but the resourceful person finds this unnecessary. Aristotle takes special note of the belief that the happy need nothing else by citing a line from Euripides: "When fortune favors us, what need of friends?" It is clear, however, that he has taken this conventional wisdom into account only to set it aside.[9]

Aristotle's response to the question is threefold. First, he says, if we attribute all good things to the happy man, why not friends, since they are the greatest of external goods? Second, since it is the mark of a friend to give more than he receives, the good man will need friends on which to bestow his beneficence. Third, Aristotle thinks that it is very strange to see the happy man as *recluse*. No one, he argues, would choose to have all possible goods on the condition that he enjoy them alone. On the contrary, man is a social, political being and designed by nature to live with others. The happy man, in short, must have society and hence he needs friends. No great stretch of the imagination is needed in order to see the intimate bearing of all this on Nietzsche's life and thought. Zarathustra invariably appears *alone* on a lofty height above ordinary mortals, and Nietzsche was often nothing if not lonely.

Anyone who has read Nietzsche at any length knows the difficulties to be encountered—the irony, his speaking through the mask of Zarathustra and in aphorisms to boot, special twists given to the meaning of German words—and it is to be expected that differences in interpretation cannot be avoided. The best approach is not to fight against these difficulties, but to accept them as what we must go through if we want to lay hold of Nietzsche's insights, many of which are quite profound. My main aim is to present Nietzsche's ideas about the nature of friendship and to draw some of the comparisons mentioned in the discussion of Aristotle. I shall be most explicit about the basis for friendship, the place of self-love in the relationship, the meaning of nobility, and the connection between friendship and community.

There is some consensus among the commentators that before seeking Nietzsche's pronouncements on any particular matter — his critique of morality and of religion, his ideas about nobility, friendship, or the doctrine of the eternal recurrence — it is necessary to be clear about the nature of his *higher morality*. For all of his insistence on being the "immoralist," this "higher morality" stands as the touchstone for his attack on Western morality and its conceptions of good and evil which the higher morality must go "beyond." Josiah Royce argued in a little-known, posthumously published essay that Nietzsche's new ethic poses three questions: 1) Who am I and what do I want? 2) What does the will that seeks power really desire? 3) How should a noble self seek perfection in relation to the surrounding universe?[10] While one rarely finds in Nietzsche's writings anything stated as clearly as Royce's questions, students of Nietzsche's works will recognize them at once as going to the heart of his main concern. In answering these questions, it is of the utmost importance to take into account what we may call the "prospective" character which these answers must take. By that I mean that Nietzsche's ideals are not descriptive of any beings now in existence, but point instead to a new type of being — the "over-man" — for whom these ideals are *tasks* to be achieved through heroic effort, suffering, and the will to *become* an individual, noble self. It is in this sense that the self is said to be *created*. Nietzsche repeatedly subordinated the individual as a *creature* to the power of the self to be a *creator*.

The answer to the first question is found in Nietzsche's central notion of "the will to power." This notion has often been misunderstood because of a failure to see that the will in question is Nietzsche's *own* will and not a will to have power over other men. The will to power is the power of self-determination, of self-mastery to be measured by the ideal of the over-man who must reject all mediocrity and not be satisfied with anything "merely moderate."

That is Nietzsche's answer to the second question. In this paramount emphasis on will, Nietzsche is, of course, breaking with the Aristotelian tradition of the "rational animal." The third question —

How is the self to achieve perfection?—will concern us only in part, since the full answer involves the idea of the "eternal recurrence" and that is a topic unto itself. The main point is that the self must have the courage to face a world in which it is no longer possible to find the purpose of life in heavenly joys, the will of the gods, Nirvana, or the beatific vision. For Nietzsche these are all gone. What we are left with is his basically fictitious doctrine of the endless return of all that has been in cycles that ever recur.[11] The over-men, however, will have the fortitude and endurance to live their lives in that sort of universe, since they are convinced that only in this way can the complete life be expressed.

Walter Kaufmann's book on Nietzsche illuminates Nietzsche's praise of friendship by exploring the figure of Richard Wagner, who was the most important friend in Nietzsche's life. Nietzsche continued to acknowledge his indebtedness to Wagner even after their friendship came to an end. From his earliest days, Nietzsche was greatly attracted to Wagner's music, in which he felt the force of creative genius—in an artistic medium which Nietzsche loved above all others. "It was Wagner's presence," Kaufmann writes, "that convinced Nietzsche that greatness and genuine creation are still possible, and it was Wagner who inspired him with the persistent longing first to equal and then to outdo his friend."[12] The great historian Jacob Burkhardt was one of the first to take note of what he called the "agonistic" character of Greek friendship in which friends, starting as equals, seek to enhance themselves and their friendship through efforts to outdo each other. We saw this point earlier on in Aristotle's idea of the noble self seeking to outdo the other in deeds of virtue. It is clear that, while their friendship lasted, Nietzsche was fully aware of the agonistic relation in which he stood to Wagner.

The key to understanding Nietzsche's idea of friendship is found in his praise of the friend and his critique of "neighbor-love" and especially of the pity that he invariably associated with love of that sort. To begin with, for all of Nietzsche's attack upon Christianity, he had the highest regard for the sayings of Jesus, especially the Sermon on the Mount. It seems that in subordinating the love of neighbor, Nietzsche was condemning *insincere* Christianity, since he believed that the true legacy of Jesus was his stress on sincere practice. Nevertheless, even sincere regard for the neighbor—what Nietzsche often referred to as "altruism"—is not enough, since on his view all the great philosophers from Plato to Kant agreed that *self-perfection* is the goal of morality and that precludes "altruism." Nietzsche sought for something that, in his own terms, would be more heroic than that.

In his work *The Dawn*, Nietzsche criticized the modern emphasis on love between the sexes as detracting from friendship between man and man. Under the heading "Friendship" Nietzsche wrote:

> In classical antiquity, friendship was experienced deeply and strongly. . . . In this consists their head-start before us; we, on the other side, have developed idealized love between the sexes. All the great virtues of the ancients were founded on this, that *man* stood next to *man*, and that no woman could claim to be the nearest, the highest . . . or the only one whom he loved. . . . Perhaps our trees do not grow so high because of the ivy and the vines.[13]

Nietzsche would have had to go no further than to his beloved Wagner's operas to find ample evidence of this "idealized love between the sexes."

According to Kaufmann, who regarded Nietzsche as "most eloquent" in his praise of friendship, Nietzsche's next work, *The Gay Science*, written in 1882 one year after *The Dawn*, contains a passage that serves as a transition from the previous quotation to what Nietzsche says in *Zarathustra*. Nietzsche begins by saying that the rest of the world seems pale and worthless to the lover ready to make any sacrifice, but once again he inveighs against the supposed superiority of the love between man and woman. "One may indeed marvel," he writes, "that this wild greed and injustice of love between the sexes has been so glorified and deified . . . yes — that one has taken from this love the conception of love as the opposite of egoism, although it is perhaps the most candid expression of egoism. . . . There is apparently here and there on earth, a kind of continuation of love where this greedy desire of two persons for each other has given way to new craving and greed, a *common* higher thirst for an ideal that stands above them: but who knows this love? who has experienced it? Its true name is *friendship*."[14] The higher ideal of love, or friendship, stands above both individuals and points beyond itself to the over-men where it becomes the means whereby the self-perfection of two human beings can be achieved.

Although Nietzsche was fully aware that the commandment to love the neighbor means loving the neighbor "as oneself," he believed that for the most part this does not happen. What happens instead is that we have a bad love of ourselves and flee to the neighbor because we cannot stand ourselves and yet hope to make a virtue of that. Nietzsche's criticism is of the *false* neighbor-love. Zarathustra counsels: "Do love your neighbor as yourselves, but first be such as *love themselves*."[15] Nietzsche is concerned with the same problem raised by Aristotle about the two kinds of self-love, and by the Christian tradition in its recognition that there must be a proper form of self-love — as distinct from selfishness — if the measure of love to the neighbor in the Commandment is to be on a par with our love to ourselves. For Nietzsche, love can be a virtue if two persons strive to perfect themselves and each other. Such love is, in fact, the highest relation between two human beings. If, however, we go to the neighbor in order to have a witness when we speak well of ourselves, that is not a virtue but a weakness that does not benefit the neighbor either.

Nietzsche was most opposed to pity, by which he often meant Schopenhauer's reading of the Buddhist idea of *compassion*, because he thought it inferior to both love and forgiveness. Nietzsche tells us that we can suffer with a friend who is suffering by being a "resting place," but a "hard bed" will profit him most because the aim is to help the friend achieve self-mastery. This cannot be done through sentimentality and indulging weaknesses. The great store Nietzsche laid by self-mastery can be seen in his perceptive comment on forgiveness. If a friend wrongs you, he says, "then say, I forgive what you did to me, but that you should have done it to yourself — how could I forgive that?"[16] Thus all great love aims at helping to create self-mastery in the beloved. In *Beyond Good and Evil*, Nietzsche takes up the assessment of pity again. There he tells us that we are all both creatures and creators, but that those who pity another deal only with the *creature*, when the task is to foster the *creator* in the other.

Not unlike Aristotle, Nietzsche took into account the difference between the powerful and the less powerful. Not everyone can attain the self-determination that defines the over-man. The strongest find happiness in self-conquest; "asceticism becomes in them nature, need and instinct"; "difficult tasks are a privilege to them." Being strong, however, is not without its obligations. In a passage cited by Kaufmann from *The Antichrist*, Nietzsche writes: "When the exceptional human being treats the mediocre more tenderly than himself and his peers, this is not mere courtesy of the heart — it is simply his duty."[17] Nevertheless, since humanity for Nietzsche is a perpetual self-overcoming, helping others must always be a secondary consideration. He sought to justify this consequence with the claim that helping others is always easier than trying to make something of oneself.

For Nietzsche, friendship was always seen in the light of his ideal of individual self-perfection. Friendship enhances the mastery of self because one does not flee from oneself in going to a friend; nor does one exert one's will to power by indebting oneself to the other. In friendship jealousy is sublimated and friends vie to make something of themselves which will both delight and inspire the other. In *Zarathustra* Nietzsche says, "You cannot turn out too beautifully for your friend: for you shall be to him an arrow and a longing for the *Übermensch*."[18] Friendship continually points beyond itself to Nietzsche's ideal of the over-man, "the creating friend who always has a completed world to give away."[19] The completed world is, of course, the perfected self who has the power to give *himself* to the other, something that goes beyond both wealth and power.

The story of Nietzsche's friendship with Wagner is long and well known, but Nietzsche's decision to end the friendship throws some light on what he meant by a friend. Nietzsche had, to be sure, other friends — Overbeck, Gast, Rohde, Malwida von Mysenburg — but no one exerted a greater influence on him than Wagner and his music. It seems clear that Nietzsche was ultimately turned away by Wagner's idealization of romantic love between men and women because this meant a subordination of his ideal of friendship between man and man. From all that Nietzsche says, he doubted that the man/woman relationship could allow for the mutual enhancement of self-mastery which was for him the heart of friendship. There were other reasons for his break with Wagner: his interweaving of Christian themes with German mythology, which Nietzsche saw as an exploitation of genuine Christianity, and his mounting anti-Semitism, to mention but two. But as far as Nietzsche's conception of friendship is involved, nothing was more important than Wagner's portrayal in grand operatic style of human relations that Nietzsche regarded as *lower* than friendship. Nietzsche saw no prospects in Wagner's romantic lovers for the development of the discipline of self-mastery which was Nietzsche's ideal.

Aristotle and Nietzsche agree in the belief that true friendships are rare because people of virtue are rare. Friendships of the highest order are not for everybody. The only difference between them on this point is in the perspective. Aristotle is describing friendship in terms of what he saw as the *best* according to the existing Greek *ethos*, while Nietzsche was appealing to his ideal of the over-man, a being to be *created* in friendship, the higher man of the future.

They agree again in the belief that it is not possible to have many friends. For Aristotle this is determined by the time needed for intimacy and by the impossibility of having many selves, since he regarded the friend as a second self. Nietzsche found it impossible to have many friends because of the rigorous self-discipline he demanded both of himself and his friends. To have many friends in Nietzsche's sense could mean nothing less than moral exhaustion.

They are in accord on the matter of *equality* in true friendship and both saw the obstacles posed by great disparities in wealth, honor, and virtuous disposition. In this connection you will recall that Aristotle said that we cannot wish for our friend that he become more than human because we would lose him as a friend. Nietzsche's demand here is for something higher, in the sense that the over-man *surpasses* human beings as they presently are.

On the matter of *community*, the two diverge quite sharply, and since Aristotle is very clear about the importance of society, we can put the question to Nietzsche. Can he have any place for community in the senses both of seeing friendship in the context of society and of a community of friends? Nietzsche certainly does not stress the social dimension and he distanced the noble self from ordinary mortals. As regards a community of friends, Nietzsche does speak of new *species* of higher men, but in the end it is the solitude that prevails.

There is some overlap in their views about ending a friendship. Aristotle said that it might be impossible, but that it should happen if we have reason to believe that the other has become a bad person. This appears to have been the ground on which Nietzsche decided to end his friendship with Wagner. Nietzsche came to have serious reservations about Wagner's character in comparison with his own ideal. Nietzsche came to believe that Wagner was betraying aesthetic ideals in pandering to the popular tastes of his time.

Both agree that there is a *proper* type of self-love that is essential for friendship, and a false kind of self-love that is detrimental to true friendship. Both say: love the friend, but love yourself as well.

Cutting across the entire discussion is an enormous difference between the two thinkers. Nietzsche would not accept Aristotle's insistence on the intellect as the best part of the person and even as identical with the person. For Nietzsche the self is one of will, passion, and the drive toward realization which he called will to power. In this regard Nietzsche joined a number of other philosophers in the attack on the intellectualism which has been so great a part of the legacy passed on to us by the Greek philosophers.

Finally, no greater contrast can be drawn than between Aristotle's argument for the need of society and Nietzsche's Zarathustra who time and again appears *alone* and speaking from a great height to those *beneath* him. The over-man is a solitary being.

NOTES

1. A historical note is germane to this important point. Decades ago such scholars as J. H. Randall and Paul O. Kristeller, in their studies of the role of Aristotle's thought in the Renaissance, pointed out that the *dynamism* that runs throughout Aristotle's philosophy in its original Greek is lost in Latin translation because Latin stresses noun substantives which are *static* and these are used to translate Aristotle's *verbal* phrases which he used as nouns. The best example is Aristotle's use of the expression "The what it was to be" to express the nature of something. That expression invariably appears in Latin as either *substantia* or *essentia* which obscures the idea that something is what it can *become*.

2. I cannot deal with the gender question beyond pointing out the well-known bias against women running throughout Greek society. Aristotle always refers to "men" and does not speak about friendship between women. When he does consider relations between men and women it is in connection with husbands and wives where the relation is *not* that of equality, a condition he thought necessary for friendship of the highest type.

3. Aristotle *Nicomachean Ethics* 9.3.

4. Ibid., 8.2.

5. Ibid., 8.4.

6. Ibid., 8.6.

7. Ibid., 8.7.

8. Ibid., 8.9.

9. Ibid., 11.6.

10. Josiah Royce, "Nietzsche," *Atlantic Monthly* 119 (1917): 321–31.

11. It is not always emphasized as it should be that the eternal recurrence is Nietzsche's ultimate defiance of the biblical worldview in which history is not *cyclical* but *linear* in its development, and governed not by fate

but by providence. The dominant tendency in Greek thought about history was to interpret it after the patterns of nature where the seasons return, day turns into night and again into day, and everything comes around again. The ancient Hebraic view of history as a development in the revelation of God's will through linear time came to replace the cyclical conception.

12.   Walter Kaufmann, *Nietzsche: Philosopher, Psychologist, Antichrist*, 3d ed. (Princeton, N.J.: Princeton University Press, 1968), p. 30.

13.   Friedrich Nietzsche, *The Works of Nietzsche*, vol. 4, *The Dawn of Day*, trans. Johanna Volz (London: T. F. Unwin, 1910), p. 503.

14.   Friedrich Nietzsche, *The Gay Science*, ed. and trans. Walter Kaufmann (New York: Vintage Books, 1974), sec. 14, p. 87.

15.   Nietzsche *Zarathustra* (trans. Kaufmann) 3.5.

16.   Ibid., 2.3.

17.   Kaufmann, *Nietzsche*, p. 370.

18.   Nietzsche *Zarathustra* 1.16.

19.   Ibid.

PART II

Friendship in Various Cultures

Confucian Friendship:
The Road to Religiousness

DAVID L. HALL
ROGER T. AMES

WE WILL INVOKE TWO PROMINENT figures in these remarks, each representative of a long and rich tradition of reflection, feeling, and institutionalized practice. One — Confucius — is named in our title. Since Confucius is at best an unfamiliar exotic whose shallow, stodgy, and oppressive presence in Western intellectual culture serves mainly to call into question the Chinese taste in heroes, we will spend some time elaborating upon this figure, bringing him into a more impressive focus.

The second figure — that of Plato — would need no introduction were it not for the complexity and many-faceted character of his thinking, overlaid by centuries of ramification, celebration, and excoriation which interpret and obfuscate the received Plato.

Ours will be a habilitated Confucius and a rehabilitated Plato. And, of course, one cannot comment upon Plato without, tacitly or explicitly, invoking his mouthpiece and mentor Socrates, the other half of what Emerson called "that double star which even the most powerful of lenses cannot separate."

Three thinkers, then — Plato, Socrates, and Confucius — will figure prominently in our remarks. But the theme is friendship and there are two of us — friends, in fact — making this presentation. It would be indecent to ignore the relationship that serves as the basis of our collaboration and that has led us to this place. A sixth individual, the convener and editor of this series, and a seventh, our lecture commentator, both friends of ours — and allies, too, of Plato and Confucius — will join this motley society.

Seven of us together in this piece. But after a brief introduction of the alien Confucius and the somewhat estranged Plato we shall be concerned not with the individuals but with the relationships forming this community. The explicit concern will be with the possible relationship of Plato and Confucius and the manner in which that relationship might qualify and enrich the understanding of those implicated in this project, as well as those entertaining these words.

Our ultimate subject is Confucian friendship and its relation to the kind of spirituality which might be termed *religiousness*. But experience has shown us that discussions of Chinese thought and culture addressed to Western audiences are best served by rehearsing collateral themes drawn from the resources of both cultures. This effort allows us to raise to consciousness some of the biases that militate against our understanding an exotic sensibility, thereby performing the task John Dewey claimed defined true philosophical endeavors—namely, "to help get rid of the useless lumber that blocks our highways of thought."

I. BEGINNING WITH PLATO

If one were considering friendship in its most general sense within the Western tradition, one could hardly omit, as we shall, reference to Aristotle. But if one focuses upon the relation of friendships to spirituality, Plato is the obvious place to begin. Specifically, we shall begin with Plato's *Phaedrus*, a dialogue whose discussion of the uses of rhetoric and philosophy serves as the basis of the emerging friendship of Socrates and Phaedrus.

When we first encounter Phaedrus he is under the influence of the rhetorician Lysias, having just heard him speak on the topic of love. There can be no relationship between Phaedrus and Socrates until the former is freed from his attachment to the persuasive power of rhetoric and raised to the level of dialectic. The dialogue tells how Socrates achieves this end. His first move is a lateral one: he seduces Phaedrus away from Lysias by constructing a superior rhetorical discourse on love. Then, in a second, philosophical speech, Socrates illustrates the employment of dialectic and dialogue, encouraging Phaedrus to accept the role of a fellow enquirer.

You may recall that this dialogue ends with a prayer of Socrates:

> Beloved Pan and all the other gods who dwell here, grant me to be beautiful within. Let me believe that it is only the wise man

who is rich. Let the mass of my gold be only what the temperate man, and no other, can make his own.[1]

Phaedrus responds:

Please include me in your prayer, for friends hold everything in common.[2]

It is Socrates' desire for temperance, wisdom, and inner beauty which qualify him to be a friend. And it is Phaedrus' sharing of this quality, the *eros* — the desire for temperance, wisdom, and beauty — that guarantees his friendship with Socrates.

The Platonic message, we all know, is that the noblest quality is to be found in none of the static, stable qualities or virtues, but in the erotic motive force that sometimes leads us, sometimes drives us, toward completeness of understanding, the presupposition of all the virtues.

This view of friendship, a variant of Platonic love, entails the consequence that the bond of friendship lies beyond either person in a common desire that can exist only by virtue of a transcendent goal: Truth, Beauty, the Good. A common purpose, a common end, a shared project — provided that project, end, or aim is a noble, refined one — is the basis of friendship.

But this raises a problem that has vexed the tradition from the beginning, doubly so after the collision of Hellenic and Hebraic sensibilities. The problem is how to distinguish the kinds of love appropriate to the differing sorts of relationships, human and divine, available to rational creatures, most of which (the earth-dwellers) are beset by disqualifying passions which compromise, if they do not cancel, any chances for true relatedness.

At one level we are embarrassed by the notion that friendship is a kind of love. It is an embarrassment born of the intuition — and here the Hebraic and Hellenic aspects of our natures coincide — that love is always tinctured by sexuality. In the standard Platonic reading, friendship is a kind of love; and in the modern Hebraic-Christian version of Platonism, it is a kind of love from which distinctly sexual feelings must be effectively absent.

We are given some assistance by appeal to Aristophanes' myth of the round men in *The Symposium*.

In the beginning the sexes were not as they are now, but originally three in number; there was man, woman, and the union of the two. . . . The primeval man was round, his back and sides forming a circle; and he had four hands, and four feet, one head and two faces, looking opposite ways, set on a round neck and precisely alike; also four ears, two privy members, and the remainder to correspond. . . . Terrible was their might and strength, and the thoughts of their hearts were great, and they made an attack upon the gods.

After much deliberation, the gods decided—it was Zeus himself who made the decision—to punish them by dividing them in two. In this manner their power was halved while the number of sacrifices they were made to perform was doubled.

Now they were divided beings, each seeking their sundered half, but with disastrous results. Once a pair was reunited, they refused to let go, becoming tangled together. They began to die of starvation and self-neglect. Zeus realized the problem and set about to solve it in a most proactive manner. He invented the sexual orgasm.

Zeus in pity of them invented a new plan: he turned the parts of generation round to the front . . . and they sowed their seed no longer upon the ground like grasshoppers, but in one another; and after the transposition the male generated in the female in order that by mutual embraces of man and woman they might breed, and the race might continue; or if man came to man they might be satisfied, and rest, and go their ways to the business of life.

The message couldn't be clearer and—with proper adjustments which take into account Plato's slightly different use of irony—couldn't be more Platonic. Love (*eros*) is for union; sexuality is for disunion. Love promotes interdependence; sexuality promotes autonomy. Love drives toward physical accord; the gift of physical sexuality allows us the freedom "to go about the business of the day."

The conclusion of the *Phaedrus* is that friends hold all things in common, and when what they hold in common is an *eros* directed toward the transcendent Good, they are true friends. The conclusion of the myth of the round men reinforces the moral of the *Phaedrus*; namely, if love, as opposed to sexual intercourse, remains at the physical level, denied any common transcending other as the basis for the search for unity, it cancels autonomy. This autonomy is rewon only for those who can employ sexuality in a recreative rather than a procreative manner. If we ask what friendship is in Aristophanes' terms, it can only be that relationship which permits one's partner to express autonomy and independence, allowing him or her to "go about the business of the day" unhindered by unsatisfied desires.[3]

Plato's principal point drawn from the *Phaedrus* and the *Symposium* seems to be that friendship is the necessary condition for realizing the Good. The passion, the *eros*, the sublimated sexuality is a condition not of the friendship, but of the common desire for the rational ideals which the friendship augments and sustains.

We said at the beginning that we would offer a rehabilitated Plato as a means of preparing for a discussion of the Confucian idea of friendship. The received Plato needs rehabilitation with respect to the notion of friendship, due to the manner in which the mystical and meditative traditions of the Hebraic-Christian sensibility have stressed the private, personal, individuated character of spirituality. Granted that the institutions of monasticism and congregational worship for the most part perpetuate this understanding of friendship as the ground of spirituality, there is the prominent belief among many of us that the sole relationship essential to the ends of spirituality is that between the individual and her God. It is this belief which leads to the interpretation of friendship as merely an instrument for the attainment of spirituality. The *philia* which binds friends doesn't really bind them at all; it is the means whereby the *eros* driving each separately toward the Good is augmented and sustained. Friendship allows friends to go about the business of being spiritual, which means seeking a personal, individual relationship with that which lies beyond.

So far, we have raised two Platonic questions as a means of anticipating our discussion of the Confucian understanding of friendship. The first question is whether friendship can promote spirituality. On the Platonic model we have sketched in the simplest terms, this is clearly so. A second question is whether by so serving it is denied any intrinsic value and is rendered merely instrumental. The evidence seems to lead us to that conclusion insofar as we rely on Plato.

We are at last prepared to address the topic announced in our title. We intend to focus upon this question: Does the Confucian understanding of the relationship of friendship and spirituality make friendship instrumental to the ends of religiousness as the spiritualized Plato seems to do?

II. CONFUCIAN FRIENDSHIP

The *Hsun Tzu* recalls a conversation between Confucius and several of his disciples on the central virtue of classical Confucianism, *jen*, conventionally translated "benevolence," "humanity," and "goodness":

> Tzu-lu came in and Confucius asked him, " . . . What does it mean to be a *jen* person? He replied, " . . . A *jen* person is one who causes others to love him." Confucius remarked, "Such is called a refined person."
>
> Tzu-kung came in and Confucius asked him, " . . . What does it mean to be a *jen* person?" He replied, "A *jen* person is one who loves others." Confucius remarked, "Such can be called a consummately refined person."
>
> Yen Yuan came in and Confucius asked him, " . . . What does it mean to be a *jen* person?" He replied, " . . . A *jen* person is one who loves himself." Confucius remarked, "Such can be called the truly enlightened person."[4]

This passage invites considerable commentary. At least for the *Hsun Tzu*'s interpretation of Confucius, the "love" originated in the project of becoming an authoritative person is a ground of mutual incorporation between oneself and other. Since the kind of love referred to in this passage requires consideration of the other person, it is not entirely surprising that the term that translates it, *ai*, also means "to grudge" or "to be sparing with." A person who loves another and assumes that person's concerns as her own, respects the uniqueness and integrity of the other, takes her on her own terms, and is circumspect in any demands she might make. She values the person's difference as the basis for their friendship, and wants the other to remain fully herself, without being distorted or reshaped in the relationship. Hence, in this classical Chinese sense of love, to love another is to be sparing of her.

The first and lowest level of personal achievement indicated by the first response entails conducting oneself in such a manner as to occasion other people taking one's concerns as their own. While this in Confucius' eyes is praiseworthy conduct, it is still one-directional, focusing as it does upon the satisfaction of one's own needs. As such, there is a residual selfishness in this espoused goal.

The second level of personal cultivation requires that one take the concerns of others as one's own. While this is perhaps a higher level of development than the first, it is again only one-directional, focusing on the needs of the other rather than one's own. Such altruism, while admirable, is unfortunately self-abnegating: one's own legitimate concerns are not properly served.

The highest level, then, is necessarily reflexive, incorporating in one's own person the entire field of self-other concerns. *Jen* here does not refer to an isolatable agent or action; rather, *jen* describes a cultivated and mutually beneficial relationship between self and other. It indicates a complementarity grounded in the resolutely unique and specific conditions of one's cultivated relationship with another person.

The cultivation of *jen* is thus a sociological phenomenon rather than psychological: it is irreducibly other-entailing. One cannot become *jen* in Descartes' closet. The relationality of *jen* — a graph comprised of "person" and the number "two" — is underscored repeatedly in the *Analects*:

> Confucius said, "To overcome the self-other distinction and engage in ritual practice is to become authoritative as a person. If for the space of one day one were able to accomplish this, the world would turn to one as an authoritative person. Becoming an authoritative person emerges from oneself — how could it come from others?"[5]

Ritual practices (*li*) are the repertory of those formal roles, practices, actions, and institutions that continue the living culture. They are meaning-invested behaviors which, when properly enacted, conduce to communal harmony. They are a central concern in becoming *jen* because of their capacity to locate a person socially and culturally within a community.

Important here again is this notion of reflexivity. Ritual practice, like love (*ai*), is bidirectional. Ritual or "propriety" requires that cultural meaning be recovered in the formal role and performance, and also that the role be personalized and "made one's own" by investing it with oneself and one's own importances. Ritual is enacted by one person, and invokes a reaction in the community in which it is performed.

This brings us to a potentially problematic passage repeated in the *Analects* which helps us focus the peculiar conditions of Confucian friendship. It is because of the fundamental importance of "other" in this existential project of becoming *jen* that Confucius can say repeatedly: "Take as friends only those who are better than yourself."[6] This exclusionary notion that a friend to qualify as a friend must be better than oneself seems to be contradicted in other passages in the text, such as:

> Confucius said, "Having three kinds of friends will bring personal improvement; three kinds will bring injury. To have friends who are straight, who are true to their word, and who are well-informed is to be improved; to have friends who are ingratiating, foppish, and plausible is to be injured."[7]

On the surface of it, it would seem that ingratiating friends are still friends. But it is not really so. Ritual practice and music, in the absence of personal achievement, is hollow and meaningless; in fact, such conduct cannot be properly called ritual practice and music. As Confucius observes,

> What does one who is not achieved in his person (*jen*) have to do with ritual practice or with music?[8]

That is, ritual performed by a culturally vacuous person is not really ritual. Similarly, a Confucian "friend" — a *yu* — who is not better than oneself is not properly a friend. Unlike the English word *friend*, *yu* for Confucius cannot be used loosely for mere acquaintances or strangers, or as a mark of goodwill or kindly condescension. The term conventionally translated as "friend" (*yu*) in classical Chinese is homophonous with *yu*, meaning the "right hand" as opposed to "left." "Friend," like the right hand, is valorized as the place of honor. As such, "friend" in classical Chinese is resolutely hierarchical — an occasion to grow personally — and can only be assigned to the *jen* relationship in which one is able to express deference to another. Friendship is based upon appreciated differences between oneself and another person which present themselves as specific occasions for one's character development, rather than upon perceived commonalities with the other person.

Yu is also homophonous and used interchangeably in the classical corpus with *yu* ("having at hand"). It is having someone at hand to whom one can defer, and take as one's model. *Yu* is going "hand-in-hand" with someone from whom one can benefit and learn, deriving as this term originally does from a graph comprised of "two hands."

That Confucius insisted upon this restricted and specific use of *friend* (*yu*) is suggested in a discussion on the meaning of *friend* which involves two of Confucius' closest disciples, Tzu-hsia and Tzu-

chang. In the years following the death of the Master, these two disciples had matured into patriarchs in their own right with their own
interpretations of what Confucius had said and meant.

> The disciples of Tzu-hsia asked Tzu-chang about friendship (*yu*).
> Tzu-chang queried, "What has Tzu-hsia told you?" They replied,
> "Join together with those from whom you can learn; spurn those
> from whom you can't."

It would seem from Tzu-hsia's definition of *yu* that he is retaining
the strictness with which Confucius wants to use this term. But such a
narrow reading does not go unchallenged. Tzu-chang says,

> This is different from what I have heard. The exemplary person
> exalts the worthy and is tolerant of the common, praises those
> who are capable and is sympathetic to those who are not. If in
> comparison with others I am truly worthy, who am I unable to
> tolerate? If I am not worthy in the comparison, and people are
> going to spurn me, on what basis do I spurn them?[9]

In evaluating these two very different interpretations of Confucius' attitude toward friendship, it is helpful to recall the profile of
these two disciples that emerges from frequent reference in the *Analects* and elsewhere. Tzu-chang with his free-wheeling altruism was
repeatedly rebuked by Confucius for paying more attention to ap-
pearances than to substance, and for using language without due care.[10]
Tzu-hsia, on the other hand, is credited more than any other disciple
for his scholarship, and played a major role in the transmission of the
Confucian Classics.[11] On this basis, then, we can speculate that it is
probably Tzu-hsia who is transmitting the more literal understanding
of Confucian friendship (*yu*).

In the peculiarly Confucian conception of friendship, then, we
have certain conditions. First, a friend is a necessary condition for becoming authoritative in one's person (*jen*). Hence, when asked about
how to become *jen*, Confucius replies,

> When living in a particular country, serve the most worthy of the
> high officials, and make friends with those scholars who are
> most *jen*.[12]

One must love a friend as a complementary aspect of one's self, yet at
the same time, allow such friends to retain their integrity. Again,

although Confucius is clear that one cannot demand all-round perfection in a single person,[13] the friend must on balance and in important respects be qualitatively superior to oneself—an object of personal deference.

Given the central importance of *jen* in Confucian thought, the decidedly underdetermined status of this notion as it is presented in the *Analects* has been a source of concern for commentators over the centuries. On six different occasions, Confucius is called upon to define *jen* and six times he gives a different answer. The best that Confucius can do in stipulating the content of *jen* is to point to historical exemplars. If we interpret classical Confucianism as an aestheticism which begins from the coordination of insistently particular details, the vagueness of *jen* can be explained as the same uncertainty that attends any aesthetic achievement. Like any ritual or role (*li*) in the Confucian world, friendship is fundamentally aesthetic in the sense that it emerges as a harmony through the fruitful collaboration of unique details. Its formal aspects are always qualified and made contingent to specific social, cultural, and natural conditions by the investment of personal interest. Given these particularistic demands of *jen*—the mutually enhancing coordination of *this* person with *this* friend—friendships are always unique relationships which cannot be captured in the language of formula or replication.[14]

Jen is conventionally translated "benevolence," "humanity," and "goodness." The problem with *benevolence* is that it individuates and psychologizes *jen*, reducing a holistic and relational conception of person to someone's particular moral disposition. *Humanity*, a broader and hence more adequate term, still fails to do justice to the profoundly religious dimension of *jen*. In fact, it tends to set up the opposition we find in the contrast between religion and humanism. Friendship, for Confucius, is grounded in *jen*, and is, at the same time, the road to religiousness. Confucius, rather than appealing to transcendent beings or principles as the ultimate reference for spiritual growth, describes the process of personal cultivation in terms of "starting from what is most basic and immediate, and penetrating through to what is most elevated."[15]

What is the relationship, then, between Confucian friendship and religiousness? Confucian religiousness begins from the assumption that there is a continuity and interdependence between what has been translated as "Heaven" (*t'ien*), and "the human being" (*jen*). This correlativity between Heaven and the particular person is often captured in the claim that *t'ien-jen ho-yi* (literally, "Heaven and human beings are continuous") used to summarize religious sensibilities during this period.[16] Hence, the *Mencius* observes:

> For a person to realize fully her heart-and-mind is to realize fully her nature and character, and in so doing, she realizes Heaven.[17]

Heaven and the Way (*tao*) are often associated if not used interchangeably in the classical Confucian corpus. And Confucius insists that "it is the human being who broadens the Way, not the Way that broadens the human being."[18] The continuity and interdependence between Heaven and the human being precludes the notion of transcendent deity familiar within the orthodox theology of the Judeo-Christian tradition, cast as it is in the language of *creatio ex nihilo*, independence, self-sufficiency, determinative and absolute power, and so on. The One-Many model of cosmic order — cosmos as universe — in which Godhead is the residence of Truth, Beauty, and Goodness, and in which all is to be ultimately explained by reference to divine will, is not operative in the classical Chinese world. The fundamental question is not: "What is the underlying cosmic unity which explains plurality?" but rather, "In a world in which a continuous and interdependent plurality of things (*wan-wu*) is all you've got — a world of self-originating, self-construing, and self-renewing things (*tzu-jan*) — where does a particular thing begin, and where does it end?" The *Mencius* thus says that "all of the myriad things are here in me."[19] We can explain this claim in the following way.

Persons are always persons-in-context, inhering as they do in a world defined by specific social, cultural, and natural conditions. Persons shape and are shaped by the field of things and events in which they reside. A person is fluid and multivalent in the sense that, in any particular situation, he or she is open to redefinition in many different ways — as mother, as brother, as student, as lover, as Chinese, as tall, and so on. Articulated and brought into focus in any one of these roles, a person expresses the community from both a focal and a local perspective within the extended field of relationships. An analogy might help here. Consider the value of any particular note in a symphony — a symphony which is always entertained through one note or another. The value of any one note can only be assayed by understanding its place in the entire piece of music and its performance. Any one note thus has implicate within it the entire score. The note has a holographic quality, bringing the field of relationships into focus from one particular place or locus. Important here is that the field of relationships is not circumscribed or holistic, but an unbounded reservoir of particular detail that remains open and available for further inclusion. The field of relevant detail for the particular note can be extended to include a movement in another piece by the same composer, or that composer's entire corpus, or the musical product of a particular era, and so on.

Returning to "persons-in-context," they, like the note, are multivalent, bringing the human community and its natural surrounds into focus from their particular perspective. As such, they are more or less distinguished, more or less articulated, more or less representative of the values and cultural importances of their communities.

This language of focus and field provides us with a way of talking about the continuity and interdependence of the human being and Heaven presupposed in the Confucian worldview. Heaven is the field — the social, cultural, and natural context — in some sense greater than the particular person ("Heaven grows the virtue here in me"),[20] in some sense implicate within and brought into focus by the particular person ("all of the myriad things are here in me").[21] Heaven is frequently described in anthropomorphic terms: it is temporal, geographical, at once physical and psychical. But the relationship is bidirectional, and works the other way as well. The human being is also theomorphic. That is, when a person is successful in focusing culture and its institutions in a manner that is exemplary, and emerges as a model for his community and future generations to which they defer, he has extended himself through their patterns of deference, and has become the object of reverence. Hence, in the Confucian vocabulary, cultivation enlarges one's person (*ta jen*), so that one becomes describable in nothing less than cosmic terms, locating one squarely as Heaven:

> Chung-ni (Confucius) is the sun and moon, and there is no way of climbing beyond him. . . . The Master is unreachable, just as the sky cannot be divided and scaled.[22]

By contrast, a failure to cultivate oneself on the part of a person who enjoys both opportunity and power results in moral retardation— the "small" person (*hsiao jen*) who appears as a foil throughout the *Analects*.

An analysis of the character *shen* restates this analysis in religious terms. It gives us the entire picture. *Shen* means both human spirituality and divinity. Etymologically, its root meaning is "extension." As persons become increasingly spiritual through the effective performance of communal life forms (*li*), and become increasingly inspirational for their communities, they are exalted, and move in the direction of divinity. As the *Mencius* observes,

> The admirable person is called "good." The one who has integrity is called "true." To be totally genuine is called "beautiful," and to radiate this genuineness is called "greatness." Being great, to be transformed and transforming is called "sageliness." And being sagely, to be unfathomable is called "spirituality/divinity."[23]

Cultural heroes, perhaps dead, yet culturally alive and well, ascend to become gods. Ancestors, long entombed, are the cultural resource for tradition, and thus its continuing object of respect.

Where, then, is the friend (*yu*) in this process of religious realization? Persons in this tradition seek spiritual growth in the community of other persons who are themselves living (although at times dead) repositories of culture and the tradition's claim to Truth, Beauty, and Goodness. Only those persons from whom one can learn and "increase" (*yi*), and who, through inspired deference, provide a source of meaning for oneself, are thus conducive to spiritual growth. Early in the quest, such friends are undoubtedly many. But one's spiritual extension absorbs these persons into one's own field of selves, and those remaining persons representing the quality of difference necessary for continuing growth become more difficult to find.

We can survey the *Analects* and ask the question: Whom would Confucius—on his strict terms that a friend must be better than oneself—call friend? The *Mencius* is of some assistance here:

> Mencius said to Wan Chang, "The best person in one village will make friends with the best person in another village; the best person in one state will make friends with the best person in another state; the best person in the empire will make friends with other people in the empire like him. And not content with making friends with the best people in the empire, he goes back in time and communes with the ancients. When one reads the

poems and writings of the ancients, can it be right not to know something about them as persons? Hence one tries to understand the age in which they lived. This can be described as "looking for friends in history."[24]

Confucius' first friend, then, is the Duke of Chou:

> The Master said, "My, but I am in a state of decline. How long has it been since I have visited with the Duke of Chou in my dreams!"[25]

Beyond such "friends in history" as the Duke of Chou and Kuan Chung and King Wen and Wu, it is a real question as to whether Confucius could have any friends so defined.

Confucius, as he is portrayed in the *Analects*, is peerless and, hence, friendless in this restricted Confucian sense of the term. To assert that Confucius had friends would diminish him. He is described as learning from everyone and from no one:

> Kung-sun Ch'ao of Wei asked Tzu-kung, "Who did Confucius learn from?" Tzu-kung replied, "The culture (*tao*) of King Wen and Wu has not yet fallen to the ground. It resides in people. While none remain unaffected by it, those who are worthy have got it in great measure, while those who are not still have a modicum of it. Who then did Confucius *not* learn from? Again, how could there be a single, constant teacher for him?"[26]

Another way of viewing this peculiarly Confucian notion of friendship is to appreciate the extent to which family relationships dominated the social and political structure. An argument can be and has been made that *all* relationships were ultimately construed in familial terms.[27] This meant that success within one's various social circles would eventually establish one as a patriarch, a position which would not reduce to friendship relations. It is significant that while D. C. Lau has Confucius referring to his disciples as "my young friends," the expression more literally translated is "my little masters/sons [*hsiao tzu*]." This paternalism was pervasive in the culture, and has remained unchanged as a model of order throughout the whole history of Confucianism.

If there is any exception to the observation that Confucius had no friends, it was his favorite disciple, Yen Hui, who most likely in death became available to Confucius as a friend. Confucius rarely and reluctantly used the term *jen* to describe anyone, including himself. In fact, he repeatedly sidestepped the use of *jen* to characterize people around him.[28] Yen Hui was the exception:

> As for Hui, in his heart-and-mind he would go three months without offending against *jen*. With the rest of them, they only achieve *jen* occasionally.[29]

Perhaps most telling was his comment to Tzu-kung which repeats the same language as "Take as friends only those who are better than yourself":

> You do not measure up to Yen Hui. He is better than both you and me.[30]

While Confucius himself had no friends, it would seem to be the case that all who knew and loved Confucius took him as friend in the proper sense. The exclusiveness with which Confucius is willing to use the term *friend* (*yu*) does not preclude other very positive relationships through which one expresses nurturance and caring. The Mencian dictum "Try your best to treat others as you would be treated"[31] means that the category *yu* does not exhaust the people to whom one owes affection in the Confucian world.

III. PLATO AND CONFUCIUS

It is difficult to think of two more distinct conceptions of friendship than those of Plato and Confucius. For Plato, true friendship is based upon the equality expressed by the need to hold all things, most particularly the search for Beauty, Truth, and Goodness, in common. For Confucius friendship is a one-directional relationship in which one extends oneself by association with one who has attained a higher level of realization. Further, the ironic self-effacement used by Socrates to permit an equality where none might otherwise exist is absent from the Confucian tradition. The negative assessment of sexuality with respect to the idea of true friendship that looms so large in Platonism is absent from Confucius. Indeed, the theme of sexuality itself is effectively absent at the level of intellectual discourse.[32] There is a clear reference to transcendent ideals in the Platonic understanding of true friendship, but no such transcendence is present in the Confucian tradition. The norm of Confucius is sagehood—the urgency of becoming coextensive with the tradition. Such a realization, which at its extreme would be tantamount to becoming *t'ien*, remains an immanent norm, for *t'ien* itself is immanent.

For Confucius, friendship has more the quality of Platonic *eros* than *philia*. It is not only one-directional, but it is directed at that which is higher, more realized. The mutuality of joint inquiry is a presupposition of the individual attainment of the Good. Insofar as that inquiry is stressed above ecstatic realization of the Good—and with respect to Confucius, insofar as the road to sagehood is held to be a process, a path, a way, rather than the realized status of Sage (insofar, that is, as both Confucius and Plato believe that "the road is better than the inn")—there is a commonality of perspective in which friendship may be said to be noninstrumental. But, to the degree that both Platonic and Confucian perspectives stress the state of realization, there is surely a sense in which friendship may be said to be instrumental in both instances. In any case, friendship is an indirect route to the Good for Plato, while it serves as the direct path in Confucian thinking.

There is a poignancy in the conclusion that Socrates and Confucius could not be friends. Confucius, at an early stage of his development, might seek friendship based upon a perceived superiority in Socrates, while Socrates would solicit Confucius' participation in the joint inquiry after the Good. Socratic irony would not allow the inequality Confucius requires as a means of self-betterment. Confucius would not permit himself and Socrates to hold all things in common.

NOTES

1. Plato, *Phaedrus*, trans. W. C. Helmbold and W. G. Rabinowitz (Indianapolis: Bobbs-Merrill, 1956), p. 75.
2. Ibid.
3. The sexist implications of these accounts have been rehearsed often in the past decades and are not the primary focus here.
4. *Hsun Tzu* 105.29.29ff.
5. *Analects* 12.1. See also 6.30, 3.3, and 15.39.
6. Ibid., 1.8. See also 9.25.
7. Ibid., 16.4. See also 19.3.
8. Ibid., 3.3.
9. Ibid., 19.3.

10. D. C. Lau, pp. 258–60.

11. Ibid., p. 256.

12. *Analects* 15.10.

13. Ibid., 13.25; 18.10.

14. We have argued for the particularity of *jen* at some length in David L. Hall and Roger T. Ames, *Thinking Through Confucius* (Albany, N.Y.: State University of New York Press, 1987), esp. pp. 110–30.

15. *Analects* 14.35.

16. See Hall and Ames, *Thinking Through Confucius*, chap. 4, esp. pp. 241–46, for our argument that this is a fair characterization of Confucian religiousness.

17. *Mencius* 7A.1.

18. *Analects* 15.29.

19. *Mencius* 7A.4.

20. *Analects* 7.23.

21. *Mencius* 7A.4.

22. *Analects* 19.24 and 19.25. See also 2.1 and 8.19, and *Mencius* 3A.4.

23. *Mencius* 7B.25.

24. Ibid., 5B.8.

25. *Analects* 7.5.

26. Ibid., 19.22.

27. See Ambrose King, "The Individual and Group in Confucianism: A Relational Perspective," in *Individualism and Holism: Studies in Confucian and Taoist Values*, ed. Donald Munro (Ann Arbor: University of Michigan Press, 1985).

28. See, for example, *Analects* 5.8.

29. Ibid., 6.7.

30. Ibid., 5.9.

31. *Mencius* 7A.4.

32. The absence of verbal reference to sexuality in friendship or in any other relationship in the classical Chinese tradition might be explained in the following way. In the Great Preface to the *Book of Songs* it states:

> Song is the result of dispositions. It resides in the heart-and-mind as dispositions and is articulated in language as song. One's feelings stir within one's breast, and take form in words. When words are inadequate, they are voiced in sighs. When sighs are inadequate, they are chanted. When chants are inadequate, unconsciously, the hands and feet begin to dance them.

Language, song, and body are three levels of discourse which differ in that as we move from words to music to dance, the discourse becomes increasingly personal and decreasingly referential. It is an investment of self. Dance or other bodily expressions, including sexual relations, cannot be reduced to language without profound depersonalization. People don't say "I love you" in Chinese because such a disposition is expressed in so many ways that the language, far from reinforcing the love relationship, depersonalizes it and brings it into question. Sexual relations, when articulated in language, invite other people into the act — sexuality becomes pornography.

An Indian View of Friendship[1]

BHIKHU PAREKH

HUMAN BEINGS STAND IN different kinds of relationship with each other: parents and children, siblings, husband and wife, neighbors, fellow-ethnics, fellow citizens. As we generally understand it, friendship, although sharing features in common with some of these relationships, constitutes a distinct kind of relationship.

First, it is nonbiological in the sense that unlike parents and children or siblings, it is not based on the ties of blood or heredity. This is not to deny that parents and children or brothers and sisters may become friends, but rather that their natural relationship sets limits to the quality and depth of their friendship and that the latter is irreducible and autonomous in nature.

Second, friendship is a voluntary relationship. Although it is not based on conscious, let alone rational, choices, and often grows unconsciously and involves an elusive "mental chemistry," it contains elements of deliberation, choice, and decision. The parties involved are aware of the development of their relationship, and freely decide whether or not to sustain and intensify it by required acts of reciprocity. Since it is entirely voluntary and neither embedded in a network of other relations nor reinforced by social sanctions, friendship is one of the most mortal of all human relationships.

Third, friendship is a relationship between two individuals. One might have many friends, but one is a friend of each of them individually. Friendship is not and never can be a mass or collective relationship.

Fourth, since friendship has no basis outside of itself and is a free creation of two individuals, it is entirely dependent on what they care to make of it. It takes whatever form they choose to give it, has such content and depth as they succeed in putting into it, is a unique expression of the kinds of persons they are, and reveals their individuality to a much greater degree than most other human relationships.

95

Fifth, friendship is open-ended and admits of degrees. One person is "just" a friend; another is a "good" friend; yet another is a "close" or an "intimate" friend—a "fast" friend, as Indians call it. Friendship covers a large spectrum ranging from a perceptible degree of warmth to a near total merger of two selves, and often occupies a place somewhere between the two extremes.

Sixth, friendship is reciprocal and involves mutual acknowledgement and a shared understanding. I cannot be your friend unless you are my friend. Friendship cannot come into being and last unless the parties involved acknowledge its existence, are broadly agreed on what it means and entails, and behave towards each other accordingly.

Finally, friendship involves mutual liking and good will. Friends are well disposed to each other, wish each other well, and help each other in times of need. They help each other not because they think they *ought* to help their fellow humans, but because they care for each other's well being and wish to be of mutual help. And they care for each other not because they cannot bear to see *human beings* suffer but because they are attached to each other and cannot bear to see *their friends* suffer or feel unhappy. As friendship deepens, mutual liking generates affection and perhaps even love. Since friendship is based on mutual liking, it is an unmediated relationship between two unique individuals. Friends are friends because, for some reason, they have "hit it off" and enjoy each other's presence. Although their common interests, temperaments, background, and so forth throw some light on why they became or remain friends, these do not determine and explain why their relationship took a specific form, acquired a specific measure of depth, and survived changes in interest and circumstances.

Friendship then is a nonbiological, voluntary, open-ended, informal, uninstitutionalized, and mutually acknowledged relationship between two individuals based on their good will and fondness for each other. Given these and its other constitutive features, it is only possible under certain conditions. Friendship presupposes a society or a culture in which human relationships are not totally structured and formalized, and leave adequate space for informal and self-generated relationships. It also presupposes that individuals are able to rise above their socially defined roles, are willing and able to undertake the adventure of new and unpredictable relationships, and have the courage and the disposition to share their intimate thoughts, feelings, and vulnerabilities with others and mortgage their happiness to others' inherently precarious feelings. It also implies that individuals have the patience, constancy of contact, and emotional energy required for a slowly maturing relationship; that they share enough experiences in common to have something to talk about; that they have the capacity to rise above their narrow self-interest and establish noncalculative relationships with others; that they have the emotional and moral maturity to understand and to adjust to each other's moods and eccentricities; and that they do not take so narrow a view of morality that it leaves no room for partiality and preference. These and related conditions do not obtain in all societies, and hence friendship is not a universal phenomenon. Some societies, such as the tribal, have only a limited space for friendship; some others, such as the modern liberal societies, encourage it up to a point but not beyond; some others such as the communist societies frown on it and prefer the collectivist ethos of comradeship based on dedication to a common cause. Many religious communities discourage friendship because it detracts from the love of God and breeds pockets of deep personal attachments. For the Stoics the wise man had no friends, and Kant had difficulty reconciling friendship with the principle of universal impartiality.[2]

I intend to inquire if Indian thinkers identified a form of relationship analogous to that of friendship as described above, how they analyzed its nature and structure, and what value they placed on it. Indian thinking on the subject goes as far back as the *Rigveda* composed around 1000 B.C.E.[3] The *Rigveda* uses three terms to describe the relationship of friendship, namely, *sakhā*, *mitra*, and *suhṛd*.[4] None of these is the exact counterpart of the modern conception of friendship, but none is wholly dissimilar either. Although sometimes the *Rigveda* uses the three terms to characterize different forms of friendship, on other occasions it uses them interchangeably. Indian thinking on friendship was further developed in such subsequent texts as the *Athervaveda*, the two epics of the *Rāmāyana* and the *Mahābhārata*, *Panchatantra*, the *Purāṇas*, and the classical literary works of Kalidasa, Bana, Bhavabhuti, and other eminent writers. Since I cannot summarize and trace the development of the Indian view of friendship developed over several millennia, I shall mostly but not entirely concentrate on the epics.

Although the two epics were composed many centuries ago and are in that sense dated, they have been reverentially read over the years, and remain an abiding source of moral inspiration and norms. They were revived and became a source of political and cultural inspiration during the Indian struggle for independence. They were also recently serialized on the state-controlled television, the *Rāmāyana* being shown for seventy-eight weeks, and the *Mahābhārata* for over ninety weeks. Each installment lasted for nearly three-quarters of an hour, was regularly watched by millions of Indians of all religions, and brought most of the country to a standstill. The concept of friendship that I shall discuss is therefore not at all a historical curiosity but very much alive and influential.

The traditional Indian thinking on friendship was enriched by the contributions of Islamic and Western civilizations, which between them exercised a considerable influence on the country for nearly seven centuries. They introduced new conceptions of friendship that shaped and were in turn shaped by the traditional Indian conception of it. For reasons of space I shall ignore these two influences.[5] Since India's independence in 1947, the regional literature, the regional and Hindi cinema, the radio and television, and so on have all been engaged in developing a shared popular culture on such a wide variety of subjects as the state, citizenship, the caste, the family, and friendship. As a result several new conceptions of friendship, eclectically derived from different traditions and often combining incompatible elements, are gaining popularity and giving rise to a bewildering vocabulary and discourse on the subject. For reasons of space as well as because of the sheer unmanageability of the material, I shall not analyze these new developments.

One last point of clarification is in order. No discussion of friendship in the Indian context can overlook the pervasive reality of caste and gender. Although the dominant ideology disapproved of the friendship between the higher and lower castes, such friendships did develop in practice and were discussed in the literature; for example, the friendship between Karna and Duryodhana in the *Mahābhārata* and that between Rama and the monkey-king Sugriva in the *Rāmāyana*. Although such unconventional friendships had their own peculiar dialectic, much of what I shall say about friendship applies to them as well.

Almost all the examples of friendship in the two epics and the other religious and literary texts relate to men. Friendships between men and women are discussed, but they are either between two lovers or, more often, between husband and wife, as in the case of Kalidasa's *Meghdūt* and *Ajavilāp*. In both of these the separated husband desperately misses his wife, who is described as a friend (*sakhi*). As for friendships between women, they too are noted and analyzed in Indian literary texts. The term used to describe such friends is *sakhi*, and their relationship involves mutual caring, fondness, support, and above all exchanging and keeping confidence. Female friendships are generally presented as more intimate, reliable, and durable, more easily made, and less self-conscious than those between men. However, in most other respects they are like male friendships. What I shall say about the latter therefore applies to female friendships as well, albeit with some qualifications.

I

Almost from the very beginning, the Indian discussion of friendship took place at two levels, which for convenience I shall call metaphysical and social. At the metaphysical level, Indian thinkers asked what should be the proper human orientation, disposition, or attitude (*bhāva*) towards the rest of the universe. In contrast to the anthropocentric and theocentric views of the universe dominant in the West, most Indian thinkers took a cosmocentric view of it. For them the universe was an internally articulated and ordered whole whose constituents were all its equally legitimate "co-tenants" enjoying the right to exist and avail themselves of its resources. Human beings therefore had a duty of universal friendliness and goodwill (*maitri*) towards the other orders of being. Rather than grudge their existence and destroy them in pursuit of their narrowly defined species-interests, they are enjoined to cherish them and take delight in the infinite beauty and diversity of the universe. A remarkable prayer to Gods in *Sukla Yajurveda* reads: "Mitrasyāham caksusā sarvani bhūtāni samikse" ("I look upon all living beings with the eyes of a friend"). In *Taitiriya Samhita*, the author wishes "peace" to earth, trees, plants, waters, and indeed to all sentient beings and prays that he may not unwittingly injure even the root of a plant. As the *Mahābhārata* puts it, "he verily knows the substance of *dharma* who is always the friend of all." Friendship to all living beings leads to non-violence (*ahimsā*), meaning not only abstention from harming them but also the absence of a wish to harm them (*vairatyāga* or *avaira*). As Vyasa defines it in one of his *Bhāsyas*, it is "sarvathā sarvadā sarvabhūtānām anabhidroha" ("absence of malice or hostility to all living beings in every way and at all times").

While being oriented to all other human beings and the rest of the universe in a spirit of friendliness, the individual also stands in specific relationships (*sambandha*) with specific individuals based on the ties of blood, caste, marriage, kinship, and so on. Friendship is one such bond or *sambandha*. For Indian thinkers it has several distinctive features, which mark it off from other types of relationship.

Friends are *suhṛd* or "good-hearted" towards each other. The *Mahābhārata* defines a friend as one who "gives his heart." As Bharata puts it in the *Ramāyāna*, "sauhardāj jayate mitram apakarorilakṣaṇam" ("from good-heartedness is born friendship; harm is the sign of enmity").[6] Heart is considered to be the seat of both feeling and soul. The idea of shared feelings and a shared self is central to the Indian conception of friendship. My friend is someone who instinctively feels for and with me, and participates in my joys and sorrows. Our hearts are bonded; our relationship is based on hearts or rather we are related "at the level of heart," and our hearts converge, know, and communicate with each other (*hridaya samvād*). In the classical Indian literature heart is often the seat of instinctive or inductive knowledge. A charioteer who knows the moods and understands the movements of his horses is said to have the heart of the horse (*ashvahriday*). Friends understand each other without speaking and anticipate each other's moods and thoughts. Friendship breaks down the barriers of selfhood or "ego-consciousness," such that the friends "flow" into each other and create a common or shared state of being. It is one way of partially overcoming the burden of particularity, and coming to feel at home in the world. Since friendship at its highest involves as close a merger between two individuals as is possible without losing their separate identities, many religious texts—especially the Vaishnavite—conceptualize human relationship to God in terms of friendship. God is *sakhā* (the "dearest friend") and is best realized through *sakhitva* (devotion or *bhakti* in the spirit of friendship).

For Indian thinkers, those enjoying the closest possible friendship share a common soul or self and "feel as one." This is how Kriṣna describes his friendship with Arjuna in the *Mahābhārata*. "Let it be understood that Arjuna is one half of my body." Elsewhere he says that they are really "one self that has been made twofold." When Garuda announces his friendship to Rama in the *Rāmāyana*, he says, "aham sakhā te kākutstha priyah prāṇo bahiscarah" ("I am your dear friend, Rama, your external self").[7] The complex concept of *prāṇo bahiscarah* (or what is also called *bahisprāṇa* or the externalized self) implies that friends reflect and manifest each other's self, spirit, life-breath, or soul (*prāṇa*) such that each discovers himself in the other. Friendship is a uniquely free relationship created voluntarily by those involved, and reveals to them and to the world at large the kinds of persons they are.

In the Indian conception of friendship, *sauhrda* or good-heartedness is associated with the three related ideas of *ānanda* ("delight"), *sahāya* ("help"), and *abhaya* ("fearlessness"). Friends are dear (*priya*) to each other and give each other *ānanda* ("pleasure," "joy," or "delight"). In the *Mahābhārata* Yudhishthira refers to Karna as *suhrdā-nandavardhana* ("one who enhances the joy of his friends").[8] In the Indian classical literature friendship is often associated with fun, merry-making, playfulness, agreeable and "amusing" conversation, escapades, and disregard of social conventions. Indeed friendship is the only relationship in which these things are permitted, and those involved released from the stern demands of duty characteristic of other relationships. In the *Mahābhārata* Kriṣna and Arjuna are always alone when they talk about their military and romantic adventures (*vikrāntani ratāni cha*), get drunk, or behave unconventionally.

Since friends care for each other, they render useful services (*sahāya*) to each other and make uncalculating sacrifices of time, energy, money, and even life. True friends are tested in adversity, and both the classical and popular literature are full of false friends being exposed in times of need. Although friends help each other, the help must spring from good-heartedness if it is to count as an act of friendship. In the *Rāmāyana* both Sugriva and Vibhisana render valuable assistance to Rama. When Bharata welcomes them all at the end of the war, he calls Sugriva a friend (*mitra*) and a brother (*bhrātā*) and says, "Tvam asmākam caturnam tu bhrata Sugriva panchamah" ("Sugriva, to us four brothers you are the fifth").[9] As for Vibhisana, he calls him his brother's "ally" who had rendered "assistance" (*sahāya*) and "done difficult things" (*kritam karma suduṣkaram*).[10] The different modes of address arise from the different ways in which the two men were related to Rama. It was Rama who had asked for Sugriva's help, which the latter rendered without knowing Rama's prowess; his help was very considerable and crucial to Rama's victory; it was born out of his *sauhrda* (good-heartedness) towards Rama; and he subsequently showed great devotion (*bhakti*) and loyalty (*dāsabhava*) to Rama. By contrast Vibhishana had gone to Rama in full knowledge of the latter's prowess and was largely interested in forming an alliance with him.

Friendship also involves fearlessness (*abhaya*). Friends not only pose no threat to each other but also know that they can always count on each other's affection, support, and loyalty. They can trust each other and be completely at ease and fearless in each other's company. In the *Mahābhārata*, Krisna describes Karna as *mitrāṇam abhayamkarah*, one in whose presence his friends know no fear or anxiety.[11] The concept of fearlessness (*abhaya*) is taken to imply that when friendship comes under severe strain, those involved may not speak to each other, but they must never betray each other, divulge information obtained during their friendship, or behave *as if* they had never been friends. "If a friendship breaks, a true friend's feelings towards that former friend undergo no change, as a lotus stalk, though cut, holds its shape," says the *Hitopadeśa*. Friendship is supposed to entail lifelong commitments, and while it may be loosened, suspended, or even ended, it can never be "broken" and its obligations violated.

Loyalty to friends does not imply that one may not criticize them or point out and protest against their wrongdoings. Indeed, in the Indian discussion of friendship, friends are almost invariably described as sources of sincere advice and each other's conscience and critic, and those acquiescing in their friend's mistakes and misdeeds out of blind loyalty, self-interest, or cowardice are condemned. Friendship is one of the few relationships in which honest and fearless criticism is both permitted and required. Friends must "speak truth" (*satyam vada*) to each other; otherwise their friendship rests on untruth and is "false." While friends should be open and honest with each other, they are required to refrain from gossiping or saying unpleasant (*apriya*) things behind each other's back, revealing their limitations to outsiders, and doing things likely to harm or demean them in others' eyes. Critical when alone, friends are expected to present a loyal and united front to the world. The two are complementary. It is precisely because friends can count on each other's good feelings and loyalty that they enjoy the privilege of fearless criticism, and vice versa.

For Indian writers, then, friendship is a distinct kind of relationship. It is a voluntary bonding of hearts, and involves both shared feelings and shared selves. It is a source of joy and claims to mutual loyalty, care, and assistance, and creates an island of socially sanctioned asociality in which one may disregard normal social conventions. Since friendship involves bonding of hearts, which is also what characterizes familial and kinship relations, the Indian thinkers have as a rule conceptualized friendship in familial terms. A friend is a "brother" (*bhrātr*) or "kinsman" (*bandhu*), and friendship is often called "brotherliness" or "brotherly disposition" (*bhrātrabhava* or *bandhutva* in Sanskrit; *bhāibandhi, bhāichairo,* and so forth in the regional languages). A close friend *is* a brother; one not so close is *like* a brother. In either case friendship is assimilated to kinship. A friend is an adopted member of the family. As we saw, Bharata welcomes Sugriva as his fifth brother. In the *Mahābhārata*, Karna and Duryodhana, Arjuna and Kriṣna, and many others call each other brothers. In several parts of India ceremonies have existed for centuries in which friends cement their relationships by taking appropriate vows and emerge as brothers. Whether or not friendship is formalized, a friend is viewed as "more or less" a brother and is expected to regard his friend's family as his own. He addresses his friend's parents, grandparents, uncles, brothers, and so on in the same way as the latter does or by their nearest equivalents. He shares food with them, an important privilege in a caste society with its rigid taboos, helps with the household chores, comes and stays with the family, enjoys more or less unrestricted access to it, and is generally given more or less equal love. Even the caste restrictions on marriages are slackened and occasionally waived in relation to friends.

Since friendship is recognized as an important social relation, several authors of moral treatises (*dharmaṣātras*) took cognizance of it and gave it a ritual status. As we saw, some of them called betraying friends (*mitradroha*) a sin (*pāpa*). According to Manu, one of the most influential Hindu lawgivers, a person guilty of betraying a friend is barred from participating in a *sraddha* ceremony involving offering oblations to dead ancestors; killing a friend is as much a sin as giving false evidence in a court of law or reviling the *Vedās*, the most sacred religious texts; having sex with a friend's wife is as much a sin as having sex with one's own sister; and when one's intimate friend dies, the impurity is supposed to last for a whole day.[12] According to *Vishnu Purāṇa*, those guilty of betraying friends invariably go to hell.[13]

Friendship also carries spiritual merit and is a source of spiritual power. In the *Mahābhārata*, when Arjuna is about to kill Karna with an arrow suggestively entitled *anjalika* (a respectful tribute), he puts all his spiritual merit behind it and invokes, among other things, the power of his friendship. Uttering *satyakriyā*, he says: "If I have sincerely practiced all the austerities, pleased the gurus, and if all that I have desired of my friends has come true, may that truth give this arrow the power to behead Karna."[14]

While Indian writers recognized that friendship was a valuable relationship, they were also troubled by several aspects of it. One might be required to bend rules or violate moral norms to protect a friend in trouble. The loyalty to a friend might require one to acquiesce in his misdeeds and even to assist him. Even if friendship involved no such partnership in evil, it morally privileged some and was fatally infected with partiality. What was more, it involved deep personal attachments, involved one in the lives of others, and stood in the way of the highest ideal of total detachment. Indian writers were deeply troubled by all this. Most insisted that true friendship was only possible between men of equally good virtue (*samānsila*), for only such friends did not make morally unacceptable demands on each other.[15] However, they knew that even the virtuous friends might occasionally get into awkward situations and require minor acts of immorality to help them out. In the *Mahābhārata* Arjuna got into several difficult situations because of his impetuosity and arrogance, and Krisna, after suitably admonishing him, had to resort to small lies and devious moves to help him out. Although the *Mahābhārata* does not justify such actions, it condones them, and is supported in this view by most moral and literary writers.

The other problematic aspects of friendship gave Indian writers considerable difficulty. They were convinced that friendship, which necessarily involved partiality, was incompatible with justice (*nyāya* or *dharma*), which involved an impartial application of rules and norms and an equal regard for the well-being of all. They were also convinced that friendship militated against the cultivation of the spirit of total detachment (*anasākti*) from the world. Although they did not discuss the matter at length, Indian writers seem to have concluded that a truly just man or one seeking total detachment and liberation from the world of sorrow (*moksa*) can have no friends.

It is striking that in the *Mahābhārata*, Yudhishthira, justice incarnate (*dharmāvatari* or *dharmarājā* as he is called) has no friends. He has brothers, but they are all *equally* dear to him. He has a wife but he has no *special* attachment to her. And when he ascends to heaven, the fate of his stray but loyal dog matters *as much* to him as that of his brothers. Kṛiṣna does have a friend in Arjuna, but he is Lord himself and therefore presumably unaffected by the limitations inherent in the relation of friendship. It would seem that for Indian writers, every society needs both justice and friendship, and no society can be based on a morality centered on either alone. Friendship fragments society, creates countless islands of close relationships, and is too fragile to sustain society. As for justice, it is too abstract to engage human hearts and too dispassionate to generate action. Each is needed to correct the limitations of the other. In the beautiful imagery of the *Mahābhārata*, each is divine and represents a partial manifestation of the total truth. Kṛiṣna, whose friendship (*sakhitva*) for Arjuna is celebrated as the highest possible level of friendship, and Yudhishthira, the paradigm of justice, are both considered indispensable and play complementary roles on crucial occasions. Their conflicts, disagreements, and compromises on crucial occasions offer valuable insights into the Indian view of how to secure a necessarily tentative balance between the demands of cold justice and warm friendship.

II

Indian thinkers distinguished different kinds of friendship. I shall analyze three that occur often in the literature and are thought to cover most relationships of friendship.

The first kind of friendship is based on genuine affection and fondness, usually built up during childhood and adolescence. There are many examples of this in the Indian literature, but one of the best and most influential is the friendship between Kṛiṣna and Sridama. Sridama, a Brahmin, and Kṛiṣna, a Ksatriya, grew up together in the same place, were educated in the same school, and were exceedingly fond of each other. Later in life Kṛiṣna became a king, and Sridama remained a poor Brahmin eking out his livelihood as a priest. They had no contact with each other for years, until one day Sridama decided to call on Kṛiṣna for financial help. When the two met, they were just as close as before. Time had not made, and was expected not to make, the slightest difference to their friendship. They spent hours reminiscing about their shared past and the subsequent changes in their lives, and simply enjoying each other's presence. Kṛiṣna built him a lovely house in his kingdom in order that they could stay close to each other.[16]

The two men had little in common. Their abilities, wealth, social status, and power were vastly unequal, their interests were completely different, and they shared few common ideals and goals. Not surprisingly they often had little to say to each other. Yet they deeply loved and cared for each other and enjoyed being together. Their friendship rested on nothing more than the fact that, thanks to their shared childhood and adolescence, their hearts had "become bonded" and they genuinely liked each other. Although their friendship was limited, that did not diminish its depth or durability. In Indian literature such friendships either originate in childhood or adolescence, or develop out of instinctive and inexplicable mutual attachments which are then cemented by acts of mutual concern and help.

Unlike the first kind of friendship, which is based on pure feeling, the second kind is based on mutual help and gratitude. Two individuals who render each other valuable services (*upakāra*) are placed under each other's debt (*rṇa*). Such acts over a period of time create a relationship of shared mutual gratitude and pave the way for friendship. Although they have good feelings for each other, not the feelings but the accumulated weight of mutual assistance is the basis of their friendship. They may not much enjoy each other's company, but they are well disposed or good-hearted towards each other and remain friends. There are several stories in Indian literature of individuals who feel uncomfortable with and have little to say to each other, but who nevertheless know that they can trust and count on each other's help and sincere advice.

In Indian thought a favor (*upakāra*) is generally seen as a sign of goodwill, and a harm is a sign of hostility or enmity (*apakārorilaksaṇam*).[17] When someone does me a favor, especially when he is not related or in any way obligated to me, his act displays goodwill towards me, signifies his friendliness towards me, and places me under a debt. My response cannot merely consist in doing him a favor on a suitable occasion, for his initial favor was not an isolated *act*, but a form of relationship (*sambandha*), an attempt to create a new *bond* between us, and has a deeper moral meaning. To view my benefactor's favor as merely an isolated act of help or a valuable service is not only to miss its point, but also to reject his tentative invitation to forge a more or less durable relationship with him. This is fully appreciated by the parties involved, and hence the recipient exercises considerable caution in accepting the favor. He needs to make sure that the favor is a well-meaning act of friendship, and not a calculated move to trap him into an unacceptable relationship or to extract an unacceptable future price. This sometimes leads to intricate social maneuvers in which one party seeks to do a favor, which the other either declines or interprets quite differently.[18]

When a favor is sincere or is at least viewed as such by the recipient, it establishes a bond between the parties involved and forms the basis of friendship. The willing recipient does his benefactor a similar good turn in future, not in a spirit of "returning" the favor but as an obligation derived from their developing friendship. Such gratitude-based friendship is the most common in Indian literature and strongly commended by moralistic writers. The best and most influential example of it is the friendship between Duryodhana and Karna.

Karna, an illegitimate child abandoned by his mother Kunti at birth, was found and raised by a lower-caste couple. When the young Karna excelled Arjuna at archery, Duryodhana, the latter's rival and eventually an enemy, made Karna a king and accepted him as an equal. Although Duryodhana's motives were suspect, Karna had no doubt that he had been done a great favor. He felt a profound sense of gratitude to Duryodhana and over time the two became close friends. When the great war began, Kunti, his mother, urged him to desert Duryodhana and join the Pandavas led by Arjuna, her legitimate son. Karna declined on the ground that he could not be ungrateful to a close friend. Duryodhana had accepted him as an equal when all others insulted him because of his low birth, had given him his pride and self-respect, and over the years had shown him great love and affection. In return, Karna went on, Duryhodhana had asked him for nothing but "just my heart," which "has been in his keeping ever since." As a result "my heart is not mine to give to you, it belongs to my friend Duryodhana."

The third kind of friendship represents the deepest and most comprehensive voluntary relationship between two individuals, and is held up in Indian literature as its highest form. Friends here share common interests, values, ideals, and lifestyles, are totally at ease in each other's presence, and deeply love and trust each other. They are *practically* oneself, but retain enough individuality and separateness to avoid total fusion. For Indian writers such friendship is rare and divine. Not surprisingly it is regarded in the Vaishnavite literature as one paradigm for the human relation to God. It is also striking that in the best example of it in Indian literature—namely, the friendship between Kṛṣṇa and Arjuna—Kṛṣṇa is lord himself and Arjuna is semi-divine.

In the *Mahābhārata*, Kṛṣṇa and Arjuna are inseparable. They have a lot of fun together; they fight, plot, and conspire together; they adore, love, and care for each other; and they instinctively understand each other's feelings, moods, and thoughts. Kṛṣṇa helps Arjuna elope with his sister Subhadra against the opposition of his family. He reluctantly tells occasional lies and even breaks his vows to protect Arjuna in difficult situations. When he fears that Arjuna might not be able to keep his pledge to kill Jayadratha before sunset the following day, he observes that he does not wish to live in a world in which Arjuna is absent and decides to break his own pledge not to engage in active combat himself. He acts as Arjuna's charioteer during the great war, a job involving not only a high risk and a low status but also a total and instinctive understanding of the plans, strategies, and thoughts between the warrior and his charioteer. Later on when he realizes that the moment of his death has arrived and that Arjuna would be deeply distressed, Kṛṣṇa summons him in a telepathic encounter, bids him a most affectionate farewell, and consoles him with the thought that once a man's purpose in life is realized, he must not only accept but welcome and even invite death. In the *Mahābhārata* the friendship between the two men is said to be so close that they are described as "aspects [*amśa*] of one another," as "really one self," as "one self that has been made twofold." The *Karṇaparvan* refers to them repeatedly with an air of mystery as "the two Kṛṣṇas," and Karna speaks of "having seen the two Kṛṣṇas together on one chariot."[19]

Although the two friends are totally devoted to each other and love each other equally, Kṛṣṇa is a senior partner. He is a little older, wiser, more mature, better informed about the ways of the world, and more resourceful. He guides Arjuna throughout his life, is a source of strength and inspiration to him at critical periods, and acts as his critic, counsellor, protector, and philosopher. Kṛṣṇa's complex relation to Arjuna is highlighted in an intriguing episode in the *Mahābhārata*. At Kṛṣṇa's instigation Arjuna takes on Indra in a battle. Indra is Arjuna's father. Kṛṣṇa knows this, but Arjuna does not. Arjuna gives a very good account of himself in the battle, which ends with the two parties discovering their true relationship. The point of the episode is clear. Kṛṣṇa, a senior friend, helps Arjuna grow out of his father's shadow and makes him at once *both* autonomous *and* dependent on Kṛṣṇa. Arjuna is liberated from a natural or biological relationship and enters into a new voluntary relationship with another individual who, although his friend, is also his guide. Kṛṣṇa is not his surrogate father, for unlike the traditional Indian description of a father, he is not a distant, self-contained, and overpowering figure of authority. He is playful, emotionally accessible, and separated from Arjuna by only a few years. Yet he is a senior partner, enjoying the right to rebuke and admonish Arjuna. The relationship between the two is relaxed, informal, and easygoing, but it is also unequal and based on Arjuna's deference.

It would seem that for the author of the *Mahābhārata* perfect friendship is only possible between individuals who share common interests, temperaments, values, and so on, but one of whom is a little older and wiser and a great source of strength. The senior partner need not be better in the area of activity in which his junior friend excels; Kṛṣṇa is not a better archer than Arjuna. But he must be more self-contained, more familiar with the ways of the world, and of a stronger character. Both depend on each other, but one depends a little more. Only such a relationship is believed to be inherently noncompetitive and nonconflictual, and free of the traces of jealousy and comparison deemed to be characteristic of the relations between equals. In such a relationship neither party feels threatened by the other, for each derives a distinct kind of fulfillment from it. This view of friendship is not confined to the *Mahābhārata* and is to be found in the *Rāmāyaṇa*, the *Purāṇas*, and many other religious and literary texts.

I have so far identified three forms of friendship in Indian thought, especially in the two epics and the *Purāṇas*. Since the latter are deeply woven into Indian life and thought, the three forms have deeply influenced Indian attitudes to friendship. Writers in English and regional languages and producers of films and plays draw upon them and hold them up as models. A rich man who remains true to his currently poor childhood friend is praised for his loyalty to his Sridama; one who forgets, ignores, or insults him is criticized. Karna's friendship with Duryodhana is held up as a model of friendship based on gratitude, but one is often advised to avoid blind loyalty. The friendship between Kṛṣṇa and Arjuna is repeatedly reproduced in the friendships between elders and juniors in all walks of life, including those between teachers and their ex-pupils, and was evident in the relation between Gandhi and his close associates, especially Jawaharlal Nehru.

III

I began this paper with a brief sketch of the current conception of friendship and went on to show that ancient Indian thinkers identified an analogous relationship. Before concluding the paper, it would be helpful to highlight the important distinguishing features of the classical Indian conception of friendship.

First, the Indian view extends friendship to the human relationship with gods and even with God. For the Indian, a devotee can relate to God in several ways or *bhāvas*, including those of a child, a beloved, and a friend. Some schools of Indian thought reject this approach, but others such as Vaishnavism regard friendship as one of the four major forms of human relationship to God.

Second, the idea of cosmic friendliness as a desired human orientation towards the other inhabitants of the universe is distinctive to the Indian view, and has few if any parallels in the Western discourse on friendship.

Third, the Indian view of friendship places much greater stress on mutual help and loyalty than is to be found in the Western tradition. Friendship for the Indian is a bonding of hearts, and centers around active goodwill and loyalty. Friends are expected to like and enjoy each other's company, but that is not considered enough or even central. They must also care for each other, promote each other's well-being, help each other out in need, and so on. This is the vital test of friendship in the classical Indian view that we have discussed. Friendship therefore has a strong practical orientation. It is a system of mutual support, a basis of mutual favors. Not surprisingly it runs the constant danger of becoming a calculated investment in human relationships, a way of accumulating social capital by building up a network which can then be used to enhance one's social status and political power.

Fourth, since friendship is considered to be primarily a matter of heart, the head is assigned only a limited place in the Indian view. Aristotle said that the good man needs friends in order to share discussions and ideas. Such a view of friendship finds only a limited support in the classical Indian literature. Intellectual discussions do take place, but they are generally between gurus and their disciples and not between friends.

Finally, in the classical Indian view, friendship is a social relation. It is one of several ways in which individuals get bonded and acquire social obligations, and is not qualitatively different from other types of social bonds. Besides, friendship is a relation not merely between two individuals but also with the friend's family. As we saw, friendship is assimilated to kinship, and a friend is deemed to be like a brother. While such a socialization of friendship gives it considerable stability and social depth, it also subjects it to social jurisdiction and control, including specifying who should be one's friend, within what limits, and what one may expect of him or her. Such socialized friendship often has only limited independence and intensity, and is unable to develop at its own pace.

NOTES

1. I am most grateful to Professor Richard Gombrich for his detailed and helpful comments on this paper. Dhirubhai Sheth, Daniel Mariau, Andrew Mason, Terry McNeill, Subrata Mitra, Lynn Thomas, and Noel O'Sullivan also offered valuable comments, and I'm grateful to them all.

2. For the Greeks and Romans, friendship was primarily a political relationship and was largely an alliance based on mutual interest and support. The idea of disinterested friendship (*philia*) as opposed to Plato's *eros* was first fully articulated by Aristotle, but it was limited to those "who are good and alike in virtue" and united by their common or shared love of good. See Aristotle *Nichomachean Ethics* 8.3.1156a1419. For a good discussion see A. W. Price, *Love and Friendship in Plato and Aristotle* (Oxford: Clarendon Press, 1989), chap. 4. The Epicureans saw friendship as an escape from social and political relations, and based it largely on a shared intellectual life. For Saint Augustine friendship was only possible among those sharing a common faith, and even then its intensity was always suspect. In China friendship was traditionally seen not as a private relationship as in the modern West, but as a public relation subject to social constraints.

3. For a valuable discussion, see Edgar C. Polome, ed., *Homage to Georges Dumézil, Journal of Indo-European Studies* (1982), Monograph No. 3, Washington D.C. See also Mariasusai Dhavamony, *Love of God According to Śaiva Siddhanta* (Oxford: Clarendon Press, 1971), pp. 47ff. In *Rigveda bandhu* is sometimes used in the sense of a friend. For the most part, however, it means a relative, and that is how it is used in subsequent classical

literature. See P. V. Kane, *History of Dharmaṣāstra*, 2d ed. (Poona: Bhandarkar Oriental Research Institute, 1973), vol. 111, pp. 753–54.

4.   In most but not all of the Indian classical literature *sakhā* generally means a friend, but in some contexts it also implies a protector, an object of adoration. This is how, for example, Arjuna uses the term in the *Gitā*. *Mitra* implies a friendship that is not too intimate, and is often used to connote an ally, especially in a political context. *Suhṛd* is generally used to convey distinterested love.

5.   The term *dost* or *dosti*, which is largely of Persian origin and implies informality, deep emotional bonds, and total loyalty, introduces a new conception of friendship in Indian thought from around the seventeenth century onwards. The Western idea of friendship arrived towards the end of the eighteenth century and did not get assimilated into Indian thought and regional literature until the mid-nineteenth century.

6.   *Rāmāyana* 6.130.44–46.

7.   *Rāmāyana* 6.50.46.

8.   *Karṇaparvan* 8.46.9.

9.   *Rāmāyana* 6.130.44–46.

10.   *Rāmāyana* 6.130.46–47.

11.   *Karṇaparvan* 51.61.

12.   G. Bühler, ed., *The Laws of Manu* (Delhi: Motilal Banarasidass, 1984), 3.160; 5.82; 11.57; and 11.59. See also *Vishnu Purāṇa* 2.6.11.

13.   Karna accuses Śalya of being a *mitradrohi* ("one who betrays or injures friends"). He could kill him but does not. "Because you are a *sakhi*, a *suhṛd* and also a *mitra* (*sakhibhāvena sauhardanmitrabhāvena caiva hi*), for these three reasons, O Śalya, you now live." Karna has clearly in mind three different relations in which he and Śalya stand, for which he needs three different terms. It would appear that he regarded Śalya as a *mitra* because he was an ally of and supported Duryodhana, as a *suhṛd* because he was generally, though not during the great war, well disposed to Karna, and as a *sakhi* because he was his charioteer. It is striking that the *Karṇaparvan* represents one of the major occasions for the diversification and a most precise signification of the vocabulary of friendship in the classical Indian literature.

14.   Arjuna's *satyakriyā* reads: "Tapoᶜsti tapam guravasca tositā māyā yadiṣṭam suhṛdam tathā śrutam" (8.67.14). When Arjuna says that what he has desired of his friends has always been heard or has come true, he has his friendship with Krṣna in mind. It is striking that austerity, satisfaction of the gurus, and trust of friends are given *equal* importance or potency. For a further discussion, see Norman Brown, *Duty as Truth in Ancient India*, Proceedings of the American Philosophical Society (1972), pp. 252–68; and Myles Dillon, "The Hindus' Act of Truth in Celtic Tradition," *Modern Philosophy* (1947), pp. 137–38.

15. *Dhammapada* lays down that one is only to "have virtuous people for friends." See Lin Yutang, ed., *The Wisdom of India* (London: Michael Joseph, A Four Square Book, 1964), p. 343.

16. For the Sridama-Krisna friendship, see J. M. Sanyal, trans., *The Srimad-Bhāgvatam* (Delhi: Munshriam Manoharlal Pubs., 1984), vol. 11, pp. 311–12.

17. As Rama says to Hanuman, for even one of the favors you have done me, all of my life is not an adequate return (*Rāmāyana* 7.40.22). Tara tells Lakshmana that her husband is a truly good man because "he never forgets favors done to him" (*Rāmāyana* 4.35.2–5).

18. *Panchatantra*, bks. 1 and 11, discusses how friends are lost and won and sums up a good deal of popular thinking on the subject. It discusses what qualities to expect in friends and how to make, keep, and test them. That a friend should never betray a secret and engage in backbiting even after friendship ceases is a recurrent theme. See Arthur W. Ryder, trans., *The Panchatantra* (Bombay: Jaico Pub. House, 1986). The translation was first published by the University of Chicago in 1925.

19. *Karnaparvan* 8.57.48 talks of *drstvā krsnāvekarathe sametau* (having seen the two Krisnas together on one chariot).

Predatory Friendship: Evidence from Medieval Norman Histories

EMILY ALBU HANAWALT

THE SCENE IS ENGLAND, at a castle in Lincoln; the year, 1141. Many of the English nobles are in rebellion against King Stephen; but this castle remains in the control of loyalists, who protect Lincoln in the king's name. Two countesses have come for a friendly visit with the wife of the knight in charge of the castle's defense. The women spend the day in laughter and easy conversation until the earl of Chester arrives, conspicuously unarmed, to retrieve his wife. Suddenly the three knights with him snatch up weapons and expel the castle guards, as the earl's brother and armed knights burst into the castle to take their place. In a moment Lincoln Castle is in the hands of the rebels, thanks to friendship betrayed.[1]

This is almost the last scene in the *Ecclesiastical History* of Orderic Vitalis, the master work of Norman historical writing. Orderic completed the history, and described this episode, shortly before his death in about 1142. It is a good example of the exploitation of friendship, which Norman histories portray as just another weapon in the Norman arsenal.

I might have called this essay "Dangerous Liaisons." But "Predatory Friendship" was inspired by the title of Eleanor Searle's *Predatory Kinship and the Creation of Norman Power, 840–1066.*[2] Searle argued that the fundamental basis of Norman power lay in expanding kinship groups that worked together to prey on outsiders and support their chosen duke. I was drawn to the title "Predatory Friendship" because it expresses more than the essentially dangerous nature of any proximity to Normans; it also suggests a calculating use and abuse of a relationship often considered sacred and inviolate.[3]

115

Norman historians usually characterized their people as an unruly lot prone to mayhem. Medievalists will recall this much-quoted assessment by Orderic:

> The Normans are an untamed race, and if they are not kept in line by a firm ruler they are very quick to commit wrong. In all communities, wherever they may be, they seek to rule and many times collude against truth and loyalty through the restless zeal of their ambition. This the French and Bretons and Flemings and their other neighbors have frequently experienced; this the Italians and Lombards and Anglo-Saxons have endured to the point of extermination.[4]

Whenever the reins of power slacken, the Normans rise up in rebellion, as they do here in Orderic's narrative, upon the death of William Rufus. Orderic feared that this unrestrained passion was the dark legacy from the Normans' northern ancestors.[5] Immediately following Orderic's statement about the bellicose nature of Normans, he traced their lineage, as recorded in the first Norman historian, Dudo of Saint-Quentin—from Scythian to Trojan to Dane to Norman. It is no wonder, Orderic concluded, punning with *auster* ("the south wind") and *aquilo* ("the stormy north wind"), that "their bold harshness (*austeritas*) has proved as threatening to their delicate neighbors as the chilling north wind to tender flowers."[6]

Persuasive evidence supports Orderic's implication that the Normans inherited a predisposition to dangerous liaisons from their Scandinavian ancestors. Blood feuds drove Vikings to abandon their homeland and seek booty and adventure elsewhere. Scandinavians in diaspora shared a common propensity for wreaking havoc, from Byzantium to Iceland. The Byzantines, for instance, feared and hated the Varangian guard quartered in their midst, considering the Varangians especially volatile when (as was frequently the case) they had been drinking to excess. The historian Michael Attaleiates reported that drunken Varangians once even attacked the man they were employed by and sworn to protect, the emperor Nicephorus Botaneiates, as he stood on a palace balcony, killing one of his secretaries.[7] Icelandic sagas are driven by hot tempers that blaze up or ancient hostilities that fester and bring ill for generations. In *Njal's Saga*, for instance, the Njalssons had every pretext for extending an old grudge into their generation by turning against Hoskuld, whose father had refused to pay compensation for the killing of their foster father. When Njal attempted to terminate hostilities by adopting Hoskuld, "the feverishly intense friendship" which Njal encouraged between the Njalssons and Hoskuld bred the circumstances for disaster.[8] An enemy of both parties, weaving treachery toward all, could too easily persuade the Njalssons that Hoskuld's gifts and hospitality concealed murderous intentions,[9] and the Njalssons ambushed the saintly Hoskuld as he sowed seed in his own field. This murder set in motion the acts that led inevitably to the feud's fiery conclusion, as Njal and his family were trapped in their farmhouse and burned alive.[10]

It is tempting, therefore, to follow Orderic and trace Norman predatory friendship back to Scandinavian patterns. But in Normandy Vikings had settled among French and intermarried with the local people. In many ways they assimilated quickly, surrendering Norse and Danish languages for French and Latin, pagan gods and customs for Christianity. The union of Vikings and French produced a volatile combination. After all, the Franks too, like the Vikings, were a Germanic people who had inherited the fondness for feuding that the *Niebelungenlied* displays no less than *Njal's Saga*. For the historian's view of the brutality in old Frankish Gaul, we need only read the sixth-century *History of the Franks* by Gregory of Tours, whose vivid, free-wheeling Latin perfectly mirrors the chaos of his world where treachery, deceit, and murder were everyday occurrences.[11] The ruling family offers many examples; if we noted only the crimes involving the Queens Fredegund and Brunhild, we would find dozens of cases. But friendship offered a particularly dangerous situation, since it afforded the proximity of kinship without the mediating warmth of blood loyalties.

A feud at Tours offers a good case study.[12] It began one Christmas when a local priest sent a servant to invite some neighbors over for a drink. Gregory says that one of the men who was offered hospitality drew his sword and killed the servant. The people of Tours rushed to take sides, and many were killed until the matter was finally resolved by the paying of indemnities. But an ill-advised friendship between the two principals in the feud—Sicharius and Chramnesindus—caused the fighting to erupt again. Here is how Gregory tells the tale:

> After murdering Chramnesindus' kinsmen, Sicharius had become very friendly with him, and they loved each other so dearly that they often ate together and slept together in the same bed. One day toward nightfall Chramnesindus had supper prepared and

invited Sicharius. He came, and they sat down together for dinner. Sicharius got drunk with wine and started boasting to Chramnesindus, and at last he is supposed to have said: "O brother, you are sorely indebted to me for killing your kinsmen, because I paid you recompense for them, and now there is plenty of gold and silver in your house. You would be poor and living a wretched life if I had not set you up a little." Chramnesindus heard Sicharius' words with bitterness in his soul and he said to himself: "If I don't avenge the death of my kinsmen, I shall not deserve the name of man and should be called a weak woman." And immediately he blew out the lights and split Sicharius' skull with his blade. In the last moment of his life Sicharius uttered a low moan and fell down dead. The servants who had come with him fled. Chramnesindus stripped the clothes from the body and hung them on a picket fence; then he climbed on his horse and raced to find the king. . . .[13]

Surely this is a friendship which more introspective people might have avoided. But for the Franks, no such caution prevailed, and there was a thin line between friendship and violence.

A couple of centuries after Gregory, the strong arm of Charlemagne introduced some semblance of law and order. But the Franks maintained their unruly and feuding nature in the Carolingian era and beyond, as attested by literary as well as historical sources. For a famous example, consider the *Song of Roland*. The historical kernel of the tale lies in a skirmish by Charlemagne's rearguard as the Franks returned from a Spanish campaign. Over the centuries of transmission, the episode evolved into an epic of pride and betrayal. It is a French epic, of course, but Normans quickly adopted Roland as their own hero and identified with his peculiar brand of heroism. Allusions to Roland had been surfacing in Norman histories since Dudo,[14] and with increasing frequency since the First Crusade. In the twelfth-century Anglo-Norman romance-history, the *Roman de Rou*, the epic itself played a central role. Wace expressly compared William the Conqueror with Roland and had the brave jongleur Taillefer lead the Norman charge at Hastings while singing of those champions whom the Normans had adopted from the Franks' heroic age — Charlemagne and Roland, Oliver and the vassals who died at Roncevaux.[15] Not coincidentally, the famous Oxford *Roland* is a Norman document.[16]

And what sort of hero appears in this epic that Normans allegedly used for inspiration in battle? Who is the hero with whom Norman historians, when they wanted a flattering epic comparison, equated their own dukes and warriors? Roland was a man who attracted the admiration of Charlemagne, the love of his noble fiancée Aude, and the passionate friendship of his loyal companion, Oliver. Roland was also hot-blooded and self-absorbed, a man who put vengeance and pride above the survival of Oliver and his men — willing and eager to risk many lives by indulging in enmity with his stepfather, Ganelon. When finally overwhelmed by a massive enemy assault engineered by Ganelon, Roland lashed out at Oliver for suggesting he blow the horn that would signal distress and bring reinforcements from Charlemagne. Intimate friendship with Roland has tragic consequences: death in battle to Oliver and death, too, to Aude, when she learns that her beloved has perished — and grief to the aged Charlemagne, who tugs on his white beard and weeps at the thought of endless battles without Roland at his side.

When we turn to Norman histories we find ample evidence that friendship was a dangerous undertaking for Normans, as it was for their Scandinavian and Frankish kin. The Normans' volatility alone made them hazardous friends, prone to fight and to draw friends into their feuds. But they also calculated their narrow self-interest, and used old friendships and created new ones for the sole purpose of predation. Normans were notoriously proud of treachery and admired trickery; often this involved friendships deliberately created so that they could be betrayed.

Here I am defining friendship as I think the Normans defined it, in a very loose sense. Intimate friendships, I think, flourish in an environment where trust, loyalty, and allegiance are honored; that is, in an environment markedly different from the social structure and value system of the Normans. The earliest Norman histories make it clear that trust is a rare and precarious commodity in the Norman world.

In the history of Dudo of Saint-Quentin, for instance, even at the moment when they were becoming Normans, the very first Normans betrayed a unique attitude toward sworn loyalty and fealty.[17] In the ceremony in which the French king Charles the Simple granted Rouen to the Vikings, the Viking chief evaded the (perhaps humiliating) act of homage by designating one of his men to kiss the king's foot.[18] Instead of kneeling, the Viking grabbed Charles' foot and pulled it up to his mouth, toppling the king in the process. It is an image that makes us laugh, but it should also warn us that this relationship of king and vassals will not be a secure and conventional one.

Dudo borrowed or invented other scenes that show a fondness for trickery and faith abrogated. His first book featured an archetypal Viking named Hasting whom Dudo developed in order to illustrate the savagery from which Normans spring. Hasting's dream is to destroy civilization, and so naturally he aims to sack the queen of cities, Rome herself. He finds what he believes to be Rome and conceives a pleasing plan. He will trick the monks inside by pretending to desire baptism, so that they will let him into the city. All this happens, and Hasting leaves the city in peace, a nominal Christian. But soon he sends word that he is dying and wishes a Christian burial. His men bring him back to the site of his baptism, lying in state, and the monks crowd around the body. Suddenly the corpse stirs, draws a sword, and leads the attack against the monks, killing everyone he can find. Although Hasting's delight is tempered by the discovery that this is not Rome but rather a tiny village called Luna, nonetheless he has succeeded in betraying Christian friendship.

In Dudo it is not just the Vikings and Normans who betray trust. Consider, for instance, the men of Flanders who trick Rollo's son William Longsword at the end of amicable negotiations. Calling him back for one last word, the Flemings assassinate him as his men look on helplessly. In this hostile and unreliable world, however, Normans won the dubious distinction of being particularly untrustworthy. In the First Crusade, as Western troops passed through Constantinople, one by one their leaders swore allegiance to the Byzantine Emperor, Alexius Comnenus. Raymond of Toulouse held out for some time, apparently because he took the oath seriously. Once he finally swore, he remained loyal to Alexius for life. With the Normans, it was different. The young prince Tancred slipped past the Byzantine lines and boarded a ship without having to give up his autonomy. Perhaps this is a sign that he, too, honored the vows. But his uncle Bohemond, son of Robert Guiscard, seduced by imperial treasures, cheerfully pledged loyalty to the emperor, apparently without any intention of keeping the covenant. As we shall see, he reneged at the first opportunity, contriving to take Antioch for himself, rather than return it to Alexius as he had promised.

By 1097 the Western Crusaders had reached Antioch. The great walls of that formidable Syrian city resisted a protracted siege; but the Christian army dared not continue south to Jerusalem with Antioch still in enemy hands. Then Bohemond conceived a plan that would assure the surrender of the city to him. We have an eyewitness account of the unfolding drama at Antioch from an anonymous knight in Bohemond's retinue, who wrote the *Gesta Francorum*, a valuable chronicle of events from Clermont to the conquest of Jerusalem. Kept as a kind of journal along the route, the *Gesta* entered the mainstream of Norman histories as learned writers like Baudri of Bourgueil refashioned it in classier prose; Orderic Vitalis copied Baudri's *Historia Hierosolimitana* almost verbatim as Book 9 of his *Ecclesiastical History*. But here is the simpler firsthand description of the anonymous knight:

> There was an amir of the Turkish race named Firuz, who had taken up a great friendship [*maximam amicitiam*] with Bohemond. Bohemond used often to assail him with messengers, asking whether he would receive him, in friendship's name [*amicissime*] into the city and promising in return that he would freely make him a Christian and would grant him riches and great honor. Firuz assented to the words and promises, saying, "I am guarding three towers, which I freely promise to Bohemond, and I will receive him into them whenever he wishes." So when Bohemond was sure that he could enter the city, looking cool and calm and collected he came before all the leaders, and said to them cheerfully, "Most valiant knights, you see how we are all, both great and small, in terrible poverty and misery, and we have no idea how our lot can improve. So if you think it good and proper, let one of us put himself before the others, and if he can take the city or contrive its downfall by any means, by himself or by others, we will all unanimously agree to give it to him." The other leaders absolutely refused and denied him, saying, "This city shall be handed over to no one, but we will all share it equally; as we have had equal toil, so let us have equal honor." When Bohemond heard these words he looked a trifle less pleased and left right away.[19]

But the Crusaders soon learned that the feared Kerbogha, atabeg of Mosul, was leading a huge Muslim army to Antioch, and the

besiegers were about to find themselves squeezed between their enemies. The Christian leaders called an emergency council to accept
Bohemond's proposal. The *Gesta* continues: "So Bohemond now set
about sending a fawning request to his friend [*amicum suum*] every day,
making the most fawning, extravagant, and enticing promises, saying,
'See, now we have a chance of accomplishing whatever good we want,
so now, my friend [*amicus meus*] Firuz, give me your help.'"[20]

Firuz agreed to admit Bohemond's men to his tower, and he even
sent his son as a hostage. By night sixty Normans stormed a ladder to
the friendly tower; and Antioch was taken, in the nick of time, amid
great carnage. Orderic Vitalis reported that Firuz lost his own half-
brother in the melee, and there is ominous silence about the ultimate
fate of Firuz himself. But Bohemond achieved his goal, eventually receiving Antioch as the center of his Syrian principality, and abandoning
the avowed end of his journey, the holy battle for Jerusalem.

Oaths sworn only to be broken and a friendship cultivated in deliberate calculation so the "friend" will betray his companions—these
seem common Norman ploys. In such a bellicose and treacherous society, men used friendship as just another diplomatic tool, and shed
old friendships with alarming ease. It is not surprising that, in the *Ecclesiastical History*, *amicus* and *amicitia* may have an ominous
overtone, as when Christians besiege Jerusalem "as friends and sons"
to free their mother from captivity.[21] Likewise, a request for friendship may elicit hostility instead, as when Count Helias approaches his
lord, King William Rufus, to ask for a guarantee of peace while he
goes on crusade to Jerusalem: "As your liegeman I ask for your friendship . . . [*amicitiam . . . vestram*]."[22] But William Rufus responds by
demanding that Helias surrender all of Maine to him. This interchange naturally leads to hostilities, and the count forsakes Jerusalem
but takes the cross to fight enemies near home.

Orderic did make occasional positive references to friendship.
Western lords in the Holy Land bid farewell to friends and companions
("amicis atque cum suis commilitonibus") as they head for home. In
the same passage, Greeks and Syrians try to persuade other crusaders
to go home, too, by reminding them of wives and friends they have left
behind:

> We know full well that for the sake of crusade you left wealthy
> realms which, now that your vows have been nobly fulfilled, you

long to see again, especially since you are moved by the tender love of your wives and dear children and the affection of your relatives and friends [*amicorum*], whom you left for Christ's sake.[23]

Meanwhile, in Byzantium, Raymond of Toulouse has become one of the emperor's closest friends and counsellors, whom Alexius especially loved and trusted ("et inter familiares convivas eius ac consiliarios habitus est. Hunc Augustus precipue diligebat, et libenter eum audiebat. . . .")[24]

Another episode featuring friendship seemed so rare and surprising that, according to Orderic, it would long be recalled with astonishment. Recall Count Helias, who wanted to go to Jerusalem, but found himself at war with his lord, King William, instead. When Helias learned that William was dead, he returned joyfully to Le Mans, his chief city, which the king had taken from him. Orderic reported: "His friends among the citizens [*ab amicis civibus*] received him voluntarily, and he took the city peacefully."[25] Then began a friendly siege of the citadel, while negotiators mixed threats with jokes. Helias often donned the white tunic that gave him safe passage to visit the enemy, since "he trusted the good faith of men he knew to be upright and honorable. . . . Besieged and besiegers alike passed their time in banter back and forth and played many tricks on one another in a far from malevolent spirit, so that for some time the people of those parts will speak of them with wonder and delight. . . . And so when peace had been made, the bold garrison came out with their weapons and all their belongings and were received by the counts, not as conquered enemies but as faithful friends [*ut fideles amici*]."[26] It is worth mentioning that, though this was reported in a Norman history, the parties involved were not in fact Normans, and also that people were astonished at this trust and friendship.

Orderic's episodes frequently mix loyalty and treachery, friendship and enmity into a stew of alarming unpredictability. A case in point is the series of tales surrounding a rebellion against Duke Robert in 1101.[27] Norman magnates send one messenger after another to Robert's brother, King Henry of England, offering him the duchy. Though Orderic has painted Robert as a pathetic and incompetent wastrel, he decries the results of these disloyal pleas: "So both peoples were corrupted by the threatened treachery, and both plotted how to harm their lords. Some rebels took up open war against loyal neighbors and stained the bosom of their nurturing land with plundering, fires, and bloody slaughter." Orderic notes with approval that Archbishop Anselm and his clergy, the bishops and abbots, remained loyal to their secular lord and prayed "for his safety and the preservation of the realm."

But a bishop had instigated the plot. The villain, Ranulf Flambard, had won the bishopric of Durham through friendship with William Rufus, brother of Robert and Henry—or rather through sycophancy and pandering to him. When William Rufus died, the new king threw Ranulf into prison, where his friends smuggled in a rope hidden with rich food and wine that he shared with the guards. "When they were completely drunk and safely snoring," writes Orderic, "the bishop fastened the rope to a supporting post in the middle of a window in the tower and, taking his pastoral staff with him, climbed down the rope. . . . His faithful friends and loyal followers were waiting at the foot of the tower and, though terrified, had their best horses ready for him. They mounted their horses, and he fled swiftly, meeting faithful companions who brought his treasure. With them he sailed quickly toward Normandy to Duke Robert."

In Normandy Ranulf stirred up the Duke against his brother, until Robert finally sailed to England. Here Orderic makes a special point of comparing this Norman attack with the one commanded by William the Conqueror, father of the two feuding brothers. "Robert's fleet," writes Orderic, "was quite unlike his father William's fleet, for it reached Portsmouth harbor not through the courage of the army but through the contrivance of traitors." Sailors sent by the duke to attack his brother joined his fleet instead, guiding it safely into port.

Amid betrayal and instigations to war, one man "was determined to preserve his own loyalty to his friend, the king, through happy times and sad. When he saw the schemes and defections of his fellow countrymen, he quietly turned over many things in his own mind and anxiously worked to protect the stability of the realm." This was Robert, count of Meulan, a man so fondly attached to Henry that a contemporary charged him with showing more eagerness to serve the king of the English than the King of the angels.[28] In a remarkable speech, Orderic has the count urge his friend, the king, to pursue lasting peace. This speech begins with a plea for true loyalty and friendship:

> Every man who is upright and strong in his knighthood and sees his friend hard pressed by assailants ought, if he wishes to be

thought worthy of his standing, to go with all his effort to help a friend in need. In zeal of this sort the profit of future gain should not be considered so much as one should think of aiding a friend in need. But we see many acting very differently, and fouling by vile prevarication the glorious faith they have pledged to their lord. These things we see perfectly clearly, and we feel the sharp pains in our sides. We, therefore, whom God has entrusted with the provision for the common good, ought to keep a watchful eye for the safety of the realm and of the Church of God. Let our greatest concern be to triumph peacefully by God's grace and gain victory without shedding Christian blood, so that our loyal people may remain in the security of peace.

Following his friend's lead, Henry astonishes all by seeking a face-to-face meeting with his brother and making a truce.

This rebellion ends with an edifying tale glorifying friendship. But this is an exceptional story. In fact, predation and distrust were the rule among Normans. Normans believed that trickery and deceit contributed mightily to their spectacular successes; and that may well be true. But those traits worked against the long-term stability and survival of a Norman state. If we use Norman historians as the benchmark, we find compelling evidence that Normans came to exhibit varying degrees of malaise, pessimism, and anxiety. The first histories were epic works that celebrated Norman valor and conquest. But the mood changed as early as the late eleventh century. Elsewhere I have shown how the tone of the *Gesta Roberti Wiscardi* reversed in mid-course, moving from celebration of Guiscard's acquisitions in southern Italy, to anguish over his undertaking a campaign against Byzantine territory, and finally to threnody at the hero's death during that ill-starred campaign.[29] I have also argued that the anonymous *Gesta Francorum* (likewise written in the final decade of the eleventh century) similarly shifted from praise of Guiscard's son Bohemond to an implied disapproval; after Bohemond grabs Antioch and refuses to honor his pledge to proceed to the battle for Jerusalem, the anonymous author abruptly strips his former hero of all the epithets he had routinely given him up to that point.[30]

After that, the mood turns bleak. Twelfth-century histories frequently express a pessimism toward Norman heroes and a gloomy attitude toward human existence. I think the two traits are related. For a monastic example, we need only look as far as Orderic Vitalis, who repeatedly punctuates his descriptions of Norman chaos with commentary on the fragility of human life and the vanity of hope in worldly affairs. In the realm of secular history, consider the romance-history of Wace, who reckoned as supreme evils the disloyalty, treason, discord, and desertion that fill his histories and bring such disastrous consequences. Like Orderic, he stresses the unpredictable and often pathetic nature of human existence, as the first prologue to his *Roman de Rou* emphasizes:

> . . . A man dies, iron rusts, wood rots, the tower falls, the wall crumbles, the rose withers, the horse stumbles, clothing wears out, every work made by hand rots away. . . .[31]

The lingering sense of melancholy in the *Rou*, usually attributed to Wace's personality and his gloomy response to the stingy patronage of King Henry II, may be at least in part a natural reaction against the alienating uncertainties of a world in which friendship and loyalties are notoriously insecure.

I have come to suspect that the very movement from the surety of epic to the anxiety of romance — a shift that occurs over the course of the eleventh and twelfth centuries — is a natural progression for a society burdened with systemic uncertainties in their patterns of friendship. But it is also possible to see some gain in the burgeoning era of romance and romantic love. The last Norman histories, the romances of Wace and Benoit, retell the old stories of Normans and their heroes, but they apply to familiar tales a fresh spin that suggests new opportunities for a gentler, intimate friendship. Consider, for instance, a provocative episode from Wace, dealing with Duke Richard I and his bride Gunnor. Wace's distant source, the first Norman history by Dudo of Saint-Quentin, devoted fully a page of text to praise of the beautiful, nobly born, eloquent Dane, whom Richard obtained amicably (*amicabiliter*) as his concubine.[32] Wace expanded this to include an intimate scene in the ducal bedchamber. Richard's clergy and noblemen have just persuaded him to marry Gunnor upon the death of his childless first wife. On their wedding night, the duke is astonished to find his bride facing him in bed, in a position of dominance, rather than meekly turned away as she had always done before. He questions her about the change, and she answers with a smile:

> Milord. . .
> I used to lie in your bed;

I used to do your pleasure.
Now I lie in my own, I will lie
on whatever side I wish.
I am a lady; when I lie in my bed,
I will lie as I please.
It used to be that this bed was yours,
but now it is both mine and yours.
I was never confident here before
nor was I ever free from fear with you.
Now I am completely at ease.[33]

And so the duke and his duchess face one another, talking and smiling.[34]

The relationship between literature and society is difficult to assess. But as the Norman histories describe it, changing manners in the twelfth century, the rise of romance, and the supposed elevation of the status of women, offered new opportunities for friendship. And not a moment too soon. Norman principalities were about to disappear—or perhaps more accurately, the Norman identity was everywhere assimilating into something else. By the time the duchy reverted to the king of France in 1204, an Angevin king ruled England and a German reigned in Sicily. Bohemond's heirs were still holding Antioch, but no longer considering themselves Norman.[35] Sometimes their rapid assimilation is reckoned as one sign of their success.[36] But from another standpoint, it looks like Norman attitudes toward friendship and predation were poor foundations for stable and peaceful societies.

We began with the capture of a castle in Lincoln during the rebellion of 1141. And we end with the rebels' sack of the city of Lincoln itself, which inevitably followed the castle's fall. Very near the close of his *Ecclesiastical History*, Orderic (by then a tired old man) reports the desertions and treacheries of this revolt, which toppled King Stephen of England, and which culminated in the capture of Lincoln: "Earl Ranulf and the other victors then entered the city and sacked it all like barbarians; they slaughtered like cattle the remaining citizens, whomever they could find or capture, killing them in different ways without regard for mercy. . . . So troubles multiplied everywhere, far and wide," he concludes, "and England was filled with plundering and fires and massacres; and the country, which had once been so rich and overflowing with luxuries, was now wretchedly desolate."[37] To readers of Orderic's history, and evidently to Orderic himself, mayhem comes as no surprise when it erupts yet again in a society that so often abused loyalty and friendship.

NOTES

1. Orderic Vitalis, *Ecclesiastical History*, ed. Marjorie Chibnall (Oxford: Clarendon Press, 1978), 13.43; vol. 6, p. 538.

2. Eleanor Searle, *Predatory Kinship and the Creation of Norman Power, 840–1066* (Berkeley: University of California Press, 1988).

3. Meyer Reinhold has reminded me that, in classical Latin, *amicitia* typically denotes a formal alliance of friendship; for Norman authors, too, the term rarely indicates a purely personal liaison.

4. Vitalis *Ecclesiastical History* 9.3; vol. 5, p. 24. All translations from the Latin are my own.

5. The duchy has its origins in the grant of 911, when the French king Charles the Simple gave Rouen and the territory at the mouth of the Seine to a band of Vikings who were supposed to protect the upper Seine and Paris from raids by other Viking bands. All the Norman dukes descended from the Viking chief, Rollo.

6. Vitalis *Ecclesiastical History* 9.3; vol. 5, p. 24.

7. *Historiae*, ed. I. Bekker (Bonn: CSHB, 1853), 294–96. This offers another striking exception to the Varangians' usual loyalty to emperor, but Botaneiates faced considerable opposition from all sides during his brief rule (1078–81), and soon lost his throne to the rebel Alexius Comnenus. For more on the Varangians, see my "Scandinavians in Byzantium and Normandy," in *Peace and War in Byzantium: Festschrift for George Dennis, S.J.*, ed. Timothy Miller (Washington, D.C.: Catholic University Press, forthcoming).

8. Magnus Magnusson and Hermann Palsson, trans., *Njal's Saga* (London: Penguin, 1960), 13.

9. Ibid., 109.

10. Ibid., 128–30.

11. Bruno Krusch and Wilhelm Levison, eds., *Monumenta Germaniae Historica: Scriptorum Rerum Merovingicarum*, 1 (Hanover, 1951).

12. Ibid., 7.47 and 9.19.

13. Ibid., 9.19.

14. In Dudo a Roland appears briefly but significantly as the arrogant standard bearer of the Frankish war party, urging battle against the Vikings led by Rollo, future count of Normandy. Is there a mythic recollection here of the leader of the war party within Charlemagne's retinue? Dudo's Roland is an enemy to proto-Normans, but one whose sentiments they might admire; and the presence of this Roland suggests a knowledge of the mythic Roland

whom the Normans would soon embrace.

15. *Le Roman de Rou de Wace*, ed. A. J. Holden (Paris: Société des Anciens Textes de France, 1970), 3.8013–8018; vol. 2, p. 183.

16. The oldest and best version of the *Roland* is found in the Oxford manuscript Digby 23, written in the mid-twelfth century. Its French possesses many traits of the Anglo-Norman dialect and contains references suggesting composition in the late eleventh century, including probably allusions to conquests in southern Italy by the Norman Robert Guiscard.

17. *Dudo de St. Quentin: De Moribus et Actis Primorum Normanniae Ducum*, ed. Jules Lair (Caen: Société des Antiquaires de Normandie, 1865).

18. Ibid., 2.29, p. 169.

19. *Gesta Francorum et Aliorum Hierosolimitanorum*, ed. Rosalind Hill (London: Thomas Nelson & Sons, 1962), 20.

20. Ibid.

21. Vitalis *Ecclesiastical History* 9.15; vol. 5, p. 156.

22. Ibid., 10.8; vol. 5, p. 228.

23. Ibid., 10.12; vol. 5, p. 270.

24. Ibid., 10.12; vol. 5, p. 276.

25. Ibid., 10.18; vol. 5, p. 302.

26. Ibid.

27. Ibid., 10.19; vol. 5, pp. 308–20. All of the quotations from this series of tales (pp. 123–25 of the text above) are from this source.

28. Ivo of Chartres. See Chibnall's comment in Vitalis, *Ecclesiastical History*, vol. 5, pp. 314–15, n. 5. See also Migne, *Patrologia Latina* 162.157–58, esp. 154.

29. Emily Albu Hanawalt, "William of Apulia's *Gesta Roberti Wiscardi* and Anna Comnena's *Alexiad*: A Literary Comparison" (Ph.D. diss., University of California at Berkeley, 1975).

30. Emily Albu Hanawalt, "Norman Views of Eastern Christendom: From the First Crusade to the Principality of Antioch," in *The Meeting of Two Worlds: Cultural Exchange between East and West During the Period of the Crusades*, ed. Vladimir P. Goss and Christine Verzar Bornstein (Kalamazoo, Mich.: Medieval Institute Publications, 1986), pp. 115–21.

31. Holden, *Roman de Rou*, Prologue.

32. Lair, *Dudo de St. Quentin*, 4.125, pp. 289–90.

33. Holden, *Roman de Rou*, 3.634–45.

34. Ibid., 3.646–48.

35. R. H. C. Davis, *The Normans and their Myth* (London: Thames and Hudson, 1976), p. 9.

36. Charles Homer Haskins, *The Normans in European History* (New York: W. W. Norton & Co., 1915: repr. 1966), p. 247.

37. Vitalis *Ecclesiastical History* 13.43; vol. 6, p. 547.

PART III

Friendship in the Modern World

My Friend Dietrich Bonhoeffer's Theology of Friendship

EBERHARD BETHGE

I. LATE

THIS IS A LATE MOMENT for me to deal with this topic, having never included it in decades of working on, with, and for Dietrich Bonhoeffer since 1945. Only now, in my eighties, I have been asked to talk biographically about the stages of our friendship, and I do it with a certain pleasure in its personal charms.

Why so late? There are two simple reasons. First, how could one of the participants control his own vanity so that the subject could be expressed dispassionately and appropriately? Second, there used to be understandable jealousy among Bonhoeffer's surviving former seminary students from Finkenwalde. I wonder if there still is. It could possibly damage our efforts to collect and evaluate the Bonhoeffer sources. A discussion of friendship as a topic could not avoid the difference between friendship in the plural and friendship in the singular, meaning *friends* in all sorts of different historical, professional, and geographic locations, and each single "best friend." In this case there were four "singular" friends. Competition in taking care of Bonhoeffer's legacy could be both useful and harmful.

It is not only I who began to reflect on this topic late in life. For Dietrich Bonhoeffer, too, this topic was explicitly and intentionally explored only very late in his life. He was interested in *communio* from the very beginning, but that always remained for him an ecclesiological topic. At the same time, it is impossible to imagine him without his friends. For someone of his temperament, they were essential to his very life. But there is not a single page in any of his own books on

133

which he wrote a specific analysis of the place and dignity of friendship, whether sociologically, psychologically, philosophically, or theologically.

The sources we have on the subject come exclusively from his time in prison from 1943 on. They do, however, then seem to me to have a concentrated power. They speak primarily of a *topos sui generis*, meaning friendship in the singular, and not as a form of socialization among many other structures of life. He probably felt some urgency to bring intellectually formulated clarity to that which he had personally experienced and possessed so generously. Did he want, on the one hand, to learn to deal with a situation better, which in the forties had become precarious and dangerous for him and his partner? For seven months in 1943 during his interrogations in prison, he had avoided any mention of me, and no communication between us by correspondence was possible. Was there a lifegiving strength in the friendship, needed now more than ever, good fortune in the midst of misfortune, which he was trying to think through? On the other hand, just at that time a problem had arisen, which called for being objectified. Both friends had either just gotten married (that was I) or were preparing to get married (he had gotten engaged in January 1943), and our friendship would certainly have undergone a mutation of our partnership.

So we find from the time of his imprisonment four salient sources of different quality.

II. FOUR SOURCES

A. *Fiction fragments*

In the summer and fall of 1943 Dietrich tried his hand at writing a drama and a novel. Pairs of friends in the singular type of friendship play a role in both fragments. Clearly concrete autobiographical experiences have influenced both the portrayal of the friendships and the reflection on them found in the fragments. In the novel, in addition, there is the singular-type school friendship, which proceeds from a perilously competitive relationship through a tempestuous crisis to a deep responsible alliance. There is no evidence of a comparable situation to this theme of conflict found in Bonhoeffer's own biographical experiences of singular friendship.

B. *The letter*

The second source — the most important one — is a portion of Bonhoeffer's letter to me from prison on January 23, 1944.[1] It attempts to illuminate something he had not thought about at all a few years before when he was working on his *Ethics*. Now he sought a possible theological and sociological integration of friendship into the four divine mandates of Christian life (church, state, work, family) — or possibly not — by adding that "broad area of freedom," which the church was providing in 1943.

C. *Stifter*

The second and fourth sources are letters addressed to me. But the third source is a small anthology of the writings of the nineteenth-century Austrian writer, Adalbert Stifter. It was sent into the Tegel prison for Bonhoeffer to read, and then returned to his parents' home in the Marienburger Allee. It delivered news for me in the form of a message in secret code, and contained his pencil markings in the margins of Stifter passages on the uniqueness of the phenomenon of friendship.

D. *The poem*

Finally, Dietrich sent me that intensely reflective poem, "The Friend," for my birthday in August 1944. It was an unequalled birthday present for me, just at the point that our communication would reach its permanent end.

E. *A fifth source?*

In fact, there was a fifth source, written during the same winter 1943–44. Bonhoeffer called it a "small literary piece," inspired by our recent coming together in November and December 1943 on the "meeting between two old friends after a long separation during the war."[2] It cost him, as he wrote, "more time than I thought at first." At the end of February he thought he would soon have it finished. In early July he admitted that "the small piece" was "not yet quite finished." Unfortunately, nothing from this fragment ever reached us. But his

interim reports on it show at least how much the topic occupied Bonhoeffer both thematically and personally since that reunion between
us. Evidently, he was not satisfied with the descriptions of pairs of
friends in the drama and novel fragments, as well as the great passages
in his January letter and his poem. He was trying to explain it more con-
cretely and in a more nuanced fashion with this "literary" piece.
But — alas — it was lost. And I would have been *so* curious to read it!

III. HIS FRIENDSHIPS

A. *Friends in the plural*

Before we come to an interpretation of these sources, a complete treatment of the topic "friendship in Bonhoeffer" would first
have to tell about his friendships and characterize them. But I can
only do that in brief outline here.

Friendships in the plural appeared in adolescence as soon as he
moved out of his lively parental home, to begin his studies in Tübingen in 1923. From then on he steadily and unreservedly brought
home friends. Before then, I do not know of any long-lasting school
friends who remained influential for him. The circle of his many
brothers and sisters and their friends filled all needs for stimulation,
entertainment, and competition of this vigorous youngster.

But then his studies in Tübingen (from 1923 on), his placements
in the vicarage in Barcelona (1928), at Union Seminary in New York
(1930), at the German parish in London (1933), and the illegal seminary in Finkenwalde (1935) all brought him travel friends, professional
colleagues, fellow music players, like-minded allies, and coexperi-
menters in liturgical and monastic experiments. His ventures overseas
and even attempts to emigrate forged particularly deep bonds. I would
mention here Paul and Marion Lehmann, Erwin Sutz, and Jean Las-
serre. The time of the conspiracy finally created stronger trust
relationships even than the church struggle years. This could be observed with respect to Friedrich-Justus Perels and Oscar Hammels-
beck, who belonged to both periods. Dietrich's prison cell in Tegel
brought unique friendships, which had an effect for a long time after-
ward — until today, for example with the Italian co-prisoner, Professor
Gaetano Latmiral. After it was all over, these were simply transferred

to me, as was also Paul Lehmann's friendship, from which I myself enjoyed the richest advantages! In this connection, I regret that I missed finding and meeting Dietrich's guide through Harlem, Frank Fisher, before he died.

Dietrich's relationships with George Bell and Karl Barth, even the sudden but short-lived closeness to Visser t'Hooft, deserve special attention. They undoubtedly became rather like "fatherly friends" for him. Their judgment and understanding were by far the most important for him when he made his most consequential decisions, those on behalf of the conspiracy. Working for the conspiracy inevitably included abuse of his ecumenical relationships in the service of preparations to topple Hitler. He could not ask any authority within the Confessing Church about that. After 1945 Bell did not hesitate to call the much younger man his friend. For Barth, Bonhoeffer was not the kind of lifelong friend that Eduard Thurneysen was, but their relationship went far beyond that between controversial, fascinating dialogue partners.[3]

During the Nazi years, a separate category of friendship would be formed by the growing friendships within the circle of siblings and in-laws. A description of it would result in an entire short story of the resistance itself, in order to illuminate the combinations of elements of family and friendships. It would reveal a picture which would greatly transcend normal family relationships. They had geographic proximity to each other and shared a tradition, which was never interrupted, of finding pleasure in their communicative activities — even when turning points intruded, which really were anything but pleasurable, and which brought real suffering. Yes, even at just those times, they managed to pass on these values to children and grandchildren. All these things became the preconditions for concrete freedom in chains. Their flow of information, competence to give advice, and support systems all were based on reliability of competent judgment and estimates of the extent to which each one could be burdened for very different kinds of tasks. For example, they thought to organize in advance a procedure for communicating by code in case of imprisonment. Dietrich's parents, nieces, and nephews participated in it, and it successfully functioned for a long time.

I refer here not only to his explicitly friendship-like affinities with the Leibholzes, Schleichers, Dohnanyis, and his brother, Klaus Bonhoeffer's family. His relationship to his oldest brother, the physicist

Karl-Friedrich, belongs here too, although he lived further away in Leipzig. Dietrich always wanted to account for his professional and faith decisions in his letters of birthday greetings to Karl-Friedrich, particularly as he was an agnostic. But in fact, among the siblings, Karl-Friedrich was the most faithful letter-writer to Dietrich in his Tegel prison cell. Except for the letters from Dietrich's parents, his fiancée, and me, the most letters existing from 1943–44 are from Karl-Friedrich.

Absolute reliability is not an unconditional element of family relationships. But it is one of friendship, and in this they formed a unity, in which one strengthened the other: family strengthened the friendship element, and friendship strengthened the family element.

B. Friends in the singular

1. *Hans Christoph von Hase*. Hans Christoph von Hase represents a transition from these family friendships to the singular friends, of whom there were most likely four. He was a cousin a little more than a year younger, from a country parsonage. His specific relationship to Dietrich was a permanent factor the family took for granted. It continued from long contacts on vacations and by correspondence during childhood through adolescence. It grew more intensive with both of their early fundamental decisions to become theologians. Hans Christoph passed on to Dietrich his first notes from Karl Barth's lectures. And Dietrich later passed on to Hans Christoph his fellowship at New York's Union Theological Seminary. The singularity and intensity of their contact lessened when Hans Christoph entered military chaplaincy in 1935 and thus kept a certain distance from the "Dahlemite" upheaval in the church struggle, in which Dietrich was so heavily involved. During the time of the conspiracy, they were in touch only rarely.

2. *Walter Dress*. Dietrich's second singular friend was the Berlin pastor and soon professor, Walter Dress. They were in the local "Hedgehog" fraternity together during Dietrich's first year of university studies in Tübingen. Later he met Dress in the seminars at Berlin University and particularly in the State Library. Dress was almost two years older and was already working on his doctoral dissertation, and soon working on even his second dissertation, the "habilitation" re-

quired to qualify as a university lecturer. The academic and scholarly relationship turned into a family connection before long when Dress married Dietrich's younger sister Susanne in 1929.

In 1992, just in the week when Volume 10 (documents from Dietrich's time in Barcelona and the United States) of the new edition of Bonhoeffer's works appeared, we found an additional almost forty letters and postcards from Dietrich to Walter from between 1925 and 1929. They make clear what a lively theological and literary exchange they had, how they consulted each other, and entrusted each other with youthful criticism of the academic and ecclesial leaders of the time. The intensity of their exchange receded to the extent that Dietrich became involved in the ecumenical world and led a wandering life, while Walter remained true to Berlin, except for his teaching in Dorpat, Lithuania, in 1930 and after. Also, Dietrich grew to an increasing affinity with Karl Barth during the church struggle, to which Walter was not as sympathetic.

3. *Franz Hildebrandt.* Dietrich's third singular friendship, with Franz Hildebrandt, became all the more intense. Franz was from Berlin, the son of a museum director (for which reason Franz never entered art galleries later on!). It, too, began with Harnack's seminars, with their common worries about their dissertations, and with a lively exchange of quotations from Luther. Soon thereafter came a common passion for the piano. That did not lead to their becoming in-laws, but it did quickly lead to an enduring "Uncle status" for Franz with many of Bonhoeffer's nieces and nephews. Later on an emigrant in England, Franz always carried photographs in his wallet of the Schleicher and Dohnanyi children in addition to Martin Niemöller's children. The nieces and nephews were often amazed to watch how the two friends could plunge into renewed heated but humorous theological debates, without having any notion of what was meant by the positions of the supposed "nomian" Dietrich and the supposed "antinomian" Franz. With Hitler's rise to power in 1933, their joint activities and writings (a catechism in 1931) took on a more and more existential dimension. In the fall of 1933 Dietrich took Franz into his parsonage in London, just as his home church, heavily compromised by the Nazis, was about to dismiss him as a "non-Aryan." There they continued their struggle in the church and their music making. In early 1934 Franz returned to Berlin at Niemöller's request for help in the Dahlem parish and in the

Pastors' Emergency League, and Franz emigrated permanently as late as 1937 after Niemöller was arrested. His emigration brought the daily practice of their friendship to a close.

This singular friendship gave Dietrich a partner for abundant dialogue during the time he was working out what became his book *The Cost of Discipleship*, although each friend maintained his own independence in a most productive way. It led to their proving their vocational loyalty to each other during the challenges which brought such profound consequences. It fulfilled each one's desires for humor and satire. For example, Franz wrote a letter of birthday congratulations to Dietrich in 1934 in the old German style of Martin Luther.[4] It fulfilled their similar musical tastes.

4. *Eberhard Bethge*. The fourth friendship was characterized, at least, by the opportunities to live together, of which we took extensive advantage. Even during the time that I had my own apartment in the early 1940s in Berlin, I lived with him in the Marienburger Allee almost more than in my own apartment in the Burckhardthaus. From 1935 on up until the end, we also had the bond of our joint illegal existence as theologians and pastors of the Confessing Church. I have told about its stages on other occasions: church struggle, travels, music.

This "friendship of illegals" (between an urbane Berliner and a country boy three-and-a-half years younger) was silenced for almost three-quarters of a year when he was arrested on April 5, 1943, during which time I advanced in status to a member of the family by marrying his niece. After the most heated period of his interrogations (April to August) was concluded, in November 1943, that amazingly functional smuggled correspondence between us opened up, with such unanticipated consequences as are now available for all to see in the book *Letters and Papers from Prison*. It broke off permanently with Dietrich's transfer to the Gestapo prison in October 1944 and with my own imprisonment shortly thereafter. But because I survived — which he and the family had arranged behind the scenes — our friendship continued in a transformed way.

At first I hesitantly collected and published fragments of his theology.[5] Then I secured biographical and historical evidence. In doing so I involved, so to speak, the whole world in this continuation of our relationship of loyalty. The fruits have long since gone into expert and critical hands from Tokyo to Seattle to Capetown. And they still unleash new stimulation for people, as they did long ago for me. In a recent article, Michael Trowitzsch of Münster University explains this continuing stimulation as due to Bonhoeffer's "concentration and passionate insistence on getting to the heart" of the Gospel, "because here someone is wholeheartedly and passionately and rousingly seeking for what is valid today."[6] Just as I finished my short story of Bonhoeffer's concrete friendships with its audacious division into plural and singular friends, I came across some wonderful evidence for this conception from Dietrich himself: namely, a few sentences from his birthday letter in 1941, which he wrote to me at the end of the day from Ettal Monastery in Bavaria. They contain very central sentences on the question of what friendship really is. They read:

> Our letters on the occasion of today [D.B.'s birthday] are notably similar in their content. This is surely not a coincidence, and confirms that things really are the way it says in the letters. You wished me, among other things, good, stimulating friends. That is a good thing to wish, and today it is a great gift. But the human heart is created in such a way that it seeks and finds refuge in the singular rather than in the plural. That is the claim, the limit, and the richness of genuine human relationship, to the extent that it touches on the area of individuality and to the extent that it rests essentially on loyalty. There are individual relationships without loyalty and loyalty without individual relationships. Both are to be found in the plural. But together (which is seldom enough!) they seek the singular, and happy is he, who "succeeds in this great luck."[7]

The "great luck" of the last sentence refers to a line in Friedrich Schiller's famous poem from 1785, *Ode to Joy*, which Beethoven used in the finale of his Ninth Symphony, "Wem der grosse Wurf gelungen, eines Freundes Freund zu sein."

This letter is a declaration of love from a friend, who rejoices in taking note of the shape of the relationship, and who is taking pleasure in communicating it in the nocturnal letter to his partner as a wonderful reassurance. He does not undertake any theological or christological derivations, but out of the "last things" which are presupposed, he experiences in himself the full freedom of "the things before the last." Thus, he does not have to extrapolate a system from *agape*, from ecclesiological foundations, for example, from "Finkenwalde," or from "Life Together," from the "brethren house." This conception flows

from an act of acceptance of a gift and not from the arduousness of dog-
matic logical deductions or from the exegesis of biblical *philia*.

Therein lies a difference between this reflection on friendship
from 1941 and that of January 1944 from Tegel prison almost three
years later. The later one is precipitated by certain specific circumstances and issues. They force it to seek objectively and decide the
place of friendship. Here Bonhoeffer harks back to his own previous
systematic attempts at theology and ethics. But he also shows an
amazing willingness to call those attempts into question on the grounds
of this *topos* friendship, which resists being ordered into his analyses.
How did it come to this, and what do we hear about it there?

IV. WHAT IS FRIENDSHIP?
AN ANALYSIS OF THE SPECIFIC TEXTS

How did it happen that this genius of friendship—giving, as
well as receiving—came so late during his time in Tegel prison to
write out such significant reflections on the *topos*, which order and
objectify the facts just related into concepts?

One turning point is the resumption of our communication after
the interrogations were finished, after an indictment was established
and hopes were raised to get on with the trial. Then he worked on establishing the method of smuggling letters; I even appeared in the
prison one day to see him when I was home on leave from the military.
At the same time, Dietrich's hopes were raised as never before that he
would be able to meet his fiancée in freedom. Nothing came of all that.
But an approaching problem came to the surface in light of the fact that
both partners in the friendship would be newly married. This problem
does not yet appear in the portrayals of friendship in his drama and
novel attempts during the summer and early fall of 1943 in Tegel. But
with the little Stifter volume it is suddenly there in a contrast between
friendship and family and the differences between them. In that
wonderful long first letter of November 18, 1943, he wrote:

> There is so much that I would very, very much like to hear of you!
> Sometimes I've thought that it is really very good for the two of
> you [Renate and Eberhard] that I'm not there. At the beginning
> it's not at all easy to resolve the conflict between marriage and
> friendship; you're spared this problem, and later it won't exist.

But that's only a private and passing thought; you mustn't laugh at it.[8]

The Stifter quotations. In late November a little volume by the Austrian writer Adalbert Stifter was returned from the prison. It was called *Wisdom of the Heart: Thoughts and Observations by Adalbert Stifter.*[9] Dietrich wrote his thanks for it to his parents on November 8:

> Your last parcel was particularly fine. I was very surprised and pleased with the Stifter anthology. As it consists mainly of extracts from his letters, it's almost all new to me.[10]

The return of this little book revealed two bits of rather exciting news for me. First, it contained the signal for a code message according to the previous agreements in the family, which was to put a tiny pencil mark under one letter every few pages starting from the back of the book. (Since the pencil marks were not erased in this case, you can still see them in the remnant of Dietrich's library in my home.) The deciphered message read: "Letter to Eberhard with Wergin." That was the lawyer Wergin, a friend of Dietrich's brother Klaus, who was supposed to defend Dietrich in the trial they hoped for. Well, that was that first very long letter from November 18–23, that sudden reopening of the source which had remained hermetically sealed for eight months.[11]

Second, we discovered Dietrich's pencil markings at passages which were about friendship and which seemed to speak to our own situation. Here are some sentences from the most important place:

> A true and upright friend is, next to a loyal wife, the greatest property that a man can have on earth. Our parents are friends given to us by God, but as loyal and sincere as they are, they are not born equal with us. Rather they stand over us as recipients of our honor. Thus, our love for them does not dare to come to them with all the little foolishness and trifles, with which we bother a friend who is a peer, and in so bothering him find our good fortune with him. A brother is a born friend, but the blood relationship has a sort of right to love. It appears, therefore, like an obligation and does not give the unforeseen joy that love given to us voluntarily by an outsider does. However pure, great, or unselfish sibling love is, it does not completely satisfy our existence and honorable siblings often give it to us even without

our doing anything to earn it. Friendship really completes the circle of happiness and gives us (however fine and good the friend really is) the assurance of our own value. An unworthy person has only accomplices, not friends.[12]

Anyone wishing to characterize the dissimilarity between Dietrich's letters to his parents and his letters to his friend, and now an entirely different third category of the wonderful correspondence with his fiancée from Tegel prison, will find key insights here in Stifter. Oh, yes, how important it is for the fullness of life to be able to bother someone with "the little foolishness and trifles," even in a prison cell! Here we can understand Dietrich's "surprised and pleased" reaction to this discovery and empathize with him marking just this margin with his pencil. Unfortunately, he left no notes showing whether he tried to figure out for what reason or experience Stifter, a Catholic, came so close to the Lutheran doctrine of orders or to Greek antiquity's esteem of friendship, transported through nineteen Christian centuries to come to this result. I myself could never yet do the work to research this point. In any case, these sentences from Stifter—although they sound outmoded, but full of original experience—do fit our friendship in that November 1943 situation. So they are in accord with and open my further reflections, and they belong necessarily to the following experimental discussion of "mandates."

Letter of January 23, 1944. In mid-December 1943 Dietrich wrote in a letter to me, just at a time when everything was uncertain for me with the possibility of a military transfer to the Russian or the Italian front:

> You're certainly right in describing marriage as "what remains stable in all fleeting relationships." But we should also include a good friendship among these stable things.[13]

Further complicating this experience of instability was a special problem I had in following the course of Dietrich's fate—his imprisonment and perhaps forthcoming trial. I had complained to him that his letters to his parents usually were shared immediately with Maria, who was his fiancée, and with his brothers and sisters. But only rarely were they ever passed along to his friend. I had written about that to him in Tegel at the New Year 1944. That became the impetus for that great passage in Dietrich's letter about the social, ethical, and theological place of the phenomenon of friendship. In my letter of January 2 from the military base in Lissa, Poland, I had written:

You write that, after marriage, our friendship is to be counted among the stable things of life. But that is not the case, at least as far as the recognition and consideration by others is concerned. Marriage is recognized outwardly—regardless of whether the relationship between the couple is stable or not—; each person, in this case the whole family, must take it into account and finds it the right thing that much should and must be undertaken for it. Friendship—no matter how exclusive and how all-embracing it may be—has no *necessitas*. . . . Your letters of course go to Maria, and almost as automatically to Karl-Friedrich, but it takes an extra struggle to make the point that I have to have them too. . . . In the army, you also say, no one pays any attention to the fact that someone has a very good friend. Friendship is completely determined by its content and only in this way does it have its existence. Marriage does not even need to be that; its formal recognition sustains it. . . . For the sake of my marriage, the family is willing to consider some special efforts on my behalf. [For example, how they might influence my being ordered to Italy instead of to Russia. E.B.] At the same time, no one has seriously considered how to arrange our possibly being assigned to serve together [in case he would come free and at once be called into the army].[14]

This complaint about the deficit in my participation in the family's information flow from the Tegel cell brought about that letter of January 23, 1944. Later, in 1949, we included the passage from it on friendship, its freedom, and the possibility or lack thereof of integrating it into his thought on the mandates as a footnote in the first edition of *Ethics*. We did not then describe its place in time and its context.[15] Strangely enough, this passage was not noted or analyzed in the most recent edition of the *Ethics*, which was otherwise restructured with the greatest care.[16]

Dietrich Bonhoeffer's passage on friendship begins with that succinct sentence, for which we now know the cause: " . . . I will also see that you get my letters to my parents."[17]

And then follows the experiment with the doctrine of divine mandates from the time that he was writing the fragments of *Ethics* a few years before. In the experiment, he intended both to stay a Lutheran and to escape the rigid Lutheran doctrine of orders of creation. We shall see how he came to think that this mandate doctrine really needed to be revised. One can sense how he wanted to remain flexible, for example, in the number of mandates, three or four (or even five?), and how he was really still in the middle of the experiment. Here is the first introductory sentence:

> I think you made a very precise observation in this connection about friendship, which, in contrast to marriage and kinship, enjoys no generally recognized rights, and therefore depends entirely on its own inherent quality.

Thus, Dietrich Bonhoeffer sees that friendship cannot be defined according to interests, goals, and purposes, which could be institutionally codified with sanctions and then also protected, whether by professions or groups. Rather, it can only be defined by what binding content exists between two people. This content can be very different individually. The different kinds of content give friendships their individual character and intensity. For that reason, they must remain free. They regulate the length of the partner relationship. Dietrich did not say that explicitly, but I interpret him that way, and I think that was how he experienced friendships, in the plural as well as in the singular. And that is what the birthday letter from Ettal 1941 truly says.

Bonhoeffer then continues: "It is really not easy to classify friendship sociologically." This conceptual difficulty—or neglect, because it was an unaccustomed project to work on— stands in contrast to his very practical capacity in his own life to "classify" his social circumstances with an enduring and influential effect. Compare, for example, his own freedom from jealousy. Here one should observe the stages of his friendships through Finkenwalde, through the Brethren House, through the family, through patterns of behavior to each of the former friends. The letter presses on:

> Probably it is to be regarded as a sub-heading of culture and education, while brotherhood would be a sub-heading under the concept of church, and comradeship a sub-heading of the concepts of work and politics.

Bonhoeffer approaches his topic using a phenomenology of concepts. According to this, friendship is something quite different from "Finkenwalde" or "Life Together." (I wonder if those who read Jürgen Moltmann's essay in this volume, "Aristotelian and Christian Concepts of Friendship," could agree with me that he arrives at a concept of friendship which is temptingly close to a "Finkenwalde" or a "Life To-gether.") With respect to the element of comradeliness, Bonhoeffer hardly associates the soldierly military experience. Instead, he associates the "political" with the "comradely" and brings that to an impressive climax with hints of the ongoing risk of responsible conspiracy. Compare his later poem, "The Friend," from August 1944.

Now he refers back to his work on the *Ethics* two to four years earlier:

> Marriage, work, state and church have their concrete divine mandate; but what about culture and education?

Back then he had conceived his "doctrine of mandates," in order to reassure people of their own responsible empowerment in their positions and decisions, to show them their divine permission which provides order and creates freedom. It did all that without opening the sluice gates to the kind of chaos feared by the Lutherans. Instead it opened doors for individual creative flexibility. Thus, it showed freedom in obligation. How important the element of freedom is to him is shown in the continuation of this passage: "I don't think they can just be classified under work, however tempting that might be in many ways."

Why "tempting"? Because friendship naturally also possesses— has to possess—a place in the mandate of work, which includes, for example, everything related to the professional. Bonhoeffer surely has some sense of the widespread criticism against the Lutherans which his mandates doctrine will attract, for instance, from Karl Barth. Therefore, because he is now attempting to locate friendship, we find him clearly stressing how important it is in the mandates to pay attention to the simultaneity which is absolutely necessary: dialectically simultaneous interdependence *and freedom.*

And so there follows one of the especially beautiful passages by that experimenting thinker in the prison cell, who always did relish playing games, and found fault with me that, in addition to not speaking English, I did not know anything about playing chess! His prison letters are so appealing because they communicate not only his abiding self-control, but also his infectious playful joy in simply "being fully human." Now, therefore, he is looking for a "fifth" mandate of freedom for the phenomena of culture and education, and with them, also friendship:

They belong, not to the sphere of obedience, but to the broad
area of freedom, which surrounds all three (or four) spheres of
the divine mandates. Whoever knows nothing about this area of
freedom may be a father, citizen, and worker, indeed even a
Christian; but I doubt whether he is a complete person (and,
thus, a Christian in the widest sense of the term).

There we have what Bonhoeffer was driving at in his ethical theology or theological ethics: "being fully human." There are some
passages in the *Ethics* fragments which epitomize the high points of
this discussion.

Using the example of his own heritage, he then shows that much
in this has to be changed: "Our 'Protestant' (not Lutheran) Prussian
world has been so dominated by the four mandates that the sphere of
freedom has quite receded into the background." Here we can see
how Bonhoeffer was not willing to leave Luther simply to the Lutherans of his century! "Prussian world"—that extended for him from the
Grunewald neighborhood in Berlin where he grew up to the eastern
Pomerania of the Kleists, his fiancée's extended family.

After this sober analysis, there follow observations on the hope
coming from the recent church struggles, experiences of renewal with
enormous implications for the future (which were never realized). He
had already mentioned such renewal in his *Ethics*:

I wonder whether it is possible (it almost seems so today) to
regain the idea of the church as providing an understanding of
the area of freedom (art, education, friendship, play), so that
Kierkegaard's "aesthetic existence" would not be banished from
the church's sphere, but would be re-established within it? I
really think that is so, and it would mean that we would recover
a link[18] with the Middle Ages.

Here Bonhoeffer hints that he is intending to fill in the gaps on
the matter of "being fully human" in those whose mentality is closest
to his own in church and theology—the "Kierkegaardians" and Bar-
thians. This is the concern of some of his *Ethics* sketches. Today, we
know more precisely how he was moving in the same direction as the
later Karl Barth did at his desk in Basel. Bonhoeffer's discoveries in his
analysis and experiments have the particular attraction of having taken
place in the middle of his life in the conspiracy and his experiences in

the prison cell. Of course, because of that they were often painfully fragmentary, and again and again they were broken off too soon.

In this way, Bonhoeffer remembers experiences just before he was arrested, well aware of how rare they were, and of their near absurdity in light of Stalingrad and the arrests of the conspirators. He asks about what he himself had just done: "Who, for instance, in our times, can attend to music or friendship, play games or take pleasure in something with an easy mind?"

Not long before, in 1942, we had gathered in Berlin-Nikolassee, in the house of Ernst von Harnack, Adolf von Harnack's son, a coconspirator who was hanged in prison in 1945. There we had celebrated playing Bach's Brandenburg Concertos together. Ernst von Harnack played first flute, I played second flute, Rüdiger Schleicher—violin, Emmi Bonhoeffer—viola, Klaus Bonhoeffer—cello, and Dietrich—piano (after he was arrested, Renate took over the piano part). How often that had happened with a similar distribution of parts in the Schleichers' house next door to the Bonhoeffers!

Dietrich's answer to his own question reads: "Surely not the 'ethical' person, but only the Christian," and that just meant: not the person who rides principles to death and not the moralizer, whose failure Bonhoeffer had described extensively in his essay "After Ten Years" and in his *Ethics*. Rather, it meant someone "fully human," whom he saw created in and through Christ.

And then Bonhoeffer returns from his examples to the main line of his argument. We see the good Lutheran tersely indicating that he is quite eager to discuss this, and is expecting corrections and further explorations. Note the especially frequent use here of question marks and exclamation points:

> Precisely because friendship belongs to this sphere of freedom ("of the Christian person"!?), it must be confidently defended against all the disapproving frowns of "ethical" existences, though without claiming for it the *necessitas* of a divine commandment, but only the *necessitas* of *freedom*!

(In 1520 Luther wrote that great essay of the Reformation: "On the Freedom of a Christian Person.")

With this paradox of a *"necessitas* of *freedom"* Bonhoeffer designates the heart and pivotal point for his "theology of friendship." But we should take note also that Dietrich intends that his theology of the mandates should *not* fall captive to a new rigidity of the Lutheran doctrine of orders. It should be kept open in fruitful illogic. Mandates guide us to take positions, they permit responsible freedoms, and in his understanding, they mean the Gospel. But they are not everything! Doesn't Dietrich Bonhoeffer permit us to tinker with his doctrine of mandates forever after only if we include this passage from January 23, 1944—that is, if we incorporate this passage on freedom and friendship with the questions it opens anew?

Bonhoeffer closes the outline of his stance with an extraordinary praise of friendship. This passage from January 23, 1944, reads:

> I believe that within the sphere of this freedom friendship is by far the rarest and most priceless treasure, for where else is there any in this world of ours, dominated as it is by the first three mandates [marriage, work, state]? It cannot be compared with the treasures of the mandates; in relation to them it is *sui generis*, but it belongs to them as the cornflower belongs to the grainfield.

At this point we should take a look at the engagement correspondence between Dietrich and Maria von Wedemeyer, which was published in German in 1992. During the same weeks in which the phenomenon of friendship had taken hold of him, he mentions it in his correspondence with Maria. They touch on questions of upbringing in their two families. Dietrich emphasizes, among other things, how good he thinks it is for parents to remain parents and not to try to make themselves "equal" with their children as "friends" in a comradely way. In doing so, he is able to speak very positively about "the austerity in the relationship of a father to a son," and even about a "sanctity of the office of fatherhood."[19] Maria, however, contradicts him very quickly and severely. Her own father had died eighteen months before at the Russian front. She writes: "I can tell you that I have only ever had one friend, and that was Father."[20] And later: "I cannot completely accept your rejection of friendship with parents. . . . I always took it for granted that when I went riding with Father, I told him *everything*."[21]

Did she blur Dietrich's "divine orders," maybe even his entire "doctrine of mandates"? Andreas Pangritz wrote to me on January 29, 1993, out of his own pro-Barthian and anti-Lutheran sentiments, what he thinks the twenty-year-old young woman did to her then thirty-eight-year-old fiancé: "In the final analysis [she] crossed out the entire doctrine of the mandates. And it seemed to me to be no coincidence that Dietrich probably ran out of arguments."

Now I hardly think that he would have run out of arguments if the couple had been able to continue the discussion. Perhaps he would have admitted that friendship can become a good and useful element in a father-daughter relationship, can even become a particularly fortunate case. Perhaps marriage/family and friendship relate to each other in a complementary way; they may even replace each other in an enriching way. But in spite of that, friendship and fatherhood are not the same thing and simply interchangeable. For if their limited interchangeability were always valid or if the one were simply reduced to the other, then they would both lose their enriching value for each other and would become poorer.

Statements of the poem from August 1944. The cornflower in the grainfield—this analogy for friendship within other sociological frameworks—takes over the first word in the second, explicitly formulated source on Bonhoeffer's "theology of friendship." It is the word at the moment of the end of the friendship's being actually practiced. It has the most concentrated form; it is a poem. It is a birthday present to me in August 1944.

In comparison to January of that year, Dietrich's situation had changed fundamentally. In the winter of 1943–44, there were still expectations of a trial, which might turn out positively. They did not yet expect the trial to be conducted by the worst Nazi tribunal or a Gestapo court, although, of course, the Gestapo would be present. It was expected to be before the national military court, in which the family could still count on individual judges to whom they could establish connections or already had them. But now, in August, that late assassination attempt against Hitler on July 20, 1944, had failed. With its failure, Dietrich's hopes for his marriage, and also for continuing his underground contacts with friends, came to an end.

Because of all this, the tenor and the intensity of "concentrated" content changes yet again. His reflection from January 23 could still be valid for friends in the plural, each according to free choice and perception. But now he expresses almost completely the being and function of a friend in the singular. From within a deeper entanglement in the conspiracy and its fate he addresses more strongly the "comradely" part of friendship, meaning the elements of complete loyalty and the acceptance of the possibility of his own sacrifice. Pre-

pared for such sacrifice, and yet filled with comforting, strangely up-
lifting, and certain joy in *philia* at that very moment, the poem
contains Bonhoeffer's complete "theology of friendship."

The *first* verse sets "the spirit's free desires" for another spirit
meeting it over against the reality which Bonhoeffer had earlier described as "orders of preservation" and their laws.

In the *second* he characterizes the sheer and wonderful useless-
ness of friendship, in which its love lives, just as the cornflower lives
uselessly in the middle of the useful cornfield.

The *third* sings of the playmates of the wander years.

The *fourth* verse describes the longed-for companionship, when
loneliness surrounds the irreversible decisions, the deeds, and the
creative work of the grown-up person.

In the *fifth* the friend expects the deadly enmity of "poisoned
tongues," which call forth the fullness of the functions of an unlimited
trust relationship: to "reveal [oneself] fully" to each other, to "affirm,"
to "acknowledge," to "thank," and to "gain joy and strength from the
other spirit."

The *sixth* verse observes:

> Even . . . rigorous standards . . . the mature man seeks from the
> loyalty of his friend. . . . In joy or in sorrow, each knows in the
> other his loyal helper to freedom and humanity.

In the *final* section, the hope is expressed that "the danger now
is past; so danger—if the omen does not lie—of every kind shall
gently pass [the friend] by."

That our last source on this topic is such a poem as "The
Friend" makes clear that Bonhoeffer's "theology of friendship" is not
for his part the result of a lecture commission, worked out at his desk
for the next seminar session. But my presentation is that. This is a
lasting difficulty. Be that as it may, it has a place in the chain of my
lifelong work, as an answer to his work on a christological theology of
being fully human. Here is where it ends, not with conceptual clarification, but with a sermon to himself and to his partner at the moment
that the friendship is brought to its end—in order, just because of
that end, to resume a transformed life later on.

Several weeks ago I stood with my wife and brother-in-law in
the lovely new art museum in Bonn, where an exhibition was on loan

from the New York Museum of Modern Art. In it we suddenly found ourselves standing in front of an oil painting by Max Ernst from 1928, which I had not seen in New York. It is called: "The Rendezvous of Friends. The friends are transformed into flowers." On the painting one sees a confusion of brown-red clumps of undefined material. Sticking out of it one can recognize here some ears, there some snakes, a dog's head, teeth, a toad, and other such things. Spread above it all are seven white, very beautiful rose blossoms. Yes, that is the way it really is: "Friends are transformed into flowers."

NOTES

1.   Dietrich Bonhoeffer, *Letters and Papers from Prison*, ed. Eberhard Bethge, enlarged ed. (New York: Macmillan, 1972), pp. 192–93. Hereafter cited as LPPN.

2.   Ibid., p. 200.

3.   Cf. Rudolf Bohren, *Prophetie und Seelsorge. Eduard Thurneysen* (Neukirchen-Vluyn: Neukirchener Verlag, 1982), pp. 76–83.

4.   See Dietrich Bonhoeffer, *Gesammelte Schriften*, ed. Eberhard Bethge (Munich: Chr. Kaiser Verlag, 1958), vol. 6, pp. 291ff.

5.   Dietrich Bonhoeffer, *Ethik*, 1st ed. (Munich: Chr. Kaiser Verlag, 1949).

6.   Michael Trowitzsch, "Auf die Anfänge des Verstehens zurückgeworfen. Bemerkungen zu Dietrich Bonhoeffers Hermeneutik," *Neue Zeitschrift für systematische Theologie* 34, no. 3 (1992): 292.

7.   Bonhoeffer, *Gesammelte Schriften*, 2:398–99.

8.   Bonhoeffer, LPPN, p. 131.

9.   Adalbert Stifter, *Wisdom of the Heart: Thoughts and Observations by Adalbert Stifter: A Brevier* (Berlin, 1941).

10.   Bonhoeffer, LPPN, p. 125.

11.   Ibid., pp. 128–38.

12.   Stifter, *Wisdom of the Heart*, pp. 10–11.

13.   Bonhoeffer, LPPN, p. 164.

14.   Ibid., p. 181.

15.   Bonhoeffer, *Ethik*, 1st ed., pp. 223–24.

16.   Dietrich Bonhoeffer, *Dietrich Bonhoeffers Werke*, vol. 6 (Munich: Chr. Kaiser Verlag, 1989). Cf. Andreas Pangritz, "Zur Neuausgabe von Bonhoeffers *Ethik*. Erfreuliche Klarstellungen—und eine bedauerliche Unterschlagung," *Weissenseer Blätter* 5:92, pp. 25ff.

17. Bonhoeffer, LPPN, pp. 192–93. All of the following quotes of this passage are from the same source.

18. Cf. Bonhoeffer's later letter to Bethge of March 9, 1944 (Bonhoeffer, LPPN, p. 229), where he expounds on the link using Walther von der Vogelweide, the Knight of Bamberg, *hilaritas*, and the *worldliness* of the thirteenth century.

19. Dietrich Bonhoeffer and Maria von Wedemeyer, *Brautbriefe. Zelle 92* (Munich: C. H. Beck Verlag, 1992), p. 125.

20. Ibid., pp. 128–29.

21. Ibid., p. 134.

Friendship and Enmity among Nations

NINIAN SMART

THE ETHICS OF INDIVIDUALS when applied to collectivities such as corporations and nations are interesting. There are crimes and virtues by analogy, though not always. A nation cannot commit adultery, but it can steal. It can try to commit murder, though it cannot ever quite succeed. It can hate, be unnecessarily extravagant, pollute, fail to show compassion, kill individuals; but it cannot commit an abortion. It can lie, but it can hardly rape. The examples of what a nation cannot do involve literal bodies: you cannot have sex without a body, and a nation has no body, literally. We shall return to these points later. Let me say a word about nations in the modern world and so begin to lay the groundwork for a discussion of friendships and enmities between nations.

Nations are the most powerful entities, at least emotionally, in today's world.[1] They have their individual myths of identity, purveyed by histories, often colored. They demand great loyalty. E. M. Forster once said that he would rather betray his country than his friends, but this remark was not well received. You are expected to pay huge swathes of your income and often high taxes on everything you buy, and to lay down your life if necessary, all for the nation-state to which you belong. Many nations, like the Kurds, not yet having a state, fight hard and bitterly for independence. Stateless people are often in trouble. Exiles frequently mourn their lot. In the United States, by the way, a lot of this is not quite understood. It is a nation of happy exiles or immigrants, save so many African-Americans. Moreover, ethnicity takes on a different meaning in the United States, a nation framed by a Constitution and not primarily by ethnicity. (Even WASP-ness is moderated by alienations from the mother-nations in Europe.)

The power of national identity is strange since that identity can be formed in so many different ways: by language and some obscurely de-

155

fined ethnicity beyond, in the case of Czechs or Poles or Italians; by religion as with the Croats versus the Serbs; by both language and religion, as with the Turkish and Greek Cypriots; by history and prehistory, as with Egyptians over against, say, Saudis; by sub-religion as with the Saudis (namely the Wahhabi connection, as well as a fading Bedouinness); by pure and recent history, as with Singapore; by partial unity of language and long memories, as with the Chinese; by a sense of historical and partly religious identity modernistically reinterpreted, as with India; by memory and a bit by religion, as with the Scots (also a sense of antagonism, mildly felt, towards the English); and so on. The United States depends on history and loyalty to ideas, enshrined in the Constitution. The Swiss lean on history and a sense of decent federalism.

From some points of view, nations function as individuals, which no doubt is why ideas of friendship and enmity apply to them. Let me explore this "individuality." The Japanese have a useful term, namely the *kokutai* or "national substance." I think this is important. When an individual thinks of her nation, she tends to think of it as an individual with its own substance. It is a kind of great Thing of which she is a part or in which she participates spiritually. That Thing has its body, which is the national territory plus bits of hardware, such as the capital city and varied monuments, as well as its beauties and so forth. If a nation does not have a territory it had better get one. This was the drive of Zionism. Herzl even negotiated for Uganda. In those days European nations did not have to care about the inhabitants of the rest of the world: they were people to conquer, master, use. Their territory did not count for them. So Herzl could in principle have settled for Uganda; any land is better than none. Of course Israel was the ideal, and so it turned out to be. But a nation has to have territory, regarded as sacrosanct. It also has another major component—people who share in whatever the heritage is. Other people on the territory not belonging tend to become second-class citizens. Also the people may be found on other people's territory: a potent source of conflict, frequently the source of territorial claims and invasions. It is notable that the concept of *invasion* has become precise in the modern world, now that the whole land surface of the planet, except Antarctica, is divided among nation-states or putative nation-states, so that if you are not in one country you are in another. Only occasionally at sea can you evade national control of one kind or another. As we observe now, when a state breaks up and differing ethnic groups fight to establish their own nation-states, and perhaps to enlarge their boundaries, chaos ensues. That chaos ultimately will be resolved no doubt by *force majeure*, and new frontiers recognized, reluctantly or otherwise. Anyway, a nation has its people and its territory; part of the *kokutai* is a sense of its unity under a government, which hopefully expresses the will of the people or *Volk*. The people is not necessarily a combination of all individuals on the territory, but of the dominant group. In addition, the *Volk* has a certain personality, for it has a biography, its history since early times (or not so early in some cases). It will have as part of the myth of its history adherence to certain values, such as democracy or some other ideology, usually reinforced by traditional religion, suitably interpreted. During World War II, Britain thought it was fighting for democracy and Christian civilization. North Vietnam fought for independence and Marxism. Iran fought for Shi'i Islam against atheist Iraq (which since has become amazingly loyal to Islamic values, despite the secularism of the Ba'ath Party).

So a nation, having its *kokutai*, is an individual, but it is also a collectivity. It is a collective person, so to speak. But because it is a construct, it can operate at two levels. As a national Thing it may murder individuals. It can at the Thing-level fight against another state, another Thing. Of course, in actuality this means that individuals are sucked up into shooting or otherwise destroying other individuals. They may also destroy other entities such as palaces, housing, trees, animals, and so on, which pertain to the property of the other Thing. So in general, nation-states as Things operate on two levels: in relation to other Things and in relation to individuals both of their own and other nations. I simplify, of course, for a nation may act against lesser or intermediate Things, such as clans, which may be for some people the community of ultimate concern, to use a phrase modeled on Tillich's famous one. The loyalty in the eighteenth century to the Macdonalds of a Macdonald tended to outweigh his loyalty to a vaguely conceived Scotland (half of whose territory and people were in any case Sassenachs); it was a miracle that the clans rallied, in so far as they did, to the call of Bonnie Prince Charlie. So national entities often crush intermediate entities. From this point of view, socialism was a nationalist ideal: it allowed the state to eliminate multinationals and other troublesome corporations. There was always a conflict between nationalism and capitalism. It is true that in the relatively early stages of nationalism, in the first part of the nineteenth century, nationalism was important as providing big enough entities to launch industrial and other large-scale enterprises. In this way there was an alliance between nationalism and capitalism. There was debate as to whether certain countries such as Belgium were big enough, though in fact Belgium was successful as a capitalist country. The conflict between capitalism and nationalism has a contemporary replay in the resurrection of European national sentiment. There is another problem incidental to our theme. A lot of resentment about Europe is not so much nationalist as democratic. Democracy can feed nationalism, but it is something a bit different. It does not take the *Volk* as an entity, even if it may sometimes express aspects of collectivism. It does not necessarily, however, believe in the *kokutai*, since individualism transcends such thinking.

Still, the forces of the collectivity are strong. And it is clear that nations can be friendly and hostile to one another. What does international friendship amount to? Friendship is not by itself a virtue but a relationship. But it has its virtuous aspects. It is good to be friendly and to seek to acquire friends. Of course such seeking may be in the long run selfish. One may want friends because of their influence or business connections; one joins the country club out of self-interest. But selfishness of a reasonable or enlightened kind may still be virtuous.

We shall seek to define international friendship shortly, but let us first glance at its opposite, namely enmity. Hostility between groups is fostered in various ways. Most obviously the suppression of one group by another not only stimulates national feelings among the oppressed but also generates hatred. It is an obvious feature of the modern world that many enmities arise in this manner. Let me list a few: Palestinian nationalism over against Jewish or Israeli control; Abkhazian feelings under Georgian rule; Russian enmities towards Estonian speakers in Estonia; various minorities and even in some areas majorities in the former Yugoslavia; Tamils in Sri Lanka versus the majority Sinhalese; Muslims as a minority in Burma; Tibetans versus the Han Chinese; and so on. One of the major problems is to get rulers and majorities in particular to give due and happy recognition to minority peoples. Federalism is not a popular principle, and where it exists it is not always fairly administered. The results are that a minority group will feel a sense of injustice and hatred, and will in due course be likely to resort to warfare to try to assert its rights. This in turn breeds hatred on the other side, cruelty, in effect racism or its equivalent, and so on.

On this point, let me interpolate some thoughts about racism. It is a common accusation, but its meaning is unclear. This is because the concept of race is unclear. For example, anti-Semitism is taken as racism, though we are of course quite at sea about the genetic inheritance of Jews. Admittedly Judaism is a greatly, though by no means exclusively, hereditary religion. But unfortunately evil vaporings about race in nineteenth-century Europe and in *Mein Kampf* have taken a grip on most of us, and so we accept anti-Semitism as racism. Mostly racism is taken to be where ethnic groups are somewhat different in appearance: then prejudice on the part of one against the other is seen as racism. When I was living in Notting Hill in London there were riots at about the same time against West Indians and Hungarians (refugees after 1956), who had settled in the area. The one riot was racist and the other not, according to the press and politicians. But I expect the West Indians had a lot of European genes and the Hungarians lots of genes from Northern Asia ultimately. I consider therefore that it is clearer if we speak more of ethnic groupism. In fact the term *groupism* represents the most general word I can think of to describe the prejudice of the members of one group against another, and an important species is ethnic groupism. But one can also have religious groupism, as with prejudices on the part of the members of one or more religions or worldviews against those belonging to another.

Since the dominant theme these days, however, is nationalism, we may note that ethnic groupism is the most vital form of contemporary prejudice and indeed hatred. As we have noted, the construction of an ethnic group occurs in various ways, so the channels of prejudice are themselves varied. To complicate matters, there are various places, chiefly Africa, but also Papua New Guinea, parts of Central Asia, and so on, where many sub-ethnics occupy a territory which is itself involved in nation building, that is, constructing an ethnic group at a higher level than the sub-ethnics. This is somewhat analogous to what happened in Europe, though people have partially forgotten. Bismarck could sneer that Italy was a mere geographical expression (what, by the way, did he think Germany was?); but by 1870 it had become a nation, even if now in these latter days the Lega Lombarda has revived some of the older more-than-regionalism.

While African nationalisms based on the colonial boundaries are not "natural" — as if anything in the cultural sphere is — on the whole the ethnicities of Europe are more solidly based. Those of Asia vary. Those of the Middle East are rather arbitrary, but since most of the inhabitants are Arabs, they do not on the whole need as much welding as will be required in Africa. But notably some minorities, either ethnic or religious, such as the Kurds and Shi'a of Iraq, are ready to break away from the invented states. Slightly similar conditions apply in Latin America, where nearly everyone speaks Spanish or Portuguese.

To get back to the problem of minorities or dominated subgroups: if they are poorly treated, and this is not untypical, then they will resort to armed conflict from within. There are plenty of areas in the world where this is currently so. Not only will this breed cruelty on both sides, but it will create eventually ineluctable demands for autonomy or independence. Where a minority belongs to a neighboring majority (like the Hungarians of Transylvania), there is likely sooner or later to be a demand for the recasting of boundaries. But in that case the old ruling majority becomes a minority and more friction will ensue. Where inevitably a group remains a minority, something other than partition will need to be done. But what? What if a minority is mingled in, so that there is no question of creating a canton or the like? This *ex hypothesi* will be the case if boundaries have already been drawn. I shall propose a solution a little later.

Some may think the answer is to make everyone internationalists. We are all human. We should all think as world citizens. True; but there needs to be an intermediate stage. Let me explain. Let me just for a moment turn to another form of socially significant division: between the two genders. Feminism demands equal rights for women, but it does not typically claim that the difference between men and women is nothing. In other words, the difference between men and women is not to be washed away; but given its ineluctability, then the distinction between genders should not be the basis of unequal power and other relations. Now, the difference between nationalities is also a pregnant social division. Admittedly it does not have quite the ineluctability of the gender difference, even if there are some genetic distinctions, usually trivial — so a Swede is liable to be blond but a Sinhala isn't. National distinctions are 95 per cent socially constructed. We could, by a social decision, abolish them. But we cannot do this by fiat; if people are to abandon their nationality they should do so voluntarily. An attempt to force assimilation is wrong and will in any case stimulate the very nationalism it is designed to overcome. Therefore at a preliminary level ethnic division remains a pregnant category distinction, for good or ill. How then does it remain friendly, rather than hostile? And in particular how do we deal with a distributed ethnic minority? As I have argued, because territory is the body of an ethnic group, it is best to redistribute territories to reflect ethnic majorities. But as we have already also argued, whatever happens there will end up being a minority which cannot have its own territory as a group. How then do we deal with this very pervasive case?

It seems to me that minorities should have as high as possible a symbolic participation in the state and the national community. That is, because symbols are importantly what demarcate and define the ethnicity of the minority, the state should incorporate them into the fabric of national self-expression. Let us dwell upon three kinds of symbolic expression: religion, language, and history. In all these areas a nation should exercise pluralism, within the feasibilities of community functioning. This should mean that there should be no established religion. If religious symbols are used in public life, then minority symbols should be given a place. Britain, for instance, presently entrenches representation of the Church of England in the upper house, but there should be constitutional provision for representing Jews, Sikhs, Muslims, humanists, and others. Again, full opportunity should be given for learning of minority languages. And if it is deemed necessary for all citizens to learn the majority language, for instance, Estonian, then reasonable provision should be made for Russian speakers to learn the language, or have some exemption on grounds of middle or old age, etc. (and not be summarily excluded from voting because they cannot pass a language examination). With regard to history, minority history should be taught in schools in some degree, and not ignored. Encouragement should be given to minority festivals and other means of symbolic gratification, such as football teams. Sport is a good means, often enough, of channelling enmities into friendly rivalries. In brief, a nation ought to be pluralistic and give minorities the maximum of symbolic ownership.[2] All this is on the basis of reciprocation, of course. Respect for majority symbols on the part of the minority is also needed.

In all this we should remember that symbolic wealth is often as important as economic wealth, perhaps more important. How often do oppressors say: "But look how well off they are!" It was often said in the days of apartheid that South African blacks were better off than their mismanaged counterparts to the North — as if being deprived of dignity was nothing, as if symbolic riches did not count.

So we might adopt a principle similar to that of Rawls' "maximin" notion:[3] we should maximize the minimum symbolic benefit. But the reasoning behind this is different. The problem with majority rule is that the majority may wish to control all the symbols. Minorities are left as citizens but derive little symbolic benefit. To even things out, a minority needs greater symbolic respect than it might have on the basis of numbers. It may also, of course, be economically oppressed. This is a major reasoning behind affirmative action. But it is often represented as offering something less justifiable, namely, compensation for ancestral oppression. The trouble now with ancestral oppression is its effects, by memory, on the psyches of descendants. That is to be made up by symbolic means, not by some incalculable infusion of money. In short there is a tendency in majorities to play the communal game by the rule of "Winner takes all" — that is, the majority takes all. The minority therefore needs special protection.

Sometimes the majority may think of itself as a minority, because of some neighboring juxtaposition of the minority group. For instance, Jews in Israel see themselves as a minority when they contemplate the large expanse of Arabs around them; Greek Cypriots look at themselves as a minority when they contemplate Turkey next door; Sinhala Sri Lankans see themselves as a minority when they look at over fifty million Tamils in India across a tiny stretch of water; Estonian speakers in Estonia see themselves in the same light when they look at the vastness of the Russian people, and so forth. This "majority-as-minority" syndrome is likely to make people more intransigent.

Maybe this idea of what may be called the maximization of symbolic richness for minorities has an analogue in a traditional virtue, that is the principle of hospitality towards strangers. They, being away from home and possibly therefore uncomfortable and even fearful, are to be given specially kind treatment to balance matters out.

Sometimes my maximization principle or its manifestations is met with the riposte: They have come to live here; they should abide by our rules. In a way the point is obvious. We all have to live by certain community rules. But the suggestion is that they should be homogenized. Perhaps some degree of this is inevitable, living in the same society. But minorities do not have to eat hamburgers. A decent society has to be pluralist, as I have argued, and this must be both in spirit and in the letter. In fact, a majority should be cheerful that different life-styles (food, for example) are made available. I do not ignore the point that migrants may threaten jobs in times of economic hardship. One must understand such roots of prejudice. But this merely tells us that another condition of maximum toleration is economic success. We should thus strive for this as widely in the world as possible. While we are usually all for that, however, we neglect this distribution of symbolic riches.

If these, then, are some of the conditions within a nation-state for harmony and friendship between groups, what are the sources of friendship and enmities between nations?

We may notice that the rise of nation-states in Europe was pervaded by an ethos of warfare and conquest. This was not just overseas, though in colonial connections it was even more blatant. Other continents were there to be dominated, conquered, exploited, and (as an afterthought) civilized. In Europe itself it was assumed that nations were plotting against one another — and might declare war. Even if Europe was relatively stable after 1815, it was not wholly so. The Crimean War, the Franco-Prussian War, and varied other armed conflicts punctuated the so-called peace. The unification of both Germany and Italy was not without violence, to put it mildly. And the Balkans, where ethnic boundaries were and still are not resolved, was the scene of wars, sometimes involving great powers such as Russia, not to mention the failing Ottoman Empire. So the ethos was one of warfare. And the great powers danced the deadly diplomatic minuet which led to the Great War, World War I, of which World War II was the second act. Only the advent of deadly nuclear bombs kept the peace in Europe after World War II, for so long. We must not suppose, yet, that peace is normal, as witness the many conflicts in Asia, Africa, and elsewhere.

The upshot of all this is fairly simple. Nations were expected on the whole to be hostile to one another. Even the slender framework of international law and moral ideas such as those animating both the League of Nations and the United Nations did not do too much, since they provided new occasions for moral outrage, itself easily developed into a *casus belli*. My wife, who is Italian, complains to me that the British were hypocritical in imposing sanctions on Italy over Abyssinia in 1935. "We only did what you did in Africa." My reply was of course suitably hypocritical: "You did it in the wrong century, my dear; the nineteenth century was the century for that kind of behavior." In short, the moralism of the twentieth century, welcome in some ways, also serves the causes of hostility.

What are the causes of war and what are the countervailing forces against it and on behalf of the friendship of nations? Since nations have sacred, ethnically defined space, I would nominate as a major cause the failure to define them properly and agreeably. This is a major cause of the Bosnian conflict: Bosnia was recognized without reflection that its boundaries included so many Serbs and Croatians that it was scarcely realistic. This point about boundaries is less easily understood in the United States, which does not have the same deadly ethnic definition that Europe and most of the rest of the world has. A second cause of conflict is the usefulness of war in creating the nation. Nothing binds a nation together so well as a common enemy. Moreover, the more dead you can have, killed in battle for the motherland (or Vaterland), the better—a terrible sacrifice on behalf of the nation. So wars are good for community. Third, there are economic reasons. Though these appeal to economic historians, where is the real evidence that they are important? Economic factors helped to create Hitler, let us say. But Hitler rose to power and prosecuted war for symbolic reasons. We have been too much dominated by Marxist thought in this connection.

Another cause of war no doubt is the lack of democracy. Anyone who has risen to power in a totalitarian way, that is, either as dictator or within a repressive hierarchy, is likely to be somewhat ambivalent mentally: psychopathic or megalomaniac or paranoid or ruthless or with some crazed utopia for his people. (I say "his" because we have not yet had a female dictator, even if Indira wore jackboots under her sari.) So lack of democracy and of relatively nice ways of retiring former rulers are a contributory cause of war, since crazed dictators are themselves a cause.

On the whole, democracies are relatively friendly to one another. They are not of course at all friendly, on the whole, to nondemocracies, though Great Powers such as the United States, even if democratic, may ally themselves with nondemocracies such as Chile and Somalia before it disintegrated. Still, democracies do not on the whole declare war on one another. And so a second way of developing friendship among nations, I would suggest, is democracy. Partly because democracy encourages individualism, and because it is likely to have a predominantly capitalist ethos, democracy encourages friendly exchanges of individuals between nations. An encouraging thing in today's world is the number of exchanges, touristic and otherwise, between individuals of differing nations and the consequent individual friendships, marriages, and so forth.

A third way of diminishing enmity is through economic cooperation. Here capitalist endeavors are important; transnational corporations help to bind peoples together, on the whole unknowingly. I like to cheer up people in Hawaii who complain that the Japanese are buying up too much of Hawaii by telling them that if the Japanese own Pearl Harbor, they are unlikely to bomb it again. Anyway, economic links are vital in binding nations together.

A fourth way is through other than economic bonds; the transnational spiritual corporations, which are the great religions, are important. So are agencies such as UNO, UNESCO, international charities, sports organization Olympiads, scholarly organizations, and so forth.

Although in recent times there have been recrudescences of national feeling—from warfare in Yugoslavia to suspicions among Danes and others of European institutions—on the whole, in certain parts of the world including much of Europe, a remarkable degree of international peace and friendship is in evidence. Though wars between Paraguay and Brazil or between Poland and Germany or between Tunisia and Algeria or between Japan and China are conceivable, they are also extremely unlikely. Still less likely are wars between Denmark and Sweden, or Britain and Ireland, or between Australia and New Zealand. In some of these cases the same could not have been said fifty or a hundred years ago. And so it is possible to mention areas where the war ethos no longer holds good. Most though not all of the cases I have cited point to the analysis of the causes of war and peace which I have cited above.

The experience of areas of relative peace between nations suggests that regional associations, such as the European Community, the North American Free Trade Area, and so forth, should be encouraged, as should, more particularly, the Organization of African States and the Organization of the Islamic Conference, which are very wideranging. Regionalisms are themselves a step on the way to globalism. For we should not forget that the community of ultimate concern is the human race, and maybe the community of all living beings; but surely the human race at least. Most religions and secular worldviews teach this. But nationalisms, until they become passive, like Finnish nationalism or Trinidadian nationalism, tend to devalue non-nationals. It seems all right for Americans to kill Libyans, or for Georgians Abkhas, as if the killed folk are not really *people*. Nationalism can thus dehumanize the other.

Thus we are brought to education. Certain features of education need to be prized, others deplored. Let me start with the deploring. First, history is taught in our schools as a myth of the nation. While pride in one's own group is no bad thing, it is dangerous to give it too much uncritical virtue. Second, by the same token, most histories taught in high schools are colonialist or chauvinistic and tend to justify the ignoring of other people's culture. Third, literature is often taught in the same way. Fourth, little education is devoted to cross-cultural studies and to world history. If we want to create a myth of global humanity we must greatly emphasize world history; but it must be done in a pluralistic way, with emphasis upon the diversity of the human condition. Too often our education ignores the cross-cultural dimensions; we have sociology which is about us, history which is our history, anthropology which has colonialist assumptions, minority studies about our minorities, literature which is our literature, and so on. We have little induction into empathetic explorations of other peoples and other individuals. All that is relatively bad news.

The good news is its obverse. We need heavy investment in world history, in cross-cultural explorations, in other languages, in political geography, and so forth. It will be possible also increasingly to use the cultural experience of diverse minorities to help in the process. Children and young people of other cultures than our own themselves can be a wonderful resource. But also we should look to the media, themselves in so many cultures defective. They too should look on themselves as an important cultural agency, involved therefore in education. Cultural and other affinities are also worth cultivating, to build on preexisting sympathies. For various reasons the Italians have an easier time with British people than do Germans, though from a deep cultural perspective we might expect the reverse. But history has played its part and people are taught memories which help to maintain enmities beyond any usefulness they might once have had.

Such then are the ways of fostering collective friendships. We have to recognize that nationalisms are basically rather invidious and so we have to overcome culturally entrenched hostilities as best we can.

It may be noticed that there is a paradox at the heart of my pre-scription for alleviating national enmities. But it is a paradox which pragmatically is unavoidable. I have argued that while ultimately we have to get beyond nationalism, we will have to do so through nation-alism. Ethnic groupism has to be humored to be overcome. An attempt to move straight to a sense of human solidarity without taking any account of ethnicity would involve perceived neglect of identities. So in practical terms it is better to give in to national demands, to try to make them compatible, then soften the impact of ethnic identity and eventually let cultural and sporting rivalries harmlessly take the place of war.

Not taking a realistic view can be dangerous, as present events in Yugoslavia and elsewhere demonstrate. Those will take a long time to heal, but heal they can, for other bitternesses have also been soft-ened and mostly cured. So nations will live, but may they become feeble as quickly as they can.

NOTES

1. Peter Merkl and Ninian Smart, eds., *Religion and Politics in the Modern World* (New York: New York University Press, 1984), discusses nationalisms.

2. David Chidester, *Shots in the Street* (Boston: Beacon Press, 1991), discusses the question of the ownership of symbols.

3. John Rawls, *A Theory of Justice* (Cambridge, Mass.: Belknap Press of Harvard University Press, 1971), discusses the maximin principle.

Friends and Family Values:
A New Old Song

MARY E. HUNT

SHORTLY AFTER I PUBLISHED *Fierce Tenderness: A Feminist Theology of Friendship*, when some might argue that I said all I have to say about friendship, I dutifully began a new file in order to keep thinking about the topic. The politics of the Reagan-Bush-Quayle era made clear that much of what I had proposed is anathema to the right wing. So-called "traditional family values" do not include the wide expanse of friendship, the deep reach of inclusivity. In fact, much of that rhetoric seems to run counter to anything that would encourage friendship as the primary mode, or even one of several significant relational modes.

Living "inside the Beltway," I may be overly sensitive to such matters, but it seems clear that issues related directly to friendship are making an impact far beyond what any scholars might imagine. I am not suggesting that my work, or the work of other philosophers and theologians on friendship, is enough to sway an election. But concern about the contours of relational life in the cosmos is not disconnected from how "a good society" ought to be shaped in the most concrete ways. To the contrary, we are all deeply involved in the political order, especially my feminist foresisters in the field. Late nineteenth-century feminist theologians were suffrage workers; late twentieth-century feminist/womanist/mujerista theologians struggle for reproductive rights, against racism, and in favor of a wide range of options in human relationships, all because, like the suffrage seekers, we believe that substantive social structural changes require deep shifts in theology, and vice versa.

This essay spells out a renewed understanding of friendship and how it reinforces rather than destroys what is useful about traditional family values. The "new world order" emerging when friendship and

169

not heterosexual marriage holds sway as the dominant paradigm is really an extension of some of the most admirable values — fidelity, nurture, attention, commitment.

My argument has four parts:

1. A brief review of my position on friendship, what I have elsewhere called "fierce tenderness," with emphasis on what a feminist theological perspective offers.

2. Several dangers I perceive with the metaphor and institutionalization of friendship as opposed to heterosexual coupling as the normative relationship. While this is a position I share, I want to suggest some critiques of it, as well as indicate some of my own reservations, as a way of expanding my position.

3. A look at the fallacy of the "traditional family values" debate and why I suspect those who were originally so enthused about it have backed off so rapidly.

4. A concluding comment on why and how friendship can function to ground what George Bush called a "new world order" which we need in order to move into the twenty-first century creatively.

This approach represents several sharp contrasts to my earlier work. *Fierce Tenderness* was based on a look at women's friendships; now I want to look at both women's and men's. That book was essentially a book of feminist theology; this essay is a political philosophy informed by religious feminism. The earlier work was poetic and ideological; this treatment is practical and prophetic at once as the urgency of social change calls out for such reflection.

I. FIERCE TENDERNESS EXPLORED

Friendship remains an infrequently tackled subject in Christian theology (to which I will confine my analysis for sake of brevity and competence). This is an odd situation given that a tenet of that faith includes "Love one's neighbor," "Go and make disciples/friends in all nations," and assorted other exhortations to form relationships of accountability. Further, the majority of the writings which exist are based on an Aristotelian model in which a) only men's experiences of friendship are taken into account, b) friendship is measured quantitatively, not qualitatively (numbers decreasing with increasing intimacy), c) social structures are built on marriage as the fundamental social unit, with friendship (that is, anything other than heterosexual marriage) forming an also-ran category.

The consequences of this method have been predictable in Christian theology, which is in turn the ideological framework that shapes a great deal of Western social mores; namely, analysis of and learning from women's experiences of friendship is either presumed to be the same as men's and therefore ignored on its own terms, or assumed to be so different and/or so trivial as not to merit attention at all.

The model of quantitative thinking as opposed to qualitative thinking about relationships persists, especially in areas of sexual ethics. The questions are how many, how far, how big, how long, rather than qualitative thinking which emphasizes the kind of accountability, generativity, and commitment which characterizes friendship. Rule-based sexual ethics so popular in the Roman Catholic tradition of which I am a part are but a few examples of the limits of such thinking. The current teachings and tenets are constitutionally inadequate for the range of relationships we experience, a sign that change is needed.

This leads to the third conclusion, namely, that social structures which undergird marriage and family life in a patriarchal, normatively heterosexual culture are constructed to prioritize marriage and to relegate friendship to a noble but lesser plane. While not wanting to romanticize friendship, I believe that putting friendship first — and of course permitting, even encouraging, marriage as well — is fundamentally more suited to the complex needs of our society. And that, of course, is why the political struggle over so-called "traditional family values" is raging. Note that I do not oppose the family; I simply see it in wider terms than the blood line.

Many people hear such a proposal as an attack on marriage. When it comes from a religious starting point they are sure that "godless communism" has been replaced by "radical feminism" with the end of the world as we know it in sight. Far from being the case, mine is simply an effort to reshape priorities to reflect what we have learned about how people form intimate relationships. Some people partner, some join communities, some remain happily single, some change their partnerships, repartner, and blend families. All these are ways we know good people live which are quite other than Mr. and Mrs. Forever Amen. The job of theology and philosophy is to reflect on these realities and to hint, suggest, cajole, inspire people to live with integrity and concern for the whole community.

It is in this context that I have developed a model of friendship which I call "fierce tenderness," based on women's friendships.[1] I explored women's friendships primarily because they were my widest and deepest pool of experience, and because they remain virtually unexplored in the theological and theo-ethical traditions. Similarly, I proposed four elements that make up successful friendships: love, power, embodiment, and spirituality. I did not prescribe nor even suggest their proportions. Rather I suggested that when these are in some semblance of harmony in a relationship, the resultant friendship is a rich and productive one.

By contrast, the myriad problems we have all faced in our friendships can be summed up as varying experiences of disharmony in these elements. Put bluntly, when I love you more than you love me; when John uses his power over Susan; when Karen wants to go to bed with Janice but Janice isn't interested; when Paul generally prefers opera to Tad's yen for pool, we can see that these friendships are heading for rocky times. My model is not meant to explain away all of the complexities of human loving. Nor is it meant to put therapists and counselors out of business. Rather, it is meant to serve as a starting point for understanding and encouraging friendships since it is my contention that these are the foundation of our social fabric, a tapestry ripped by racism, soiled by sexism, and wrinkled by power differences which translate into privilege and want.

There is much to explore about these dynamics, but my intention is to demonstrate that models are only helpful insofar as they illuminate and nurture real experiences. What is unique about this model is: first, that it emerges not from the Aristotelian notion of scarcity (that is, I only have so much relational energy so it needs to be more focused as I ascend the hierarchy of intimacy), but from a feminist insight into equality. It is not the myth of sameness, which has been used to discredit feminists as unable to distinguish between and among competing claims. Rather, it is the need for treating all that is, persons, animals, other aspects of nature, with the same fundamental respect, that is, in the same friendly manner. This does not mean, of course, that I need be equally attentive to my pet as to my lover. But it does mean that the fundamental way of *paying attention* which is the hallmark of friendship, as well as the generativity which comes from our common attention, is something to strive for in every relationship.

Happily, no reviewer of this work has made the reductionistic claim that I urge friendship instead of marriage as normative simply because I wish to make the world safe for people who choose not to marry. However, there would be some, albeit partial, truth to the matter insofar as I have constructed a whole model of friendship based primarily on women's friendships with women. That I include, even encourage, appropriate sexual expression in some same-sex friendships adds to the debate. Moreover, I claim that such friendships, far from being relational also-rans in a marriage-manic society, are in fact equally valid, in some instances more beneficial relationships than many marriages.

It is claims of this sort, wherein friendship *replaces* marriage as the relationship of record, that make right-wing politicians exclaim that "traditional family values" are in the balance. The fact is that in an important way they are correct. Since married people can be friends, but all friends cannot be married, the implication of taking lesbian/gay relationships seriously is to see friendships between persons of the same sex who choose sexual expression in their friendships as in fact the relational equivalent of marriage. Moves in the direction of domestic partnership bills, civil and religious recognition of same-sex relationships, happy, healthy, holy lesbian/gay families, are just what I have in mind.

These exist all over the country now, but the point is that in the absence of legal changes to accommodate, indeed to celebrate and encourage, something as traditional as a stable relational unit and attention to children, philosophical and theological space must be made first to pave the way for legal and attitudinal shifts. That is my job as a theologian, despite the unpopular reaction it may evoke from certain church officials.

Religion, especially certain forms of evangelical Christianity and other fundamentalist faiths, is used in the public forum to negate what I now call the friendship norm. Recall that in and of itself friendship does not preclude or eclipse marriage. It challenges the hegemony of heterosexual marriage as the only way to file joint income taxes, visit a spouse in the hospital, automatically inherit another's goods without a blood tie, and so forth. Sex is but a small part of any relationship. Social supports or lack of them play a large part in how and whether friendships, including heterosexual marriages, deepen, mature, endure.

Longevity is never the ultimate criterion for friendship; that would be a quantitative measure instead of a qualitative one. But duration does provide an opportunity for shared memories as well as shared newness, repetition of good experiences as well as endless novelty, in-depth knowing as opposed to more superficial awareness. Even in the sexual arena, I would argue after a dozen years with the same beloved partner that practice makes perfect. But all of this is condemned by those who oppose homosexuality *per se*, against the social scientific and biological information to the contrary that proves it to be a perfectly healthy lifestyle for upwards of 10 percent of the population, perhaps even an occasional experience for far more than that. While less is known about bisexuality, and even less about heterosexuality without coercion, conservative religious ideology which grounds the efforts of the so-called Religious Right is rooted in the rejection of any relationships but heterosexual monogamy and celibate friendships.

The Roman Catholic Church has codified such demands into a rigid sexual prescription, at least at the official level. While many Catholics ignore the teachings about birth control, masturbation, divorce, and homosexuality yet still consider themselves in full communion, a dangerous trend toward intrusion into the political arena was confirmed by a summer 1992 letter to U.S. Catholic Bishops from the Congregation for the Doctrine of the Faith.[2] The Vatican claimed that "there are areas in which it is not unjust discrimination to take sexual orientation into account, for example, in the placement of children for adoption or foster care, in employment of teachers or athletic coaches, and in military recruitment."[3] While reconciling traditional Christian teachings with any form of discrimination is a theological sleight of hand that is the ethical equivalent of the Wizard of Oz behind the screen, this is indeed what this Vatican Declaration calls for.

The document becomes quite specific on how and by whom discrimination is to be carried out: "Finally, where a matter of the common good is concerned, it is inappropriate for church authorities to remain neutral toward adverse legislation even if it grants exceptions to church organizations and institutions. The church has the responsibility to promote family life and the public morality of the entire civil society on the basis of fundamental moral values, not simply to protect herself (sic) from the application of harmful laws."[4] Catholic bishops are urged to enter the political fray on behalf of monogamous marriage and celibate friendship.

Read through the lens of a friendship norm, such pronouncements reveal a deeply rooted denial of how many of us love and how
successful we are at it! Jane Redmont in her book *Generous Lives*
names this quality of friendship aptly.[5] Such counterintuitive moves by
the bishops in the face of such generosity and the vehemence with
which they are made make me wonder why allegedly celibate men in
a homosocial hierarchy protest so much. Don't they have any friends?
But more substantively, I am persuaded by the contradictory nature of
their utterings that *something* important has set them off, and that the
something appears to be the obvious success of friendships — many
kinds between and among many people — in the face of a 50 percent
divorce rate and the crying need for children to be nurtured in responsible constellations of adults who love them regardless of the
adults' gender or marital status.

This is why as a theologian I take seriously that the religious foundations of ethics are finally determinative. No other sector of society
has as its reason for being specifically a concern with morals. Universi-
ties educate as well as shape ethics; businesses make profits as well as
shape ethics; medical workers heal as their primary work, with ethical
concerns factored in. But religious professionals, especially ethicists
and moral theologians, shape the fabric of a society's ethics as a primary
responsibility. Hence, when we jump the ship of state, turn state's witness on our co-religionists by urging into being new relational para-
digms, in this case friendship over marriage, we can expect problems.

Problems heat up when the divine or God is likened not to
Father, Mother, or even Parent, but to Friend. Then the seriousness
of the project becomes more obvious. Without wanting to overuse the
metaphor, it is this move away from heterosexual family images that
underlies the panic. When we recall that equal consternation was expressed by opponents of inclusive language in scripture, it is not hard
to imagine the wrath that awaits the explicit move to relational language which evokes equality not hierarchy, mutuality not dominance,
and even unpredictability.

A feminist theological approach involves a critical appraisal of
metaphors for the divine with a "preferential option" for inclusivity. Insofar as the language and imagery function to limit and exclude, they
are left aside; insofar as they illuminate and invite participation in the
divine reality they describe, such language and imagery are to be encouraged in worship and common life. It is on the basis of taking such

discourse seriously that we reshape laws and other social structures. To the degree that we succeed, feminist theology will have accomplished an important goal, the increased empowerment of women and men.

II. SOME PROBLEMS WITH THE FRIENDSHIP METAPHOR

Despite my heralding of friendship, which I define as "those voluntary human relationships that are entered into by people who intend one another's well-being, and who intend that their love relationship is part of a justice-seeking community," I am nonetheless critical of it as well.[6] Four problems that I perceive illustrate that my perspective is anything but romantic. I am indebted to the many reviewers of my book for attention to these matters and to Barbara Darling-Smith for her clear perceptions.

I sketch these not to retreat from my claim that friendship and not marriage is the most adequate social framework, but to acknowledge that the transition takes place in a society in the United States which is structurally flawed by racism, sexism, class divisions, and rampant homo-hatred. These are not trivial matters when one undertakes a consciousness shift of the proportions I propose. To the contrary, the very elements which make safety and well-being distant dreams for so many would-be friends in our society need attention if friendship becomes normative. In addition, the same religious foundations which underlie the opposition to a friendship norm also underlie those social elements which will finally subvert it. Hence, my focus on:

A. violence
B. racial/ethnic considerations
C. safeguards for the care/nurture of children
D. the coopting of lesbian/gay friendships into couples

A. *Violence*

Domestic violence statistics stagger the imagination. The American Medical Association, in recognition of the problem, changed the standard of practice so that patients who present symptoms which might be caused by violence must be asked if such were the case. Estimates vary but it is generally agreed that one of eleven boys and one of seven girls suffers incest; that half of all women experience violence (physical and/or psychological) in their marriages. In short, for many people "home sweet home" is really "home dangerous home," with few support systems to change the behaviors and structures literally embedded in many nuclear families.

Of course it is my hope that moving toward a friendship norm is a step in the right direction. If heterosexual marriage is about unequal power relationships in patriarchy, and if "compulsory heterosexuality" as Adrienne Rich describes it forces some people to live in situations which do not express their deepest longings, then it would seem that friendship would take care of the problem. But we are just beginning to learn about violence in same-sex relationships, something that the lesbian and gay communities understandably wish would go away. It is hard to be honest about such matters when the wolf is at the door, that is, when lesbian-gay bashing is on the rise and the AIDS pandemic is decimating our ranks. With regard to violence, we know little about cross-gender friendships which are not marriages. Whether they are more or less prone to violence remains to be researched.

Still, honesty compels me to counter that my worst fear of a friendship norm is that it will not stem the tide of violence much more effectively than the marriage norm has. We are just beginning to understand that violence is deeply woven into the Christian tradition, with some theologians suggesting that the action of a "Father God" giving up "his only begotten Son" for the salvation of the world—the Christian doctrine of the Atonement—functions as a kind of perverse legitimation for child abuse.[7] While this and the resultant deconstruction of Christianity around other issues of violence deserves further attention, the important issue for our consideration is whether such a dynamic is mitigated by friendship.

What about the dictum from the same source to "lay down one's life for one's friends"? Is this any more helpful? Does it invite yet another manifestation of the same dynamic? Is it sage advice for women and persons from racial/ethnic groups which have been discriminated against? This is the kind of feminist theological work in the 1990s which parallels the deconstruction of Christianity on the basis of gender in the 1970s and 1980s. My sense is that the currents of violence may run so deep in the Christian tradition as to mitigate any small changes that a shift from marriage to friendship may produce. Still, I urge the experiment, cognizant of the danger that lurks not in the corners but in the center of our society.

B. *Racial/ethnic considerations*

The Euro-American middle-class location of my perspective on friendship necessarily raises important questions about its grounding in and/or applicability in other contexts. The frank answer is that I do not know, nor am I persuaded that it needs to be applicable elsewhere in order to be valid in the partial, limited, and contextual situation about which I do make claims. This is a difficult problem, but it illustrates what is in my judgment the most important change in theological thinking in this century, namely, the radical contextualization of all theology.

In short, no position is valid without a clear articulation of its social location—this coming most profoundly from African-American, feminist, and Latin American liberation theologies. Further, no one person or group speaks for the whole, a decided reversal of the universal claims with which theology has been identified. Rather, my frank admission is that the limits of my perspective imply *de facto* limits on the usefulness of my insights. Far from weakening my position because I am not claiming that others must hold it, the resultant theological mix includes an explicit invitation to people from other contexts to consider, weigh, even reject my insight in favor of their own.

This is the nature of contemporary theological work, especially in feminist/womanist/mujerista circles where the survival of women and dependent children and the "hearing each other into speech" demand no less. If I were persuaded that a friendship norm would exacerbate the already hideous racism in this country, I would drop it immediately. But precisely because I am persuaded that it reflects the reality and aids the survival of many people, especially people who are marginalized because they are viciously condemned as single mothers, absent fathers, and boarder babies, I insist on its justice-seeking potential.

C. *Safeguards for the care/nurture of children*

A third concern which I put to the friendship norm is an explicit concern for how children will fare. It seems so obvious now that one major plus for a marriage norm is the clear concern for having a structure, that is, the nuclear family, in which to care and provide for children. Thus far, most discussion of friendship has passed over this dimension, something that leaves those of us who advance it vulnerable to charges of solipsism and irresponsibility.

While I do not believe that everyone must have and/or nurture children to be a whole adult in our society, I do take the care of children to be a communal and not finally an individual responsibility. Hence, I must advance the theo-ethical concern of how this is done as the paradigm shifts away from marriage. In fact, statistics, from infant mortality to abandonment, from access to early childhood education to latchkey kids, raise this question in a profound way. The current social arrangement is not doing very well. But will a shift away from the legal obligations of parents to their children take place when friendship and not necessarily blood or marital ties apply?

One can only plead ignorance about the question since data are insufficient to answer it. But there are several trends which I find helpful in countering the ghastly images right-wing defenders promote of Mom in the kitchen pulling the apple pie from the oven. One is the effort on the part of unrelated same-sex partners — call them friends for lack of a more precise legal term — to adopt children. This is especially impressive when the children have special needs; for example, friends of mine, two Euro-American women, adopted a child who was HIV-positive.

The communal effort which was extended for his care during five years of living and eventually dying from AIDS-related causes assured me that no heterosexually married couple could have done more. As this phenomenon of Shawn having two moms or Amanda having two dads spreads, we see an enrichment of the single parent pressures that one would think even the most virulent homophobe would applaud. Yet when children's books featuring same-sex parents are introduced into the curriculum, many people frown. Is it that a child could ever get too much nurture?

D. The cooptation of lesbian/gay friendships

This leads to my fourth worry about a friendship norm, namely, the degree to which it can be quickly coopted into yet another form of the same pattern. One might argue that there is really nothing new under the relational sun, that we love one another as we always did whether in same- or different-sex combinations. I am more concerned about the rapid mainstreaming of a certain number of "good" lesbian and gay friends: monogamously committed, prepared to live happily ever after, able to afford and aspire to a marriage license, with a job that has health insurance for a partner — prepared to register their china and silver patterns at the local emporium. While this caricature does not fit most of us anymore, and while everyone has a right to social trappings they desire, I would be remiss if I did not launch a critical warning on this front.

Will the move toward acceptability and assimilation of what have heretofore been different ways of "constructing a life" blunt the real contribution of a friendship norm? Will it mean that the variety, flexibility, and sometimes even changeability that have characterized other than marital relationships in our society will be lost? Will the fight over joint property and custody of the cat, not to mention children, in lesbian-gay divorces be as frequent and as brutal as in the heterosexual counterparts? Perhaps. But the point is that while there is still time, before complete cooptation has taken place, we need to think through the benefits and liabilities of adopting the prevailing customs for all relationships. Instead of moving inexorably toward lesbian-gay marriages, a friendship norm invites moving away from compulsory marriage for heterosexuals, for example, away from coupling and toward community.

III. THE TRADITIONAL FAMILY VALUES DEBATE: A SHORT STORY

The discussion of "traditional family values" tapered off quickly for two major reasons. First, the economic picture in this country and around the world is so grim that most people are content to pay their bills and have no time to speculate on how their neighbors are paying theirs. Jobs and not bedroom behavior are on top of most people's minds. Second, even in those parts of the country where campaigns against reproductive choice and relational choice find their most ardent supporters, most people have by now experienced divorce, homosexuality, and children born and reared outside of a marital relationship. In many instances they have been edified by what has followed their worst fears, namely, that life goes on and even improves when options open up and honesty prevails.

This is the direct, if by some dreaded, consequence of a friendship norm. Of course it is not to be confused with license for promiscuity, the breaking of promises, or a lack of accountability. Rather, it is simply the same old values played to a new tune. I suggest that there is a nascent intuition of this even among those who oppose it deeply.

Some cynical political philosophers may simply attribute the rapid dissipation of the debate to polls which show that lesbian and gay people vote, that unmarried heterosexuals who live together in record numbers vote, and single mothers vote. But I think this is to miss the more interesting shift that is underway, namely, a society which is groping for effective ways to embody, both personally and corporately, friendly values.

CONCLUSION

Some concrete examples of those values in place in society will hasten their arrival.

1. Friendship and not marriage is the relationship of primary importance. Hence, commitments, not weddings, are encouraged; children live with their adult friends, not only with their biological parents; families are constructed on the basis of choice, not blood line. Surely the outline allows for some falling through the cracks — what if no one chooses me for their family? — but will there be any more loss than we presently experience? I don't know, but are we willing to try? I am not sure. A small step in the direction would be to loosen up restrictions on adoption and foster care by non-married people, something that in most states is still a distant dream.

2. Government programs need to be adjusted accordingly. Tax laws, pension systems, and health care coverage would need to shift from a bias toward those who are legally married to equality for all. For example, inheritance would not pass automatically to one's blood relatives, but to the friends so named by everyone whether married or not. Wider visitation rights in hospitals and explicitly designated power of attorney would replace any such automatic rights that heterosexually married people have over the rest of us. The point is to avoid making unmarried people second-class citizens. To encourage the full range of relational options by leveling the relational playing field, by making civil rights available to all based on age not marital status, would be a step in the right direction.

3. Religious and ethical changes would include rethinking what it means to live in what Carter Heyward and others deem "right re-

lation." The "good man" of philosophical fame is redefined to resemble the friend, not the father. In this new situation the normatively good person would come in both genders, many races, and endless relational possibilities. His goodness is measured as much by how he loves his pets as his current partner, how she claims power for herself as well as with her co-workers, how he safeguards himself and his sexual partners in the AIDS pandemic, and finally how she names her spiritual commitment to social change as part of her justice-seeking life.

It all begins to sound wonderfully familiar, like an old tune with new lyrics or a new tune with old words. An ethic based on friendship, what I have called "fierce tenderness" and for now simply call relational justice, is rapidly coming into focus. It needs more work, to make it explicit, to smooth out those parts which do not enhance our common well-being. But I trust that it cannot be worse than what currently prevails, and that it probably will be a great deal better in our lifetime and in the times of today's children's children.

NOTES

1. Cf. Mary E. Hunt, *Fierce Tenderness: A Feminist Theology of Friendship* (New York: Crossroad, 1991).

2. "Some Considerations Concerning the Response to Legislative Proposals on the Non-Discrimination of Homosexual Persons," Congregation for the Doctrine of the Faith, leaked to the press on July 15, 1992, by New Ways Ministry and released (with minor revisions) by the Vatican on July 23, 1992.

3. Ibid., par. 11.

4. Ibid., par. 16.

5. Jane Redmont, *Generous Lives: American Catholic Women Today* (New York: William Morrow & Co., 1992).

6. Hunt, *Fierce Tenderness*, p. 29.

7. Joanne Carlson Brown and Rebecca Parker, "For God So Loved the World?" in *Christianity, Patriarchy, and Abuse*, ed. Brown and Parker (New York: Pilgrim Press, 1989), pp. 1–30.

When Harry and Sally Read the *Nicomachean Ethics*: Friendship between Men and Women

GILBERT MEILAENDER

IN XENOPHON'S *OECONOMICUS* Socrates and Critobulus are discussing household management, in which the wife plays a major role. The exchange goes this way:

> "Anyhow, Critobulus, you should tell us the truth, for we are all friends here. Is there anyone to whom you commit more affairs of importance than you commit to your wife?"
> "There is not."
> "Is there anyone with whom you talk less?"
> "There are few or none, I confess."[1]

Friendship between husband and wife is, of course, only one possible kind of friendship between the sexes, though an important one. But most classical thinkers—with the exception of Epicurus—were inclined to think friendship between men and women impossible.

No doubt this can be accounted for in part, perhaps large part, by social and cultural circumstances—differences in education, a public life from which most women were excluded, constant warfare which drew males away from home. In my own view, these circumstances have changed considerably, but not everyone agrees. Thus, for example, writing very recently, Mary Hunt says: "Economic, political, psychological, and other differences between the genders result in the fact that women find it difficult to be friends with men and vice versa."[2] I will suggest that Hunt is in part mistaken about the reasons, but it is true that the relation between the sexes in our society is a

tense and often anxious one. It still makes sense to ask the classical
question: Is friendship possible between men and women? Or, more
modestly put, are there reasons why friendship between men and
women may be more difficult to sustain than same-sex friendships?

When we ask this question, the first problem that comes to mind
is the one raised by Harry Burns in the 1989 movie *When Harry Met
Sally*. In the opening scene, as he and Sally are driving together from
Chicago to New York, Harry says: "Men and women can't be friends—
because the sex part always gets in the way." Harry has an important
point. And, though I do not think it is finally the deepest issue raised
by our topic, I shall devote a good bit of attention to it.

Aristotle, whose two books on friendship in the *Nicomachean
Ethics* are recognized almost universally as the most important piece
of writing on the subject, tends to agree with Harry. Aristotle recognizes, of course, that there is a kind of friendship between husband
and wife, but it is one example of what he calls friendship between
unequals. In such bonds the equality that friendship always requires
can be present only if it is "proportionate" rather than "strict"—only,
that is, if "the better and more useful partner . . . [receives] more affection than he gives."[3] Still, of the three types of friendship which
Aristotle discusses—based respectively on advantage, pleasure, or
character—the highest, based on character, can exist even between
unequals as long as this proportion is present. And Aristotle seems to
think that such a character friendship, with the necessary proportionate equality, is possible between husband and wife (cf. 8.12).

More generally, however, Aristotle suggests that a relation
grounded in erotic love will not be the highest form of friendship. He
distinguishes a bond like friendship, grounded in a trait of character and
involving choice, from a bond grounded in an emotion (8.5). And, while
there can be friendship between lover and beloved, it will not be the
highest form of friendship. It will be a friendship grounded not in character but in pleasure—and it is, therefore, likely to fade. "Still," Aristotle grants, noting how one sort of love may grow from another, "many
do remain friends if, through familiarity, they have come to love each
other's character, [discovering that] their characters are alike" (8.4).

It is important to note that *eros* and *philia* are indeed different
forms of love, even if they may sometimes go together. In making a
somewhat different point, C. S. Lewis suggested the following thought
experiment:

Suppose you are fortunate enough to have "fallen in love with" and married your Friend. And now suppose it possible that you were offered the choice of two futures: "*Either* you two will cease to be lovers but remain forever joint seekers of the same God, the same beauty, the same truth, *or else*, losing all that, you will retain as long as you live the raptures and ardours, all the wonder and the wild desire of *Eros*. Choose which you please."[4]

In recognizing the reality and difficulty of the choice we discern the difference between the loves. That difference Lewis captures nicely in a sentence. "Lovers are normally face to face, absorbed in each other; Friends, side by side, absorbed in some common interest" (p. 91). Friends, therefore, are happy to welcome a new friend who shares their common interest, but *eros* is a jealous love which must exclude third parties.

Lewis believes that friendship and erotic love may go together, but in many respects he agrees with Harry and with Aristotle that the combination is an unstable one. He suggests that friendship between a man and a woman is likely to slip over into *eros* unless either they are physically unattractive to each other, or at least one of them already loves another. If neither of these is the case, friendship is "almost certain" to become *eros* "sooner or later" (p. 99). This is not far from Harry's view of the matter. Having asserted that "men and women can't be friends—because the sex part always gets in the way," Harry adds a caveat when he and Sally meet again five years later: "unless both are involved with other people." But then, in one of his characteristically convoluted pieces of reasoning, he adds: "But that doesn't work. The person you're involved with can't understand why you need to be friends with the other person. She figures you must be secretly interested in the other person—which you probably are. Which brings us back to the first rule." A little more optimistic than Harry, Lewis suggests that lovers who are also friends may learn to share their friendship with others, though not, of course, their *eros*. Still, however, that does not address Harry's chief concern: the instability of friendships with members of the opposite sex when those friendships are not shared with one's beloved.

We ought not, I think, deny that friendships between men and women—friendships which are not also marked by erotic love—are possible. We ought not, that is, let a theory lead us to deny the reality

we see around us, and we do sometimes see or experience such friendships. Nor need we express the view shared by Harry and Lewis quite
as crassly as did Nietzsche: "Women can enter into friendship with a man
perfectly well; but in order to maintain it the aid of a little physical anti-
pathy is perhaps required."[5] Nor, surely, need we hold, as my students
sometimes do, that friendship between men and women is possible only
if at least one of the friends is homosexual—a view that will make *same-
sex* friendships difficult for those who are homosexual, unless, of course,
their experience of *eros* is in no way jealous or exclusive. At the same
time, however, there is no reason to deny some truth to Harry's claim,
even without the additional support provided by Aristotle and Lewis,
for our experience also suggests that there is something to it.

The difficulties of combining *eros* and *philia* are the stuff of our
daily life. Equalizing the relation of the sexes, bringing women into
the academy and the workplace, has not made these difficulties disappear. Indeed, in certain respects they may have been exacerbated.
Men and women are radically uncertain about how they are to meet
in such shared worlds. Friendship requires an easy spontaneity, a
willingness to say what one thinks, talk with few holds barred and few
matters off-limits—precisely the sort of thing that some will find difficult on occasion to distinguish from sexual harassment.

I have discovered, however, that college students often wish to
argue that Harry is wrong, that there need be no obstacle to friendship
between the sexes. That may be because they have great difficulty
managing erotic attachments, which are quite a different thing from
sexual encounters. Fearful of the kind of commitment *eros* asks of us,
fearful of being drawn toward one who is completely other than the
self but to whom the most complete self-giving is called for and before
whom one therefore becomes vulnerable, they take refuge in groups
of friends—hoping thereby to achieve what parents of thirty years ago
saw as the advantage of group dating: the domestication of *eros*. But
eros is a wild and unruly deity, unlikely, I think, to be tamed so easily.

It is wiser to grant the point. Friendship between men and women
will always have to face certain difficulties that will not be present in
same-sex friendships. There will almost always be what J. B. Priestley
calls "a faint undercurrent of excitement not present when only one sex
is involved."[6] This may even give to the friendship a tone not easily
gotten any other way. Thus, as Priestley again puts it: "Probably there

is no talk between men and women better than that between a pair who are not in love, have no intention of falling in love, but yet who *might* fall in love, who know one another well but are yet aware of the fact that each has further reserves yet to be explored" (p. 59). Priestley offered this opinion in a little book titled *Talking: An Essay*, published in 1926 as one of several volumes in the Pleasures of Life Series. But he might well have been describing what many viewers found appealing in *When Harry Met Sally*. Consider the scene in which Harry and Jess are talking while hitting some balls in a batting cage:

Jess: "You enjoy being with her?"
Harry: "Yeah."
Jess: "You find her attractive?"
Harry: "Yeah."
Jess: "And you're not sleeping with her?"
Harry: "I can just be myself, 'cause I'm not trying to get her into bed."

And yet, not too much later comes the party at which Harry and Sally dance together—and themselves recognize the presence of Priestley's "faint undercurrent," which we call *eros*. This is a problem for friendships between men and women, even if it may also be enriching. *Eros* always threatens; for, unlike friendship, *eros* is a love that is jealous and cannot be shared.

If we grant this, we may not agree with Mary Hunt, whom I quoted earlier. She ascribes the difficulties facing friendship between men and women to "economic, political, psychological, and other differences"—unwilling, almost, to admit the power and presence of erotic attraction between men and women in human life. Nonetheless, it may be worth thinking briefly about what she recommends: namely, "new models of mutuality" which are most easily found among women friends. We ought not, she argues, take Aristotle's model of friendship and suppose that he simply forgot to include women when he talked and wrote of it—an omission we can then easily correct. We should not take his model and then just add women's experiences "as if they should have been there in the first place" (p. 93).

What is mistaken about Aristotle's model? Chiefly, it seems, that "[h]e considered friendship something that decreased in quality as it increased in quantity; the more intense the friendship, the fewer people with whom it was possible to enjoy it" (p. 92). Thus, according to Hunt, women need not worry about classifying friendships as carefully as did Aristotle, nor need they worry about whether friends are best friends or just good friends. "Only ruling-class men whose survival is not in question have the dubious luxury of looking up and down at their friends, companions, and acquaintances" (pp. 95–96). Women, by contrast, in a society which—in Hunt's view—is oppressive, cannot concern themselves with levels of friendship. For them the simple truth is that "friends, lots of them, are necessary for . . . survival in an often unfriendly environment" (p. 95). Paradoxically, however, to the degree that Hunt's assessment is correct, her thesis can have little to do with friendship between men and women or, even, between those of the same sex. For, on her account, women would have every reason to seek as many women *and* men as possible to be friends, and men who were not "ruling-class men" would be in similar circumstances. Neither would have reason to seek the kind of close, particular, and preferential friendships which Aristotle—and many others since—have considered the highest form of friendship.

What Hunt seems not to realize is that she is, in fact, like Aristotle in at least one important way. "How," Aristotle asks, sounding very much like Hunt, "could prosperity be safeguarded and preserved without friends? . . . Also, in poverty and all other kinds of misfortune men believe that their only refuge consists in their friends" (8.1). As it stands in the *Nicomachean Ethics*, of course, this is for Aristotle only one of the received opinions about friendship which he will refine, and it will turn out that this is not for him the highest form of friendship. More important, however, for Aristotle friendship is not only a particular and preferential bond which must be limited in number. He knows also a different kind of friendship which we call "civic friendship"; indeed, for him *philia* is the bond which joins together the members of any association. The concept of civic friendship deserves more attention than we can give it here. We need to ask whether it is coherent, whether we really wish to call it "friendship," and whether—if there is a coherent notion and we do call it friendship—it is helpful or harmful in life. Those who—like Hunt—emphasize such a concept of friendship may, despite their political concerns, have difficulty explaining one of the terrible things about injustice: how it may deprive us of the "luxury" of a *private* bond like friendship. But in any case, in her emphasis upon friendship as a public, political relation, Hunt is far more like Aristotle than she realizes, but, lacking his additional interest in those more private bonds we have in mind when speaking of friendship, she can shed little light on the problems of friendship between men and women.

These problems, I want to suggest, go deeper than the presence of erotic attraction alone. They involve the very nature of the bond of friendship. The friend is, in Aristotle's influential formulation, "another self" (9.4). At several points Aristotle considers whether friendship is more probable among those who are like or unlike each other. And, although he notes defenders of each view, he holds that friendship "implies some similarity" and that in the highest form of friendship "the partners are like one another" (8.3). In arguing that a person of good character should not—and ultimately cannot—remain friends with someone who becomes evil, Aristotle again appeals to the notion that "like is the friend of like" (9.3).

Anyone who reads Aristotle's discussion of the friend as another self is likely to find it puzzling in certain respects. It grows out of a peculiar treatment of self-love (in 9.4) as the basis of friendship, of love for the friend as an extension of the friendly feelings one has for oneself. And there are, in fact, aspects of his discussion that I would not claim fully to understand. What he has in mind, however, in depicting the friend as an alter ego is something *we* might discuss in terms of the social origins of the self. The friend is the mirror in which I come to know and understand myself. I have no way to look directly at myself and must come to see myself as I am reflected by others— and especially, perhaps, by close friends. In the friend I find that other self in whom I come to know myself. That is why friendship "implies some similarity" and why, at least in the most important kinds of friendship, "the partners are like one another."

Friends wish, Aristotle says, to pursue together activities they enjoy. "That is why some friends drink together or play dice together, while others go in for sports together and hunt together, or join in the study of philosophy: whatever each group of people loves most in life, in that activity they spend their days together" (9.12). I think Aristotle is largely correct here. We want in the friend someone who cares about the things we care about; yet we want the friend to be "another" who cares about these things, another with whom we can share them and with whom we come to know ourselves and our concerns better. The friend must be "another," but not entirely "an-other." Perhaps we do not, therefore, seek from the friend quite that sense of otherness which the opposite sex provides.

This takes us beyond the issue of erotic attraction into much deeper questions about what it means to be male or female. I do not know precisely how we can make up our minds about these questions today; we have a hard enough time just discussing them openly and honestly. A child of either sex begins in a kind of symbiotic union with its mother, without any strong sense of differentiation between self and mother. But as that sense of self begins to form, it develops differently for males and females. In attaining a sense of the self as separate and individuated we take somewhat different courses. Thus, Lillian Rubin argues, boys must repress their emotional identification with their mother and learn to identify with men, while girls, though repressing any erotic attachment, can leave the larger emotional identification with the mother intact.[7] The process of becoming a self involves identification with those who can be for us "another self"—those, as it happens, who share our sex. This does not, in my view, mean that friendship between men and women is impossible. It does mean, though, that J. B. Priestley was right to say of their "talk": "It will be different from the talk of persons of the same sex" (pp. 56–57). These differences are the stuff of bestsellers—and of much humor. Thus, for example, Deborah Tannen, who teaches linguistics at Georgetown University, could write a bestseller titled, *You Just Don't Understand: Women and Men in Conversation*. Full of illustrations in which one often sees oneself, Tannen's book suggests that for men life is "a struggle to preserve independence," while for women it is "a struggle to preserve intimacy."[8] The sort of problem this creates is illustrated clearly in a story like the following one Tannen recounts:

> Eve had a lump removed from her breast. Shortly after the operation, talking to her sister, she said that she found it upsetting to have been cut into, and that looking at the stitches was distressing because they left a seam that had changed the contour of her breast. Her sister said, "I know. When I had my operation I felt the same way." Eve made the same observation to her friend Karen, who said, "I know. It's like your body has been violated."

But when she told her husband, Mark, how she felt, he said, "You can have plastic surgery to cover up the scar and restore the shape of the breast."

Where she felt the need for understanding and sharing, he discerned a problem to be solved.

If this can sometimes be disconcerting, we need not be too serious. And these differences have provided the occasion for much humor. Dave Barry, the columnist, can title a column "Listen Up, Jerks! Share Innermost Feelings with Her"—and most of us are likely to read it.[9]

Barry writes:

> We have some good friends, Buzz and Libby, whom we see about twice a year. When we get together, Beth and Libby always wind up in a conversation, lasting several days, during which they discuss virtually every significant event that has occurred in their lives and the lives of those they care about, sharing their innermost feelings, analyzing and probing, inevitably coming to a deeper understanding of each other, and a strengthening of a cherished friendship. Whereas Buzz and I watch the playoffs.
>
> This is not to say Buzz and I don't share our feelings. Sometimes we get quite emotional.
>
> "That's not a FOUL?" one of us will say.
>
> Or: "You're telling me THAT'S NOT A FOUL???"
>
> I don't mean to suggest that all we talk about is sports. We also discuss, openly and without shame, what kind of pizza we need to order. We have a fine time together, but we don't have heavy conversations, and sometimes, after the visit is over, I'm surprised to learn—from Beth, who learned it from Libby—that there has recently been some new wrinkle in Buzz's life, such as that he now has an artificial leg.

Our world is full of attempts to remove such differences from life. In Tannen's words, "Sensitivity training judges men by women's standards, trying to get them to talk more like women. Assertiveness training judges women by men's standards and tries to get them to talk more like men" (p. 297). Better, perhaps, she suggests, to learn to understand and accept each other.

In this effort, I have found Priestley's old essay quite helpful. If talk between men and women is different from talk between persons of the same sex, it will not give the same kind of pleasure. But it may, Priestley suggests, compensate in other ways. The *first* condition of such talk is, he says, "that sex must be relegated to the background. . . . The man and the woman must be present as individualities, any difference between them being a strictly personal and not a sexual difference. They will then discover, if they did not know it before, how alike the sexes are, once their talk has dug below the level of polite chatter and they are regarding the world and their experience together and not merely flirting" (p. 57). That is, to revert to the terms I drew from Aristotle, they must find in the friend another self, another individuality, but one whose otherness is not so overwhelming as to threaten to engulf or invade their selfhood. No doubt this is not always possible, for reasons we noted earlier when considering the impact of *eros* on friendship. But when, for whatever reason, "passion is stilled," men and women may meet as individualities who care about the same things or seek the same truth.

There may, however, be something dissatisfying about the suggestion that a crucial aspect of our person — our sexuality — must, as it were, be bracketed for such friendship to be possible. And this *would* be unsatisfactory, I think, were no more to be said. Priestley goes on, however, to suggest that friendship between men and women can go beyond the play of individual personalities. "Secure in this discovery" of how alike they are, men and women "will then go forward and make another one, for at some point they must inevitably discover how unlike the sexes are. . . . This double play, first of personality and then of sex, is what gives intelligent talk between men and women its curious piquancy" (pp. 57–58).

In this second movement, when individual personality no longer brackets sexuality, Priestley ultimately discerns something more fundamental still — a third factor, which goes beyond the level of individual identity to a difference between men and women. "Men frequently complain," he writes, "that women's conversation is too personal" (p. 62). And, even writing in an age that knew not Carol Gilligan, Priestley finds some truth in this judgment. He says:

> [Women] remain more personal in their interests and less concerned with abstractions than men on the same level of intelligence and culture. While you are briskly and happily generalising,

making judgments on this and that, and forgetting for the time being yourself and all your concerns, they are brooding over the particular and personal application and are wondering what hidden motive, what secret desire, what stifled memory of joy or hurt, are there prompting your thought. But this habit of mind in woman does not spoil talk; on the contrary it improves it, restoring the balance. . . . It is the habit of men to be overconfident in their impartiality, to believe that they are god-like intellects, detached from desires and hopes and fears and disturbing memories, generalising and delivering judgment in a serene mid-air. To be reminded of what lies beyond, now and then, will do them more good than harm. This is what the modern psychologist does, but too often he shatters the illusion of impersonal judgment with a kick and a triumphant bray, like the ass he so frequently is, whereas woman does it, and has done it these many centuries, with one waggle of her little forefinger and one gleam of her eyes, like the wise and witty and tender companion she is. Here, then, is a third kind of play you may have in talk between the sexes, the duel and duet of impersonal and personal interests, making in the end for balance and sanity and, in the progress of the talk, adding to its piquancy. (pp. 63ff.)

In this sense, friendship between the sexes may take us not out of ourselves but beyond ourselves and may make us more whole, balanced, and sane than we could otherwise be.

Indeed, I think this is one of the purposes of friendship—one of the purposes God has in giving us friends. We are being prepared ultimately for that vast friendship which is heaven, in which we truly are taken beyond ourselves, and in which all share the love of God.[10] Something like this understanding of friendship, though without the strong theological overtone I have just given it, can be found in Katherine Paterson's *Bridge to Terabithia*—a book about friendship which is not simply a children's book.[11]

The friendship of Jess and Leslie in the book is between a boy and a girl who are a little too young for *eros*. In different ways they are both outsiders in the world of their peers at school, and that very fact draws them together. They create—largely at the instigation of Leslie—a "secret country," Terabithia, in which they are king and queen. This country—a piece of ground on the other side of a creek, to which they swing across on a rope—is, in Leslie's words, "so secret that we would never tell anyone in the whole world about it" (p. 38). And, at least at first, it must be that way. Were they to follow Mary Hunt's advice, were no friendships of theirs to be special and particular, were they to have no secret country that others did not share, they would never come to know themselves as fully as they do. Thus, for example, Jess finds that his friendship with Leslie opens up new worlds for him. "For the first time in his life he got up every morning with something to look forward to. Leslie was more than his friend. She was his other, more exciting self—his way to Terabithia and all the worlds beyond" (p. 46).

Jess says that Leslie is his way not only to Terabithia but also to "all the worlds beyond," but he learns that truth only slowly and with great bitterness. When the creek is swollen from a storm and Jess is gone, Leslie still tries to cross to Terabithia on the rope. It breaks, she falls onto the rocks, and is killed. Grief-stricken and alone, without his alter ego, Jess can barely come to terms with what has happened. But he does, finally, and in doing so learns something about the purpose of all friendship.

> It was Leslie who had taken him from the cow pasture into Terabithia and turned him into a king. He had thought that was it. Wasn't king the best you could be? Now it occurred to him that perhaps Terabithia was like a castle where you came to be knighted. After you stayed for a while and grew strong you had to move on. For hadn't Leslie, even in Terabithia, tried to push back the walls of his mind and make him see beyond to the shining world—huge and terrible and beautiful and very fragile? (p. 126)

To learn to see beyond our own secret countries—to what is at the same time both terrible and beautiful—is, from the perspective of Christian faith, the purpose of friendship. And to the degree that friendship not only with those of our own sex but with those of the opposite sex may more fully enable such vision, we have every reason to attempt it, despite its inherent difficulties.

We should not, therefore, underestimate the importance of the most obvious location for friendship between men and women: the bond of marriage. There are many differences between our world and that shared by Socrates and Critobulus. By no means least of them is the formative influence of Christian culture, with its exaltation of marriage as the highest of personal bonds. To be sure, precisely because the husband or wife as friend is not only "another self" but as fully "an-other" as we can experience, friendship in marriage cannot be presumed. If there is any truth in Lillian Rubin's analysis, each spouse may fear the otherness of the partner and the loss of self that intimacy requires. The man fears engulfment, "losing a part of himself that he's struggled to maintain over the years" (p. 24). The woman fears invasiveness that threatens the boundary she has struggled to maintain between her self and others. Each is tempted to avoid such otherness, to settle for a friend more like the self. But if we can overcome that temptation — in this case, perhaps, with the aid of *eros* — we may find a bond that truly helps us see beyond ourselves and become more balanced and sane. With the aid of the commitment marriage asks of us, we may find that friendship is possible between men and women not only when passion is stilled but when it is satisfied and fulfilled. And it may even be true that within a life marked by such commitment we become more generally capable of friendship between men and women.

When Harry finally realizes that he loves Sally and wants to marry her, he ticks off the reasons: the way she's cold when it's 71 degrees outside; the way it takes her an hour and a half to order a sandwich; the way she crinkles up her nose when she looks at him. All these might be only the signs of an infatuated lover looking at the beloved, not of a friend who stands beside the friend and looks outward. But last in Harry's litany of reasons is that Sally is "the last person I want to talk to before I go to bed at night." And J. B. Priestley — though worrying that spouses' lives may be "so intertwined, that they are almost beyond talk as we understand it" — has a view not unlike Harry's: "Talk demands that people should begin, as it were, at least at some distance from one another, that there should be some doors still to unlock. Marriage is partly the unlocking of those doors, and it sets out on its happiest and most prosperous voyages when it is launched on floods of talk" (p. 60).

In marriage, if we are patient and faithful, we may find that "balance and sanity" which friendship between men and women offers, and we may find it in a context where *eros* also may be fulfilled without becoming destructive. Against the view of Critobulus we may, therefore, set the wisdom of Ben Sira (40:23): "A friend or companion is always welcome, but better still to be husband and wife."

NOTES

1. Xenophon, *The Oeconomicus*, in *Memorabilia and Oeconomicus* trans. E. C. Marchant (London: William Heinemann, 1923), 3.12.

2. Mary E. Hunt, *Fierce Tenderness: A Feminist Theology of Friendship* (New York: Crossroad, 1991), p. 92. Future references will be given by page number in parentheses within the body of the text.

3. Aristotle, *Nicomachean Ethics*, trans. Martin Ostwald (Indianapolis: Bobbs-Merrill Library of Liberal Arts, 1962), 8.7. Future citations will be given by book and chapter number in parentheses within the body of the text.

4. C. S. Lewis, *The Four Loves* (New York: Harcourt Brace Jovanovich, 1960), pp. 99–100. Future references will be given by page number in parentheses within the body of the text.

5. Friedrich Nietzsche, cited in Ronald A. Sharp, *Friendship and Literature* (Durham, N.C.: Duke University Press, 1986), p. 73.

6. J. B. Priestley, *Talking: An Essay* (New York and London: Harper & Brothers, 1926), p. 59. Future references will be given by page number in parentheses within the body of the text.

7. Lillian B. Rubin, "Women, Men, and Intimacy," in *Eros, Agape and Philia*, ed. Alan Soble (New York: Paragon House, 1989), p. 22.

8. Deborah Tannen, *You Just Don't Understand: Women and Men in Conversation* (New York: William Morrow, 1990), p. 25. Further references will be given by page number in parentheses within the body of the text.

9. Dave Barry, "Listen Up, Jerks! Share Innermost Feelings with Her!" *Arizona Star*, 8 June 1992, p. 3B.

10. I do not here seek to defend this view, but I have done so in *Friendship: A Study in Theological Ethics* (Notre Dame, Ind.: University of Notre Dame Press, 1981).

11. Katherine Paterson, *Bridge to Terabithia* (New York: Avon Books, 1972). Citations will be given by page number in parentheses within the body of the text.

Political Friendship

MICHAEL PAKALUK

THOMAS JEFFERSON COPIED several excerpts from Euripides on the theme of friendship into his *Literary Commonplace Book*. One of the more interesting of these is from the *Phoenissae*:

> Prize equality that ever linketh friend to friend, city to city, allies to each other, for equality is man's natural law.[1]

Here is Jefferson, the great prophet of the natural equality of human beings, quoting a fragment from a classical writer which asserts that equality begets friendship at every level of human social life. Yet one searches in vain throughout the volumes of Jefferson's writings — and also those of Madison, Franklin, and Washington — for any discussion of friendship among citizens, of what was classically known as *civic* or *political* friendship. In general it is puzzling that, in the writings of the Founders, there seems to be scant attention paid to political friendship, even though political equality is vitally important to them, and equality is closely linked with friendship.

A common explanation focuses on the distinction between virtue and rights. Classical political thought, it is said, takes *virtue* to be basic. It holds that the aim of the state is to make its citizens good. Furthermore, it presupposes a single conception of human flourishing. Citizens share the same ideal of the good life and thus have a friendly regard for one another in pursuing this ideal. Modern political thought, in contrast, focuses on the *rights* of individuals, and whereas virtue is a positive notion which can serve as the basis for a civic friendship, rights are essentially negative — they are claims against being harmed. Clearly, people can claim their rights against one another, while having little in common and even less mutual esteem. Indeed, the very language of rights seems to imply the threat of enmity and the potential for conflict among persons, rather than anything like friendship. It is not surprising, then, that the Founders speak little of civic friendship. The essentially individualistic view of the human person implicit in their language of equality and rights can hardly support the rich social unity and community which classical authors consider so important.

My aim is to challenge this line of thought. I think it is misguided and has, furthermore, given rise to an inappropriate romanticism about the past and contempt for the present. It both misjudges the role of virtue in classical accounts of political friendship and misunderstands appeals to rights and equality in modern liberalism. My thesis is that political friendship, *as it was conceived in classical theory*, has in fact been a characteristic of the American republic. Yet at present political friendship among Americans is very weak, and I shall briefly suggest some of the principal reasons why this is so. But my first task will be to explain the conception of political friendship in the relevant classical sources; then I shall consider whether and how this conception can be transferred to the case of the American republic.

I. POLITICAL FRIENDSHIP IN PLATO

Both Plato and Aristotle agreed that a state should be as unified as possible, and both agreed that this unification was accomplished through some sort of friendship. It is easy to see why they thought this. They both held that the worst evil for a state was civil strife, the natural culmination of which was the destruction of the state. Therefore, the greatest good for a state would have to be the opposite condition, and the opposite of strife, which apparently is some sort of hostility, would be friendship.

This line of thought, recapitulated by Aristotle at the beginning of his treatise on friendship,[2] would have been accepted, I think, by most classical political minds. But Plato and Aristotle had very different conceptions of the nature of the desirable friendship for a state.

Plato believed that the state should, ideally, strive to achieve the sort of unity which obtains, in our experience, between two very close friends, who are alike in character and sentiments, and who have all of their goods in common. We find this view expressed in both the *Republic* and the *Laws*. In the *Republic* we are told that the best state is the one in which the proverb that "friends have all things in common" (*koina ta philon*) is realized to the greatest extent possible.[3] And, just as two close friends seek to become, as much as possible, like a single human being, so the best governed state is that which most closely resembles a single individual,[4] in which nothing is private,[5] where even the pains and pleasures of each citizen belong to all.[6] It is with a view to producing this sort of friendship that Plato justifies the "community of wives and children" of the guardian class.[7] That he wishes to achieve this friendship in the state explains why he must be hostile to private bonds of affection between natural relatives and friends; for these can only be so many competitors of political friendship.

This conception of the state, which is as extreme as it is breathtaking, is not abandoned in Plato's last work, the *Laws*. "That city and constitution is first," Plato writes, "and those laws are best, in which the old maxim is realized to the greatest extent possible throughout the entire city, viz., that friends really hold their things in common."[8] This requires common wives and children; common possessions; and the eradication of "the private" by every means possible—even to the extent of making the sense organs and limbs of the citizens common to the state as a whole. Only then will the state be "unified to the greatest degree possible [*mian hoti malista polin*]."[9]

There is another sort of political friendship mentioned by Plato. I have so far been speaking about friendship which is supposed to obtain among all the citizens of a state; it is a relationship which each citizen has to every other. Yet Plato sometimes also uses the language of friendship to characterize the specific relationship between the rulers of a state and their subjects. This language seems to derive from Plato's analogy between demagogues and flatterers. A flatterer is someone who pretends to be a friend. Thus, if a demagogue is someone who flatters the people, a true ruler must be a friend of the people. We find Socrates drawing such a contrast in the *Gorgias*, where he likens the orator Gorgias to a flatterer and advises him, somewhat obscurely, that if he would "effect a genuine friendship with the Athenian people" he would need to acquire a natural and not merely imitative resemblance to them.[10] And in the *Republic* we find Plato worrying about how to educate the guardians so that they have friendship towards their subjects, the subordinate classes. He proposes, in fact, a precise criterion for this: the guardians should think that the same things are good both for themselves and for their subjects, and that, when their subjects do well, they themselves are doing well.[11]

Plato seems to think the one sort of political friendship depends upon the other. The friendship of all citizens for one another depends upon the guardians being true friends of their subjects. For when the guardians are true friends of the other classes, then they rule for the good of the others, and not for their own good. Thus they direct the state, properly, so that the citizens achieve the desired unity.

Why did Plato hold his strange idea that a state should have the unity of a close personal friendship? He seems to have held the metaphysical view that unity and goodness are closely related, if not the same, and he applied this view to both individuals and states. It is reasonable that he should have linked unity with goodness, by a generalization of the argument we considered earlier. The supreme evil of a thing is apparently its destruction, but this comes about through the complete separation of its parts. Hence, its supreme good, the opposite of this, would have to consist in its being a complete unity. Thus, a good individual would be a unified individual, and a good state would be a unified state. But unity is effected by friendship. In the case of an individual, this is evidently accomplished by self-friendship. But Plato seems to have held, furthermore, that the term *friendship* is univocal; that the word *friendship*, wherever it is correctly applied, signifies the very same sort of relationship. Thus the friendship that unifies the state must be the very same sort of friendship as that which unifies individuals and pairs of close friends. Consequently, Plato's project in political philosophy is creating in the state the same friendship that obtains between a good person and himself.

I have briefly described Plato's views in order to provide a contrast with Aristotle, since much of the contemporary skepticism about political friendship derives, I think, from not adequately distinguishing these very different conceptions of political friendship. It is Aristotle's account, I believe, which has application in a liberal democracy. Something like Plato's view does of course occur in modern political theorizing. Marx has a similar ideal, as does Rousseau, whose social contract reads very much like a group marriage, and whose aim is to create a "collective body" which is analogous to a single individual. Yet I shall proceed on the assumption that neither of these views of a good society is adequate to our tradition.

II. FRIENDSHIP WITHIN COMMUNITIES IN ARISTOTLE

Aristotle regards political friendship as the friendship which is inherent in the political community. Thus, in order to understand his account of political friendship, we must first try to grasp his remarkable idea that friendship exists in every community. This is a claim he develops in book 8, chapters 9–12, of the *Nicomachean Ethics*. The idea is almost paradoxical to us, because we tend to view justice and friendship as exclusive. To the extent that claims of justice upon us are increased, we think, to that extent the scope for a free and spontaneous friendship is decreased. Yet Aristotle, as we shall see, holds the opposite view, that friendship actually *increases* with justice.

Aristotle defines and classifies friendship in the *Ethics* by means of a central or "focal" case. The central case of friendship is a particular sort of "friendship between comrades" (*hetairikē philia*). A "friendship between comrades" is a friendship between two people equal in age, who have had a similar upbringing, and who therefore have similar character, likes and dislikes. Basically, it is the relationship to which we restrict the name *friend* in contemporary usage. When two such friends love each other because of their goodness of character, then a "perfect" (*teleia*) friendship results, which Aristotle calls "complete," because each friend, he thinks, is loved by the other for every possible reason for which a human being can find another human being lovable. Each friend is loved as good, useful, and pleasant.[12]

Aristotle holds that the love found in friendship is not merely an emotion. Rather, the core element pertains to the will, to a rational desire. Friends *wish* goods to each other and they do so in a habitual way, which springs from a state of character.[13] Emotions and affections are built upon this rational structure. Furthermore, this structure needs to be mutually recognized. Each friend is aware that the other wishes goods to him as well, and each is aware that the other is aware, and so on.[14] Finally, the wishing is *reciprocal*, which is to say that each friend understands the other's wishing of goods to be made in view of, or coordinated with, his own wishing.[15]

Aristotle seems to choose complete friendship between comrades as the central case of friendship because it best displays unity. Aristotle distinguishes three distinct sorts of unity: equality, similarity, and sameness. A complete friendship of comrades is the human relationship in which the members are most equal (*isoi*)[16] and most similar (*homoioi*).[17] Furthermore, each is related to the other as "another self" (*allos autos*),[18] and in this sense they are even "the same" as each other. Aristotle held, like Plato, that unity is the characteristic work or "function" (*ergon*) of friendship;[19] so, reasonably, that relationship which most achieves unity is what he considers to be a true friendship.

Aristotle counts as a friendship any relationship which exhibits mutually recognized and reciprocated wishing of goods, even if, in other respects, the relationship diverges from the central case. He distinguishes two sorts of friendships which in most respects run parallel to the central case but in which each friend loves the other solely because he is useful or pleasant — the so-called "friendship for utility" and "friendship for pleasure" (*dia to chresimon* and *dia to hēdu*). Then there are friendships between those who are alike but unequal in goodness, usefulness, or pleasure. Then again there are friendships in which the friends have complementary but distinct roles, and thus different distinctive virtues, such as the relationship between father and son or husband and wife. Finally there are friendships which arise within communities, one sort of which is political friendship.

How does Aristotle defend the view that every community contains a friendship? Unfortunately the only arguments he gives are very obscure. He tells us that "shipmates and fellow-soldiers greet one another as friends, and likewise those in other communities."[20] He also tries to invert the meaning of the proverb "the things of friends are in common." This straightforwardly means that, if people are friends, then they hold things in common. Aristotle claims that the proverb also suggests that, to the extent that people hold things in common (that is, *in a community*), to that extent they are friends.[21] These are weak arguments, which could at best serve to confirm the thesis after it was already established on other grounds.

Another argument begins with the claim that the heinousness of an injustice is directly proportionate to one's degree of friendship with the victim. Aristotle supports this claim with various examples: "It is more heinous," he says, "to renege on a loan payment to a comrade than to a fellow citizen; to fail to assist a brother than a stranger; to strike one's father than anyone else."[22] The injustices are more heinous because the relationship between wrongdoer and victim is so close. The injury violates claims of justice, which are in direct proportion to the degree of friendship. As Aristotle says, "justice and friendship by nature increase together."[23] But this argument is not very persuasive. First of all, it doesn't seem to be consistent with Aristotle's own views. He holds that the greatest degree of friendship is with a comrade, so it ought to be more heinous to strike a comrade than a father. Furthermore, Aristotle doesn't explain what it means to say that there are degrees of injustice; nor does he give us reason to think that our sense of heinousness is a reliable measure of this.

He has one last argument, which at first appears to be little more than word play: "To the extent that people share something (*koinō-nousin*), to that extent there is friendship, since [to that extent] there is justice."[24] The Greek word for community, *koinōnia*, is in fact derived from the verb "to share"; *koinōneo*, "a community," is literally "a sharing." Therefore, if sharing in fact implies justice and hence friendship, and if a community is "a sharing," as the word *koinōnia* suggests, then every community somehow involves justice and thus friendship as well.

This seems a promising line of argument. But in order to examine it more fully, we need to consider more carefully what a community is. It seems correct to say that a community consists of more than one person working together to accomplish a task which cannot be accomplished at all, or very easily, by an individual working on her own. An example Aristotle is fond of is a trading vessel. Sailors and merchants wish to make money through trade, but no one can operate a trading vessel on one's own so they must band together and form a crew, which is a community.

Now work which can only be accomplished through the efforts of several persons needs to be divided and shared in some way. Typically this is done by establishing functions, or "offices," as we may call them; on a sailing ship these might include the captain, first mate, helmsman, navigator, deck hands, and cook. Each office has its own distinctive work, and the relationship among offices is established by regulations, which will vary in explicitness and formality, depending upon the community. Finally, some scheme must be established as well for allotting the goods attained through the joint effort of the various members of the community; in the case of the sailing ship, a wage or percentage of the profits is assigned to each office. Typically communities also recognize and honor their members for exemplary performance in an office. Let us call the division and relationship of offices, the method of dividing gains, and the procedure for awarding honors the "scheme of cooperation" of a community.

Aristotle believes that the scheme of cooperation for a community constitutes justice for that community. But in order to make this idea plausible, three further assumptions are necessary. First, I think Aristotle believes that in the paradigmatic cases of communities, each member of the community freely consents to being a member. I don't think he has an argument for this assumption; I think he simply takes it as obvious that a member of a community cannot be truly seeking the goal of that community, and so cannot fully be a member of that community, unless he does so willingly. Second, Aristotle holds that no one consents to being treated unjustly.[25] Third, decisions about the division and allotment of duties, in a truly cooperative endeavor, will in each case be made with a view to what is "fair," that is, to what is just. For example, the night watch will be divided equally among the members of the crew (an instance of what Aristotle calls "justice according to number" [*kat'arithmon*]); other responsibilities may be allotted depending upon special talents (what Aristotle calls "justice according to merit" [*kat'axian*]). A consequence of these three assumptions is that the scheme of cooperation in a true community will be just.

It is an important feature of a community that the goal which its members aim at is given form by the scheme of cooperation of the community. What I mean by this is the following. A community, we have said, consists of a plurality of persons working together to achieve a goal that no one could achieve individually. It follows, then, that no member could have, as his goal, that mere good, on its own and apart from any consideration of his means of reaching it. For example, it would be absurd for a soldier in a battle to have as a goal "winning the battle (however I might attain it)". Rather, the soldier's goal *must* be something like "to contribute to winning the battle through the battle plan drawn up by the generals, etc." Likewise, in agreeing to serve in a certain office on a particular ship, a sailor agrees to seek profit *through* the scheme of cooperation proposed for that ship. The ship, then, with its various offices and terms of hire, actually gives form to the sailor's previously indeterminate aim to seek gain through sailing. Thus, although it may have been the case that before being signed to a particular ship the various sailors had indistinct and not wholly compatible goals, once they have signed on, they all share the very precise (and no longer indeterminate) goal of "seeking gain through serving on this ship with its scheme of justice." They therefore become alike in a specific sense, in pursuing the same goal, as a *consequence* of their accepting the terms of cooperation for that community.

We are now in a position to ask: Why does Aristotle claim that a community exhibits a *friendship* because of its justice? It seems to me that this is to be understood as a consequence of a community's having a scheme of cooperation that gives structure to the motivation of its participants. For a community would therefore have the same rational structure as a friendship. First, each member wishes goods to the others through the scheme of cooperation. Each member consents to the scheme, but the scheme assigns offices, gain, and honors to the various members of the community, and these things are so many goods. Second, this well-wishing is mutually recognized. Each member knows that every other member accepts the scheme of cooperation, and each knows that the other knows. Third, the well-wishing has a reciprocal character. Each member wills the very same scheme of cooperation, but each plays a different role in effecting it. Consequently each member is capable of seeing her own activity as related to that of any other member by a sort of analogy. For example, the helmsman can reason, "just as I participate in the scheme by steering, so the navigator participates by navigating." In this way two activities which are different in kind— steering and navigating— are conceived of as in some sense equivalent to and standing in for each other.

It even seems to be possible for the members of a community in this way to count the achievements and honors of other members as in some sense belonging to themselves. Consider, for example, a mountain-climbing expedition. Perhaps only two members of an entire expedition of fifty will reach the summit, yet it is common for the other members to speak of "sharing in the victory" of those two. Or consider how the members of an academic community sometimes think that they share in the achievements of their colleagues. This phenomenon of counting another's good as one's own seems very characteristic of friendship.

But what role does virtue play in "friendships within communities"? We can distinguish general from specific "virtues of community." A general virtue of community is one that is needed for playing one's part well in any community. In his curious discussion, in Book 3 of the *Politics*, of the question of whether "a good citizen and a good human being are the same," Aristotle remarks that "a good citizen must have both the *knowledge* and the *ability* to be ruled and to rule."[26] He equates the former trait with justice and the latter with temperance. These virtues indeed appear to be necessary for communities generally. A good member of any community will need to view his own actions as governed by the laws and principles of justice of the community, and, furthermore, he will need the self-control which will enable him to act in accordance with this understanding. But then there will be particular virtues necessary for certain communities, and other virtues necessary only for particular offices within a community. For example, every sailor on the trading vessel will need to have, not only justice and temperance, but also courage, because of the enduring threat of danger upon the seas.[27] And then there will also be particular virtues which would be necessary for acting well within the various offices of the vessel. The navigator will need to have certain intellectual virtues; the captain will need practical wisdom. Yet it seems correct to hold that virtue plays only an *oblique* role in friendships of community. The fact that the members of a community have the relevant virtues is a necessary condition for there to be friendship within that community, but it does not itself, in the first instance, provide a reason for that friendship.

Sometimes the question is raised, concerning the political community, of whether it is a "utility friendship" or not. It seems to me that this question is best framed with regard to friendships within communities generally. We have seen that communities form to seek some particular good (something "expedient," *sumpheron*), Aristotle says. Does it follow that the members of a community are friends with one another only "for the sake of that (expedient) good"?[28]

The question is in fact ill formed, since it attempts to apply a distinction derived from personal friendships to the very different class of community friendships. In a personal friendship, the reason each friend has for loving the other would need to be stated in the third person singular, and would refer to some feature of the friend, which she possesses prior to the relationship, such as, "Because she's funny," or "Because she's generous." A utility friendship is one in which the reason given would refer to the usefulness of the friend. However, in a friendship within a community, the reason for any member's friendly regard for another will have to refer, in the first instance, to the shared scheme of cooperation. The reason has to be framed in the first person plural: "Because we're both serving on this ship headed for Sicily," or "Because we both teach at such-and-such college."

III. POLITICAL FRIENDSHIP

Aristotle regards the *polis* or city-state as a community of communities. It coordinates, balances, and, most importantly, supplies the deficiencies of, subordinate communities, such as households, villages, tribes, and voluntary associations. It is incorrect to describe the goal at which the political community aims, without qualification, as the happiness of its members. For the subordinate communities also aim at happiness. And it is not the case that people band together in families, villages, and tribes, only to realize that some further community is necessary in order for them to be happy. Rather, the political community aims at happiness in a specific way, by completing and coordinating the goods already sought by subordinate communities. The scheme which is agreed upon for assigning offices, honors, and gain in the pursuit of this goal is referred to as the constitution (*politeia*) of the political community. According to Aristotle, a friendship comes about through this constitution, just as in any community.

Aristotle takes pains to argue that a state is not like a "horde" (*ethnos, plethos*), for a horde does not consist of offices with distinct functions, and so cannot achieve the unity of having a single form.[29] Moreover, a state is not a mere "alliance"(*summachia*), because the members of a state are capable of regarding their association as intrinsically worthwhile and noble.[30] It is important to observe that, in insisting on these points, Aristotle is simply arguing that a state is a community. The features he claims of the state are possessed by communities generally and not merely the political community. *Any* community has a unity achieved through a single and agreed upon scheme of cooperation; any community is desirable for its own sake, since as a community it necessarily displays justice, and justice is desirable for its own sake. This is of course not to claim that all of its members will succeed in desiring it for this reason. Aristotle simply needs to hold that a good man could value the association in that way. The point about activity in an alliance is that *not even a good man* can value it as intrinsically worthwhile.

Aristotle calls political friendship a sort of "consensus" or "concord"—the Greek word is *homonoia*, literally, "like-mindedness." This is noteworthy, because it confirms the reading I have been giving of friendship within a community as something essentially "intellectual," something which is constituted by agreement on a scheme of co-operation. According to Aristotle, "concord" obtains when each member of a group recognizes that the other members hold the same view about "large-scale practical matters."[31] By "large-scale" matters, Aristotle means, I think, *constitutional* matters. This is important, for political friendship does not extend to matters of policy. This is confirmed by what Aristotle says about civil strife (*stasis*), which is a failure of political friendship. Civil strife is always directed at changing the constitution of the state.[32]

Aristotle's longest continuous discussion of political friendship, in *Nicomachean Ethics* 8.9–12, involves an ingenious comparison between forms of government and relationships within the household. He begins by distinguishing three basic forms of constitution — kingship, aristocracy, and republican government — and correlates each of these to a familial community, on the basis of a general similarity in schemes of cooperation. The relationship of king to subjects, he claims, is like that of father to children. The relationship among aristocratic rulers is like that between husband and wife in governing a household. The relationship among citizens in a republic is like that among brothers. Each form of constitution, he holds, will therefore have a form of friendship resembling the friendship which arises in the household community correlated with it.

The main point of this fascinating passage seems to be the anti-Platonic conclusion that political friendship is not a unified phenomenon but rather has distinct forms. The argument is that, since household friendships differ in kind, the political friendships that are analogous to them will also differ in kind.

Yet a further lesson, which Aristotle apparently wishes us to draw, is that the various household friendships are actually the *sources* of the corresponding political friendships — an idea which he in fact asserts explicitly in the *Eudemian Ethics*: "It is in the household," he says, "that one finds the first origins and sources of friendship, of constitutional government, and of justice."[33] Aristotle does not actually describe the causal mechanism by which familial relationships are extended to the political community. Presumably he would hold that friendship must first be extended to "mediating institutions," such as the village, the tribe, and fraternal associations, before it can be extended to the state. But what seems particularly important here is the implied contrast between the origin of friendship among comrades and the origin of political friendship. Friendship among comrades seems to be an extension of self-love. "All of the marks of friendship [*ta fallacy*]," Aristotle writes, "extend from oneself towards others."[34] But friendship with fellow members of a community seems to be an extension of familial affection. Personal friendship involves extending to another the natural love one has for oneself as being virtuous and good. Community friendship, it seems, involves extending to a group of persons the natural love one has for oneself as being naturally related to another, for example, as daughter, as sister, as mother. That is, it is in a family that one can acquire love for oneself as someone whose nature is to be in relation to others, and it is this sort of self-love which is extended to the political communities — so that one can regard oneself as *phusei politikon*, "by nature in a political relationship with others."

IV. POLITICAL FRIENDSHIP IN THE AMERICAN REPUBLIC

Is the classical conception of political friendship, as expressed in Aristotle, even potentially applicable to the American republic? I believe it is. Such a conception of political friendship would have to be limited in character, and we have seen that Aristotle's view is indeed limited, since it extends only to the sharing of goods and activities within a community. Indeed, it *must* be limited, since it is understood as the extension of a love for others that begins within the family and voluntary associations.

We would also want this friendship not to be *weaker*, because it is thus limited; that is, it would be preferable if we did not have to hold that political friendship would be *stronger* in an absolutist or totalitarian regime. And indeed the Aristotelian conception apparently has no such consequence, for the strength of the friendship is meant to depend upon the degree of justice of the constitution of that community. There is no reason for thinking that an absolutist regime, as such, is more just.

I have also been arguing that political friendship, as understood by Aristotle, depends only indirectly on virtue or on conceptions of virtue; that it could indeed be applied to communities of citizens who have different "conceptions of the good" — and even to persons who have very little in common but for a shared understanding of the political constitution. These are clearly features that make it suited for application to a liberal regime.

Given, then, that the conception in principle admits of application, we can now ask: *Has* the American republic in fact exhibited political friendship, according to this conception? It seems to me that we must answer yes, on very general considerations. As we have seen, according to Aristotle, every community constitutes a friendship; the American republic is indeed a political community; hence it constitutes a friendship.

The American republic is a political community because its citizens share the goal stated in the preamble to the Constitution: "to form a more perfect union, establish justice, insure domestic tranquility, provide for the common defense, promote the general welfare, and secure the blessings of liberty," and this goal is sought through the scheme of cooperation stipulated in that Constitution. It is no objection that American citizens do not necessarily have warm feelings for one another; as we saw, political friendship is a sort of "concord," a shared agreement. This conclusion can be confirmed by reflecting on the fact that the American republic has been remarkably stable for over two hundred years and troubled by constitutional civil strife only twice during that time. The classical mind would reason that such stability would be impossible without political friendship, and this seems to me correct. That we typically do not *think* of consensual agreement over the Constitution as amounting to some sort of friendship does not, of course, keep it from being so.

But I must insist on an even stronger claim: political friendship finds a particularly clear expression in our form of government. For the U. S. Constitution, besides being a marvelous piece of statecraft, is in fact a *written* constitution, which acts as fundamental law, marking the boundaries of licit action of the various offices of government. A result of this is that the *content* of consent, that is, of the "scheme of cooperation" consented to, is very clear, so that citizens can easily conceive of the activity of the government as an expression of their agreement and have a greater assurance that it is so. The written U. S. Constitution marked a shift from the classical conception of a constitution as being, in the words of John Adams, "a frame, a scheme, a system, a combination of powers,"[35] to the notion of an absolute limit on the power of government as issuing from a constitutive agreement. The latter conception vividly places the cooperative character of political society before the minds of the citizens.

Yet another important feature of the American republic, which has contributed, in the past at least, to its exhibiting political friendship in a very striking manner, is the role played by the Declaration of Independence in providing the ideology of republican government. The important question, I believe, is this: Is it possible to interpret a political society as, in some sense, giving expression to, or serving as an example of, the universal society of all human beings? Can the bond which links citizen to citizen be reasonably interpreted as the universal love of humankind, or *philanthrōpia*, as given a concrete embodiment at this place and in this time? Plato held that Greek was naturally friendly only to Greek, whereas Greek and barbarian were by nature at enmity.[36] Aristotle holds essentially the same view, though he flirts briefly with the idea that "every human being is near and dear to every other."[37] There is nothing about the natural friendship of all humankind in the Declaration. Nonetheless, a society which affirms the existence of rights prior to political society, rights which derive simply from the fact of one's humanity, thereby expresses a fundamental regard—if not love—for the interests of every human being, and its actions in securing those rights within its own borders can then be interpreted as an expression of regard for humanity generally. Now this, I contend, makes for a very stable political friendship, because each citizen thereby has a fundamental regard for every other, and the basis of this regard, namely, the humanity of the other, is unalterable.

Indeed, it is not uncommon to hear sentiments expressed such as, "If one person is oppressed, all are," or "The attack on the rights of one is an attack on the rights of all of us." This "meddlesome" concern to root out injustice; this intent to identify with, rather than ignore, a victim of injustice, on the part of someone who may be separated from the victim by vast distances—such sentiments, which require a radical identification of the other's interests with one's own, were entirely unknown in the ancient world, but they are part of the fabric of political friendship in the United States.

Yet if the American republic has exhibited political friendship, then why has it not been much talked about? Why does the notion of friendship play so small a role, it seems, in political reflection, both ordinary and systematic, in this country? The reasons the Founders said little about political friendship, I think, is that they took it for granted. It is a background assumption of their political thought, which might be revealed, I think, through a careful study of their references to "peace," "tranquility," and "comity"—through a study like Harvey Mansfield's examination of the rich language of virtue embedded in the Federalist papers.

Then, at particular times in our nation's history, political friendship has *indeed* received much attention. The principal idea of Lincoln's "House Divided" speech—which was a novelty at first, but which came to be the view of the Republican party—was that the Kansas-Nebraska Act, in overturning the Missouri Compromise, had placed the nation in a condition of civil strife, which, from that point on, admitted of only two possible solutions: either the nation would become entirely free or entirely slave.

But that political friendship *now* receives little thought seems to me to be another example of the impoverishment of our moral and civic discourse, which was documented by Robert Bellah and others in *Habits of the Heart*[38]—an example of our lacking the vocabulary even to express any ideals and aspirations other than individualistic ones. The causes of this seem to me to be complex and obscure.

This leads me to my final question: If we grant that the Aristotelian conception has application, and that, furthermore, there are reasons for thinking that the American republic can, in principle, exhibit such friendship in a clear and noteworthy way, is it in fact the case that political friendship is strong in this country, or weak? And if it is weak, what explanations might the Aristotelian theory give of this?

This opens up a vast topic of discussion, but there are some obvious explanations that follow from the account I have given. For, if Aristotle is correct, then the *sources* of political friendship dry up when the household is weakened. The *extension* of friendship within the household to the political community is hindered, to the extent that voluntary associations and mediating institutions flag and wither. And the *content* of political friendship is diminished, to the extent that citizens are poorly educated about the traditions and constitutional principles of the nation. It seems to me that these three causes are acting in concert at the present time.

NOTES

1. Douglas L. Wilson, ed., *Jefferson's Literary Commonplace Book*, The Papers of Thomas Jefferson, 2d series (Princeton, N.J.: Princeton University Press, 1989), p. 71.
2. Aristotle *Nicomachean Ethics* 1155a22–26.
3. Plato *Republic* 424a1–2, 451d6.

4. Ibid., 462d7.

5. Ibid, 462b.

6. Ibid, 462b-d.

7. Ibid, 451d.

8. Plato *Laws* 739c.

9. Ibid.

10. Plato *Gorgias* 513b.

11. Plato *Republic* 412d4–7.

12. Aristotle *Nicomachean Ethics* 1156b19–24.

13. Ibid., 1157b28–36, 1156a9–10.

14. Ibid., 1155b34–1156a2.

15. Ibid., 1156b35–1157a6.

16. Ibid., 1157b35–1158a1.

17. Ibid., 1156b22.

18. Ibid., 1166a31–32.

19. Aristotle *Politics* 1280b37–39, 1262b8–11.

20. Aristotle *Nicomachean Ethics* 1159b27–29.

21. Ibid., 1159b30–32.

22. Ibid., 1160a6–7.

23. Ibid., 1160a7–8.

24. Ibid., 1159b29–30.

25. Ibid., 5.9.

26. Aristotle *Politics* 1277b14–18.

27. Cf. Aristotle *Nicomachean Ethics* 1115a29.

28. Ibid., 1160a10.

29. Aristotle *Politics* 1261a26–33.

30. Ibid., 1281a3–4, 1280b5–7.

31. Aristotle *Nicomachean Ethics* 1167a28–29.

32. Aristotle *Politics* 1301b7–20.

33. Aristotle *Eudemian Ethics*, 1242a40–b1.

34. Aristotle *Nicomachean Ethics* 1168b5–6.

35. John Adams, cited in B. Bailyn, *The Ideological Origins of the American Revolution* (Cambridge, Mass.: Harvard University Press, 1967), p. 175.

36. Plato *Republic* 470c.

37. Aristotle *Nicomachean Ethics* 1155a23.

38. Robert N. Bellah, et al., *Habits of the Heart: Individualism and Commitment in American Life* (Berkeley, Calif.: University of California Press, 1985).

Author Index

215

Subject Index

217